LONDON'S
PARKS &
GARDENS

Robbi Atilgan & David Hampshire

Survival Books • Bath • England

First published 2013

Copyright © Survival Books 2013
Cover design: Di Bruce-Kidman
Cover photo: © Dmitry Naumov (shutterstock.com)
Maps © Jim Watson

Survival Books Limited
Office 169, 3 Edgar Buildings
George Street, Bath BA1 2FJ, United Kingdom
☏ +44 (0)1935-700060
✉ info@survivalbooks.net
🖥 www.survivalbooks.net

British Library Cataloguing in Publication Data
A CIP record for this book is available
from the British Library.

ISBN: 978-1-907339-95-0

Printed in China by International Press Softcom Limited

Acknowledgements

The authors wish to thank all those who helped with research and provided information for this book, unfortunately too many to list here. Special thanks are due to Peter Read for research and editing; Alex Browning for proof-reading; David Woodworth for final proof checking; Di Bruce-Kidman for DTP, photo selection and cover design; Jim Watson for the superb maps; and the authors' partners for continuing with the pretence that writing is a proper job (that pays a proper salary).

Last, but not least, a special thank you to the many unnamed photographers who provided images – the unsung heroes – whose beautiful images add colour and bring London's parks and gardens to life.

NOTE

Before visiting anywhere mentioned in this book, it's advisable to check the opening times, which are liable to change without notice.

Information Boxes

The notes below refer to the general information provided for each park and garden.

◆ **Address:** Includes the phone number and website (if applicable). You can enter a park's postcode to display a map of its location on Google and other map sites. If you're driving you can enter the postcode into your satnav.

◆ **Opening hours:** These sometimes vary, so confirm by telephone or check the website, particularly when travelling a long distance. Note that parks that officially open at dawn usually open between 7 and 8am and those that close at dusk/sunset may actually close around 30 miniutes earlier. Some private gardens and parks are closed in winter or at other times, which should be indicated on their website.

◆ **Cost:** Most parks are public and provide free entry, while charges for private parks and gardens are liable to change. If applicable, ask about concessions and family rates. Where a park or garden is combined with a house or museum, it may be possible to pay a reduced fee to visit just the grounds. Many parks and gardens have cafés and shops, which can often be visited independently of the garden or park, i.e. without buying a ticket (where applicable).

◆ **Transport:** The nearest tube and rail stations are listed, although in some cases there may be a lengthy walk. You can also travel to most venues by bus. Some parks and gardens are best reached by car, although parking can be difficult or impossible (or very expensive) in some areas, particularly central London.

◆ **Attractions & amenities:** Special attractions such as an arboretum, parks with formal gardens, lakes/ponds, house, museum, gallery, sculpture/artworks, café/restaurant, bandstand, playground, concerts, animal attractions/farm/zoo, sports facilities, etc. have been noted. Most public parks provide WCs, although they may not be wheelchair accessible.

ACCESS

All parks and gardens provide wheelchair access unless noted otherwise. Note, however, that this doesn't always apply to buildings within parks or WCs. Contact parks and gardens if you have specific requirements. The Disabled Go website (⌨ disabledgo.com) provides more in-depth access information for some destinations.

Contents

CHAPTER 5 - SOUTHWEST LONDON   159

CHAPTER 6 - SOUTHEAST LONDON   251

APPENDICES   302

INDEX OF ATTRACTIONS & AMENITIES   305

INDEX   313

Readers' Guide

The notes below refer to the general information provided for each park and garden.

◆ **Catering:** All major parks and gardens have cafés and/or restaurants, many of which are excellent (where applicable we have also made alternative local suggestions). Where there are no catering facilities you can usually take a picnic.

◆ **Green Flag Award:** Green Flags (🖳 greenflag.keepbritaintidy.org) are awarded annually by Keep Britain Tidy to recognise and reward the best green spaces in the country, and are the benchmark national standard for UK parks and green spaces. We have indicated parks and gardens that have been awarded a Green Flag.

◆ **Dogs:** Most parks and gardens welcome dogs, provided they're kept under control and/or on a lead, and some have special dog runs where you can let Rover run free. Places where dogs may not be so welcome include formal gardens, nature reserves, playgrounds, city farms/zoos and some cemeteries – always check before visiting. Make sure you clean up after your dog or you risk being fined.

◆ **Cemeteries:** Many of London's cemeteries – including the Magnificent Seven of Abney Park (1840), Brompton (1840), Highgate (1839), Kensal Green (1833), Nunhead (1840), Tower Hamlets (1841) and West Norwood (1836) – were designed as garden cemeteries – now cemetery parks – and are among London's most beautiful parks. These (and a number of other attractive and interesting cemeteries) are included in this book.

◆ **Registered Parks and Gardens:** The English Heritage 'Register of Historic Parks and Gardens (🖳 english-heritage.org.uk/caring/listing/registered-parks-and-gardens) of special historic interest in England' was established in 1983 and identifies over 1,600 sites judged to be of national importance. These include many in London.

◆ **Listed Buildings:** Many London parks and gardens contain buildings of special architectural and historic interest (noted where applicable) that are protected from development or major alterations. Listed buildings are placed on the 'Statutory List of Buildings of Special Architectural or Historic Interest', which in England is maintained by English Heritage (🖳 english-heritage.org.uk/caring/listing/listed-buildings). There are the following three grades of listed buildings:

- Grade I: buildings of exceptional interest;
- Grade II*: particularly important buildings of more than special interest;
- Grade II: buildings of national importance and special interest.

OPEN LONDON

Visit gardens which are usually closed to the public on special days, when residents of private gardens, squares and estates open their doors to the public. The main events are Open Garden Squares Weekend that takes place in June (🖳 opensquares.org), when, for example, the garden of 10 Downing Street is among those unveiled, and Open House London in September (🖳 londonopenhouse.org).

Introduction

Britain is renowned for being a green and pleasant land, and nowhere in the British Isles has such a rich diversity of beautiful green spaces as London. The capital's green bounty includes magnificent royal parks, historic garden cemeteries, majestic ancient forests, breath-taking formal country parks, expansive commons, tropical greenhouse collections, elegant squares and enchanting 'secret' gardens, many of which are known only to insiders and locals.

London is more verdant than any other world city of its size – green spaces cover almost 40 per cent of Greater London – and provides a wealth of places where you can play, relax, exercise and commune with nature year round. There are around 400 green spaces in the City of London alone and over 1,000 in Greater London, ranging from famous public parks to semi-private gardens, city farms to converted church yards – each with its own unique character. This book gathers together over 250 of London's parks, gardens and squares, including all the major ones, and many that are lesser known but often just as glorious – most of which can be visited free of charge!

For London's largest, best-known (royal) parks we must thank – somewhat surprisingly – Henry VIII. Not that the Tudor monarch ever intended his lands to be opened to the *hoi polloi*; when he appropriated them in the 16th century it was so he and his friends could hunt deer in private. Bushy Park, Green Park, Greenwich Park, Hampton Court Park, Hyde Park, Regent's Park, Richmond Park and St James's Park all owe their existence to the royals' passion for chasing deer.

The vast majority of London's public parks were founded by the Victorians from the 1840s onwards (the first was Victoria Park in Hackney, created in 1845) as part of a range of measures to improve the living conditions of the

Kyoto Garden, Holland Park

working classes by providing 'green lungs' where they could enjoy exercise and fresh air. It's thanks to the foresight and dedication of those visionary Victorians that modern London is the greenest of green cities; their work is continued today by an army of volunteers ('friends'), who toil selflessly to restore, maintain and improve the city's green spaces.

London's living network of parks and gardens, commons and woodlands, canals, rivers and reservoirs, is vital to the health and well-being of Londoners (and visitors!) and makes an invaluable contribution to the quality, character and economy of the capital. It also provides food and refuge for the city's flora and fauna, which – despite living alongside some 8.25m people – is extraordinary in its abundance, variety and scope.

There's nothing pristine or precious about London's parks and gardens, no multitude of signs saying, 'Keep off the grass' – heaven forbid! The city's green spaces are there to be enjoyed by all as places to sunbathe, nap, play, picnic, read, listen to music or just chill out. They attract all kinds of sportsmen and women, from walkers to joggers, cyclists to horse-riders, frisbee throwers to rollerbladers, kite flyers to model boat sailors, tai chi practitioners to yoga enthusiasts. They also provide a stage for all manner of organised sports including swimming (in lidos, lakes and ponds), tennis, soccer, rugby, cricket, hockey, skateboarding, basketball, bowls, golf and much more.

So, whether you're a nature lover or a history buff, a horticulturist or a fitness fanatic, or just a deckchair dreamer looking for a bit of peace and quiet, you'll find your perfect spot in London. All you need is a comfortable pair of shoes, a sense of adventure – and this book!

We trust you'll enjoy discovering London's profusion of amazing parks and gardens as much as we did.

Happy hunting!

Robbi Atilgan & David Hampshire
June 2013

CHAPTER 1

CENTRAL LONDON

1   HYDE PARK

Address: Hyde Park, W2 2UH (☎ 0300-061 2000, 🖥 royalparks.org.uk/parks/
hyde-park).
Opening hours: Daily, 5am to midnight.
Cost: Free.
Transport: Lancaster Gate, Marble Arch, Hyde Park Corner or Knightsbridge
tube.
Attractions & amenities: Restaurant, café, refreshment kiosks, boating lake, lido,
tennis club, horse riding, playgrounds, mobility buggies, parking (fee).

Serpentine

The largest of the four great royal parks that run like a ribbon of green through central London, Hyde Park is a major London landmark, attracting some 7m visitors a year. In past times it has hosted exhibitions and celebrations, witnessed protests and executions, and provided respite from the noise and discomforts of the city – as, indeed, it still does.

Covering an area of 350 acres (142ha), the park is bordered by Bayswater Road to the north, Kensington Road/Knightsbridge to the south, and Park Lane to the east. To the west is Kensington Gardens (see page 20) which, although it appears to be a seamless extension of Hyde Park, has been separate since 1728. Hyde Park takes its name from the manor of Hyde which was owned by the monks of Westminster Abbey, until Henry VIII seized it in 1536 for his favourite sport of deer hunting. It remained a playground for royals and gentlefolk until 1637, when it was opened to the general public. It quickly became a refuge and rallying point: Londoners camped in the park in 1665 in the hope of escaping the Great Plague and later gathered to celebrate major victories such as the Battle of Trafalgar and Waterloo.

Successive monarchs have shaped Hyde Park to suit their needs. In 1689, William and Mary had a private drive laid across the southern edge to their new residence at Kensington Palace. The 'King's road' or *Route du Roi* became known as Rotten Row, a fashionable place to ride out in the 18th and 19th centuries; the Household Cavalry still exercise their horses there. In the 1820s, George IV ordered a makeover of the park, and commissioned Decimus Burton to design new railings and gates, including the monumental gateway at Hyde Park Corner, now called the Queen Elizabeth Gate. It included an ornate triumphal screen which can still be seen today, although the massive Wellington Arch which accompanied the gate was later moved to the centre of the Hyde Park roundabout.

Many major events have taken place in Hyde Park. In 1851 it was the venue for the Great Exhibition – Joseph Paxton's Crystal Palace (see page 258 was first built here – and more recently has hosted concerts, from the Rolling Stones to Pavarotti, and also provided a venue for sporting events at the 2012 Olympics.

Hyde Park has a wide variety of flora and fauna. Robins and tits nest among the trees and in herbaceous plantings, such as the Rose Garden, while in the centre of the park a wilderness meadow attracts butterflies to its wildflowers, and waterfowl share the Serpentine with pleasure boats and swimmers.

The park is full of unexpected treats – memorials, statues and works of art; but its best-loved attractions include the following:

 The Serpentine: This long and lovely stretch of water gets its name from its sinuous shape, although only the eastern stretch is called the Serpentine – the western end beyond the bridge is the Long Water. It was created in 1733 when Charles Bridgeman (1690-1738) undertook a major landscaping project for Queen Caroline (wife of George II). He created the Serpentine by damming the Westbourne stream that flowed down from Hampstead at the then astronomical cost of £20,000. It's a popular spot for

---

🍴 FOOD & DRINK 🍸

The Serpentine Bar & Kitchen: Situated at the eastern end of the lake, the Serpentine serves modern English and French cuisine. The all-day menu from 8am to 8pm includes classics such as eggs Benedict and wood-fired pizza. Wonderful views from the terrace.

The Lido Café: Licensed café with outdoor seating, 8am to 7pm (10am to 4pm in winter); child-friendly and a great spot for people-watching.

Kiosks: You can buy ice cream, drinks and snacks at kiosks dotted around the park or take your own food and enjoy a picnic.

birding, boating and swimming – the Lido is open from May to September although the hardy souls of the Serpentine Swimming Club take the plunge all year round, including on Christmas Day.

🔍 HIDDEN CORNER

In the garden of Victoria Gate Lodge, just off Bayswater Road, is one of Hyde Park's curiosities: a pint-sized cemetery full of miniature headstones. It's the last resting place of over 300 much-loved pets – mainly dogs – buried between 1881 and 1967. The first dog interred, a Maltese called Cherry, belonged to friends of the gatekeeper, Mr Winbridge. The epitaphs are heartfelt, even if some names are strange: 'residents' include Fattie, Tally-Ho and Pomme de Terre! Sadly, the cemetery can only be viewed through the railings or by appointment.

◆ **Speaker's Corner**: Close to Marble Arch and the former site of the Tyburn gallows, this is London's best known area for free speech. Hyde Park has always been a magnet for marchers and protestors, from the Chartists in

Speaker's Corner

the 1830s to the anti-war rallies of recent years. Since 1872, people have been allowed to protest and preach at Speaker's Corner, provided they don't cause offence, and Karl Marx and George Orwell are among the many who have spoken here. To gain attention, speakers would stand on wooden crates used for shipping soap – hence the term 'to get on your soapbox'.

◆ **Diana Memorial Fountain**: Designed by Kathryn Gustafson and opened by HM The Queen in 2004, this sweeping oval fountain south of the Serpentine is dedicated to Diana, Princess of Wales, who died in 1997. It was designed to express Diana's spirit and approachability, and visitors are welcome to cool their feet in the water when the fountain is open (from 10am to between 4pm and 8pm, depending on the time of year).

◆ **7th July Memorial**: This permanent memorial honours the victims of the London Bombings on 7th July 2005. It comprises 52 stainless steel pillars, each representing one of those killed, grouped together in four inter-linking clusters reflecting the four locations where the bombs exploded. A plaque listing the names of the victims is sited nearby.

The first-ever Victoria Cross investiture took place in Hyde Park on 26th June 1857, when 62 heroes of the Crimean War were decorated by Queen Victoria in the presence of Prince Albert and other members of the royal family.

◆ **Holocaust Memorial**: Just east of the Serpentine, two boulders surrounded by silver birch trees mark the first public memorial in Britain to victims of the Holocaust. It's inscribed with the words: 'For these I weep. Streams of tears flow from my eyes because of the destruction of my people.'

◆ **Achilles Statue**: This 18ft (5.5m) statue of the Greek hero stands near Hyde Park Corner and is dedicated to the Duke of Wellington. Sculpted by Richard Westmacott in 1822 on the orders of George III, it's made of bronze

Achilles statue

from cannons captured in military campaigns by the Duke, including Waterloo. It was London's first public nude statue and caused considerable controversy, despite the fig leaf preserving its subject's modesty.

◆ **Boy and Dolphin Fountain**: This charming Pre-Raphaelite marble sculpture of a cherub and dolphin by Alexander Munro dates from 1862, and sits in the centre of the Rose Garden. Look carefully and you'll see that the water flows from the nostrils of the dolphin, not its mouth.

◆ **Weeping Beech**: Tucked away in the Dell, this is one of the park's living curiosities; also known as the Upside Down Tree because its branches descend from the crown and look like roots making it look like a shady green tent.

Sports fans are well catered to in Hyde Park. Joggers, skateboarders and people practising tai chi are part of the scenery; there are also cycle tracks and ample space for ball games. As well as swimming at the Lido, there are a tennis centre, putting and bowling greens (☎ 0207-262 3474), while several stables offer horse-riding in the park. Children have a choice of playgrounds, plus the Lookout, a former police observation point which is now an education centre. The park also has excellent facilities for the disabled, including Liberty Drives mobility buggies, which provide half-hour tours of the park and neighbouring Kensington Gardens from seven different pick up points (🖥 hyde parkappeal.org).

2   KENSINGTON GARDENS

Address: Kensington Gardens, W2 2UH (☎ 0300-061 2000, ⌨ royalparks.org.uk/parks/kensington-gardens).
Opening hours: Daily, 6am to sunset (check website for exact times).
Cost: Free. There's a fee to see Kensington Palace.
Transport: Lancaster Gate, Queensway, Bayswater or High Street Kensington tube.
Attractions & amenities: Restaurant, café, palace, art gallery, lakes, adventure playground, bandstand, mobility buggies.

Kensington Palace

The quieter, more refined neighbour of Hyde Park, Kensington Gardens strikes just the right balance between culture and nature. It was once the 'back garden' of Kensington Palace (see below), one of the great royal residences, although its 270 acres (111ha) are now open to all. Divided from Hyde Park in the 18th century, Kensington Gardens has a more formal atmosphere – it's hard to imagine a rock concert taking place here – and the gardens, fenced off and closed at sunset, feel more private.

Kensington Gardens has had close links with royalty since 1689 when William III and his wife Mary moved to Nottingham House – later Kensington Palace – to escape the grime of Whitehall. While William commissioned Sir Christopher Wren to upgrade the house, Mary landscaped the palace gardens in Dutch style to please her Dutch husband. When her sister Queen Anne took over the throne in 1702, she created an English-style garden and added an Orangery next to the palace.

However, it was Queen Caroline, wife of George II, who fashioned today's Kensington Gardens. She appropriated a large slice of Hyde Park and separated it from Kensington Gardens with a ditch, called a ha-ha – an idea which was copied all over England. She appointed Charles Bridgeman to design a new landscape, which included two lakes: the Round Pond, which has centre stage in front of the palace, and the Long Water/Serpentine. The bridge where the waters meet marks the border with Hyde Park.

👁 DON'T MISS!

Art lovers should stop at the Serpentine Gallery (☎ 020-7402 6075, ⌨ serpentinegallery.org), just north of Mount Gate. One of London's most important contemporary art galleries, it has exhibited work by Henry Moore, Andy Warhol and Bridget Riley, among many others. Open daily, 10am to 6pm, free entrance.

The royal connection carried on through Queen Victoria, who was born in Kensington Palace, up to current royals. Princess Diana lived in an apartment in the palace and would jog incognito in Kensington Gardens; thousands of tributes were laid on the lawns after her death in 1997.

Elephant sculpture

In the 18th century, Kensington Gardens was the place to see and be seen on Saturdays, when the gates were opened to respectably-dressed citizens. Its proximity to the palace gave it an edge over Hyde Park – at least until the late 19th century – and it still has a more rarefied air. With its formal avenues and carefully planned water features, mature trees – plane, chestnut, lime, sycamore, beech – and neat lawns, the gardens are a place for relaxation and contemplation rather than sports and games. There are paths set aside for cyclists and skaters, but it seems to suggest more low-key activities, such as feeding the ducks, model boating and flying kites. Organised activities include bandstand recitals in the summer, while guided walks take place throughout the year exploring the park's horticulture, wildlife and history.

The main attraction in Kensington Gardens is **Kensington Palace** (☎ 0844-482 7777, 🖳 hrp.org.uk/kensingtonpalace, daily 10am to 6pm – 5pm in winter). Re-launched in 2012 following a £12m facelift, it's a charming and well-presented stately home, particularly if you're interested in grand décor and the intrigues of the Georgian court. It features a magnificent sunken garden planted in 1908 to recreate the splendour of the original 17th-century gardens. Vibrant colours and exotic planting surround an ornamental pond with fountains formed from old water cisterns retrieved from the palace. An arched arbour of red-twigged lime, known as the Cradle Walk, surrounds this intimate oasis. You can access the palace gardens from Kensington Gardens without paying to visit the palace itself.

Other must-see attractions include:

◆ **Round Pond**: Octagonal rather than round, this lake's lack of corners has made it popular since Victorian times for sailing model boats, and it's the home of two model yacht clubs. It's also a draw for waterfowl and you can see ducks and swans dodging the pint-sized dinghies.

◆ **Italian Gardens**: The ornamental water garden at the head of the Long Water was built in the 1860s to a design by James Pennethorne, and is said to have been a love token from Prince Albert to Victoria. Featuring four fountains and an array of classical sculptures, carved in Carrera marble and Portland stone, it's Grade II listed and provides an elegant resting place among the water lilies, yellow flag iris and flowering rush. Look for

The Orangery

Albert and Victoria's initials carved on the wall of the pump house, which once contained the steam engine that powered the fountains.

◆ **Peter Pan Statue**: South of the Italian Gardens is the famous bronze statue of Peter Pan, one of the city's most popular statues. The park is the setting of J M Barrie's book *Peter Pan in Kensington Gardens*, a prelude to Peter's adventures in Neverland, and the statue, sculpted by Sir George Frampton, was commissioned by Barrie in 1912 for the enjoyment of children visiting the park.

◆ **Albert Memorial**: On the southern edge of Kensington Gardens, facing the Albert Hall, this grand high-Victorian Gothic extravaganza commemorates Queen Victoria's adored husband, who died of typhoid fever in 1861, aged just 42. It was designed by Sir George Gilbert Scott and opened in 1872 by Victoria. As well as a gilt-bronze statue of Albert, the memorial celebrates the achievements of the Victorian age and empire, with massive marble sculptures of the continents and a delicately carved frieze of painters, poets, sculptors, musicians and architects. Tours provide a close-up view and take place at 2 and 3pm on the first Sunday of the month from March to December (adults £6, concessions £5).

🔍 HIDDEN CORNER

South of the Diana Memorial Playground, there's a rather odd tree stump entombed in a cage, but look closely and you'll see it's carved with fairies, elves and small woodland animals which appear to be living in the bark. This is the Elfin Oak, a 900-year-old tree stump, which was installed in the gardens in 1928 and restored in the '60s. It's now Grade II listed and encapsulates the charm of the gardens.

Other memorials within the park include **Speke's Monument**, which

View from the Italian Gardens

Henry Moore Arch

Peter Pan statue

commemorates John Hanning Speke (1827-1864), the explorer who discovered Lake Victoria, and a statue of **Edward Jenner** (1749-1823), pioneer of the smallpox vaccine.

🍴 FOOD & DRINK 🍷

Orangery Restaurant: Queen Anne's former greenhouse, alongside Kensington Palace, serves good food and is a popular spot for afternoon tea. Open daily, 10am to 6pm (5pm in winter).

    Broadwalk Café & Playcafé: Next to the Diana Memorial Playground, this informal eatery has flatbread pizza, soups, sweet treats and a menu for children; open all day.

    Kiosks: Drinks, pastries and ice cream are available from kiosks near both the Italian Gardens and the Albert Memorial.

◆ **Diana Memorial Playground**: Opened in memory of the late Princess of Wales in 2000, this is an innovative adventure playground, with a huge wooden pirate ship as its centrepiece. The gardens are also the starting point for the **Diana, Princess of Wales Memorial Walk**. This 7-mile (11km) stroll takes in four parks and many places associated with Diana (see 🖥 royalparks.org.uk for a map).

◆ **The Arch**: One of several artworks in the gardens, this 19.6ft (6m) marble sculpture was donated by Henry Moore in 1980 and recently restored. Sited alongside the Long Water, it perfectly frames a view of Kensington Palace.

3   REGENT'S PARK

Address: Regent's Park, NW1 4NR (☎ 0300-061 2300, ☐ royalparks.org.uk/parks/the-regents-park).
Opening hours: Daily, 5am to sunset; see website for seasonal closing times.
Cost: Free.
Transport: Baker Street, Regent's Park or Great Portland street tube.
Attractions & amenities: Formal gardens, restaurant, café and refreshments, London Zoo, wildlife garden, bird walk, lake, bandstand, sports centre, playgrounds.

Home to London Zoo, a vast swathe of parkland and some of the most exquisite Georgian terraces in the UK, Regent's Park is the largest of central London's five royal parks. It was created in the early 19th century for the Prince Regent – later George IV – and is officially titled **The** Regent's Park. These days, it's better known for its sporting and entertainment facilities, and its wealth of birdlife, although the glorious architecture which surrounds the park is a constant reminder of its noble heritage.

Regent's Park is well documented in literature and film. It features in Dodie Smith's novel *The One Hundred and One Dalmatians* as the park where the canine protagonists would take their human family (the Dearlys) for a walk. Trevor Howard took Celia Johnson boating on the lake during their illicit romance in David Lean's *Brief Encounter* (1945) and Hugh Grant's character chatted up young mums in Queen Mary's Gardens in *About a Boy* (2002).

Regent's Park covers 410 acres (166ha) and is bordered by Marylebone and Paddington to the south and west, and Camden and St Pancras to the east. To the north, the park is encircled by Regent's Canal, built to link the Grand Union Canal to the London docks, which offers a peaceful towpath stroll to Camden Lock (east) or west to Little Venice. The canal divides the main park from **Primrose Hill** (see page 45), officially part of Regent's Park but considered by many Londoners (and the authors) to be a separate park.

Regent's Park has an unusual layout consisting of two ring roads: the Outer and Inner Circles. The Inner Circle encloses formal gardens and an open-air theatre, while the Outer Circle surrounds the wilder reaches of the park and its many amenities, which include gardens, a lake, sports pitches, playgrounds and, of course, the zoo.

Like many of London's important parks, the land which now forms Regent's Park was appropriated from

its ecclesiastical owners – in this case the nuns of Barking Abbey – by Henry VIII who used it for hunting deer. When hunting fell out of fashion in the mid-17th century, it was leased out as farmland. It wasn't until 1811 that the architect John Nash (1752-1835), commissioned by the Prince Regent, came up with a grand plan to transform the area into a suburb within a park, creating the stylish neighbourhood we see today.

Nash's original plans were very grand indeed and included a summer palace for the Prince and over 50 villas for his courtiers and friends. By the time building began in 1818, two years before George IV became king, the scheme had lost some impetus; his majesty's attention was diverted to rebuilding Buckingham Palace, so plans for all but eight villas were shelved, and Nash focused on the terraces which line the edges of the park.

Important organisations such as the Zoological Society and Royal Botanic Society moved into the spaces set aside for the villas and laid out formal gardens, but the park remained an exclusive estate until 1835 when the public were finally allowed access to selected parts. Today, most of the park is open to all, although it retains its cachet as one of the most elite addresses in London – home to the US Ambassador and Sultan of Brunei, among others – and somehow achieves the near-impossible feat of being a country park in the heart of the city.

Regent's Park has some glorious formal gardens, including **Queen**

Gorilla, ZSL London Zoo

Mary's Gardens which occupies the Inner Circle (for more information, see page 43), the Avenue Gardens in the south eastern corner and the **Garden of St John's Lodge** (see page 38).

 FOOD & DRINK

Boathouse Café: With a large terrace overlooking the Boating Lake – from where you can watch the antics of the water fowl – the Boathouse serves pizza, pasta and other family favourites (9am to 6pm).

The Hub Café: Soups, toasties and cake with a 360º panorama of the park.

The Honest Sausage: Free-range sausage or bacon butties in organic bread. Find them at the top of the Broad Walk near the zoo.

The park's other main attractions include:

◆ **Open-air Theatre**: Founded in 1932 and refurbished in 1999, this is the only permanent professional outdoor theatre in Britain. Located within the Inner Circle, it stages four productions annually between May and September, from Shakespeare to musicals. Its steep auditorium seats 1,240 people and it also boasts the West End's longest 'bar'. For tickets and information, see the website (⌨ openairtheatre.org).

◆ **Bandstand**: Alongside the lake is an old-fashioned bandstand where visitors can enjoy a variety of lunchtime and evening concerts. Look for the memorial to the seven bandsmen of the 1st Battalion of the Royal Green Jackets who died here on July 20th 1982 when the Provisional Irish Republican Army (IRA) detonated a bomb under the bandstand during a performance of *Oliver!*.

◆ **Boating Lake**: The lake is a tricorn shape with bridges crossing each 'corner'. It's a great place to hire a boat or pedalo (charges start from £4 for 30 minutes) but equally good for bird watching. Regent's Park is home to a waterfowl breeding centre, where birds are raised to populate other royal parks, with over 650 waterfowl on the Boating Lake, including 260 pairs of ducks. There's also a heronry with over 20 nesting pairs – one of the largest grey heron colonies in London.

Chester Terrace

The park's varied terrain – ranging from formal gardens to scrub, woodland and rough grassland with wildflowers – makes it one of London's richest sites for bird watching; over 200 species have been spotted, including owls, kestrels, woodpeckers and peregrine falcons. There's a dedicated bird walk starting from Clarence Gate off Baker Street (see 🖳 regentsparkbirds.co.uk for information).

FOR THE ZOO, BOOK TO REGENT'S PARK OR CAMDEN TOWN

👁 DON'T MISS!

Everyone should visit London Zoo at least once. Opened by the Zoological Society of London in 1828, it's the world's oldest scientific zoo and houses over 750 species – one of the largest collections in the UK. Favourite residents include penguins, gorillas and the family of meerkats, plus iconic architecture such as the Mappin Terraces (1913) and Lord Snowdon's Aviary (1962). For more information and ticket prices see the ZSL London Zoo website (🖳 zsl.org/zsl-london-zoo).

South of the Inner Circle, the park's **Wildlife Garden** is a haven for a range of animals, from bats and hedgehogs to butterflies and newts.

◆ **Georgian Terraces**: Walking around the Outer Circle of Regent's Park is an architectural treat. Between Gloucester Gate in the north-eastern corner and Hanover Gate to the west of the lake, there are ten fine terraces of elegantly proportioned white stucco houses, many Grade I listed, all designed by John Nash or one of his protégés. The longest and possibly best known is Chester Terrace, a row of 42 houses which stretches for 280m (920ft). After Chester Terrace, take a detour south to peek through the railings at Park Square, one of the largest private squares in London. An unusual and original feature is the Nursemaids' Tunnel (to enable nannies to take their charges to the park without having to negotiate the busy road), an early example of an underpass, linking the square with Park Crescent beneath busy Marylebone Road.

◆ **The Hub Sports Centre**: This is the largest outdoor sports facility in London, complete with underground changing rooms and a café. As well as outdoor exercise classes and children's activities, it maintains pitches for soccer, rugby, lacrosse, softball and cricket. The park is also popular with cyclists who ride around the Outer Circle (the local cycling club is the Regent's Park Rouleurs). The Regent's Park Tennis Centre near York Bridge has both tennis and netball courts, and there are also three playgrounds and a miniature boating pond.

4   ST JAMES'S PARK

Address: St James's Park, SW1A 2BJ (☎ 0300-061 2350, 🖳 royalparks.org.uk/parks/st-jamess-park).

Opening hours: Daily, 5am to midnight.

Cost: Free.

Transport: St James's Park, Westminster or Victoria tube.

Attractions & amenities: Restaurant and refreshment kiosks, lake, bandstand, deckchairs.

St James's Park is the oldest of the royal parks. Surrounded by three of London's great palaces – the Palace of Westminster (now the Houses of Parliament), St James's Palace and Buckingham Palace – it's at the heart of royal history. It's also a glorious urban landscape, providing relaxation and recreation for the workers of Victoria and Whitehall – the writer Hunter Davies once described it as 'the haunt of civil servants' – and for tourists drawn to the area's pomp and pageantry.

The park is quite small – just 57 acres (23ha) – but it packs a lot into its space and it's easy to find your own quiet corner – no mean feat considering 5.5m people tramp through it each year. Its centrepiece

is a tranquil lake with a small island at either end, surrounded by lawns and trees, plus the requisite bandstand and deckchairs. It's bounded by the Mall to the north and Birdcage Walk to the south, with Buckingham Palace at its western end and Horse Guards Parade to the east. As well as its proximity to these London landmarks, St James's Park is also famous for its splendid views and self-important pelicans

The park takes its name from St James the Less, one of the 12 Apostles, to whom the first building on this site – a leper hospital – was dedicated. The land was acquired by Henry VIII in 1532 to use as yet another deer park, this one conveniently close to Whitehall Palace, his main London residence. It was Henry who built St

James's Palace, which is still the official residence of the British Sovereign, even though no king or queen has lived there since 1837!

FOOD & DRINK

Inn the Park: Overlooking Duck Island, this innovative Oliver Peyton restaurant serves a wide-ranging British menu and opens from 8am to 11pm (last dinner orders 8.30pm). It also offers a 'grab and go' menu, so you can take away treats for a picnic.

Kiosks: These can be found at Marlborough Gate, Horse Shoe Bend, Artillery Memorial, and the playground – serving sandwiches, snacks, ice cream, coffee and cold drinks.

When James I came to the throne in 1603 he set about transforming Henry's boggy deer chase into a suitably regal garden. It was drained and landscaped, and became home to the king's menagerie which included crocodiles and an elephant, while aviaries of exotic birds lined the southern perimeter, now named Birdcage Walk. Charles II had the park redesigned in the 1660s, probably by André Mollet, to resemble the formal gardens of France with neat lawns, avenues of trees and a half-mile long ornamental canal. Charles used his creation to entertain guests and court mistresses – the diarist John Evelyn spotted him here in 'familiar discourse' with 'Mrs Nellie [Gwyn]' – but allowed the public in.

The park was remodelled again in 1826-7, this time on the orders of the Prince Regent (George IV) and overseen by the architect and landscaper John Nash (1752-1835), who also worked on the enlargement of Buckingham Palace. Charles' canal was converted into a more naturally-shaped lake, and formal avenues became winding pathways. There were more changes at the western end of the park between 1906 and 1924, when the area outside Buckingham Palace was enlarged to make room for the Victoria Memorial, but St James's Park remains much as Nash intended.

Plantings include the Nash shrubberies and the 'tropical' border, both on the north side of the lake. The majority of trees in the park are plane trees, which are known for their flaking bark and resistance to pollution. Other species include the Black Mulberry Tree (*Morus nigra*), which was associated with James I's failed attempt to build a British silk industry, and fig trees, which border the lake.

It's undoubtedly a park for relaxation. You can hire a deckchair by the bandstand – there are free concerts on summer evenings – or take the circular stroll around the lake, part of the Diana Memorial Walk which begins at Kensington Palace. Children are catered for with a playground near Australia Gate.

Highlights unique to St James's Park include:

◆ **The Blue Bridge**: The views from the bridge which bisects the lake are among the most stunning in London. Look west to see Buckingham Palace and the Victoria Monument framed by trees. Then turn east to see the roofs of the Horse Guards building, the Old War Office building and Whitehall Court, the Foreign and Commonwealth Office, London Eye and The Shard. The original elegant suspension bridge was built across the lake in 1857, but was replaced a century later by a concrete crossing.

◆ **The Pelicans**: There has been a resident group of pelicans in St James's Park since 1664, when a Russian ambassador presented the birds to Charles II. They are sociable creatures who act as if they own the park, often perching on the benches alongside visitors; feeding time is between 2.30 and 3pm each day. As well as the pelicans, there are some 15

varieties of waterfowl, including ducks, geese and grebes on the lake, using the nesting sites on Duck and West islands. Look for **Duck Island Cottage**, built by John Burges Watson in 1840 to accommodate the park bird-keeper, a position which still exists today. The cottage, resembling a Swiss chalet, is now home to the London Parks and Gardens Trust.

👁 DON'T MISS!

A morning visit to St James's Park is an ideal opportunity to catch the Changing of the Guard at Buckingham Palace – or the Guard Mounting, as it's officially called. This ceremony, which dates back to the 17th century, involves a New Guard exchanging duty with the Old Guard, the handover accompanied by a Guards band. It's a timeless London experience and takes place at 11.30am each morning in summer and on alternate days in winter (see ⌨ royal.gov.uk).

◆ **Horse Guards Parade**: At the eastern end of the park is the wide parade ground used for annual ceremonial events such as Trooping the Colour, which marks the Queen's official birthday,

Pelican

and Beating Retreat, a musical spectacular by the bands of the Household Division which recalls the ancient ceremony of closing and securing the castle gates. Both take place in June. Polo tournaments are sometimes also held on Horse Guards Parade, which hosted the beach volleyball tournament during the 2012 London Olympics.

♦ **Victoria Memorial**: At the other end of the park, outside Buckingham Palace, stands the Queen Victoria Memorial which celebrates the glory days of the British Empire. At its centre is the marble statue of Victoria, surrounded by the glittering figures of victory, courage, constancy, charity, truth and motherhood, created between 1906 and 1924 by Sir Thomas Brock. The Queen Victoria Memorial Gardens were fashioned by Sir Aston Webb in 1901, the year of Victoria's death, and feature a broad semi-circular sweep of flowerbeds enclosed by a low stone balustrade. In summer they're often planted with scarlet

Victoria Memorial

geraniums to reflect the tunics of The Queen's Guard at Buckingham Palace.

> The Mall, and nearby Pall Mall, get their name from a game which Charles II introduced from France, which was played on courts in St James's Park. *Pele Mele*, a forerunner of croquet, was played on a long fenced court, using a mallet to hit a ball through a hoop.

5   GREEN PARK

Address: Green Park, SW1A 2BJ (☎ 0300-061 2350, 🖵 royalparks.org.uk/parks/green-park).
Opening hours: Unrestricted access.
Cost: Free.
Transport: Green Park or Hyde Park Corner tube.
Amenities: Refreshments, deckchairs.

Topiary crown for Queen's Diamond Jubilee

The smallest of the royal parks, Green Park may appear to be an extension of St James's Park, but the two have very different characters. If St James's Park is an urban garden, Green Park is lush pasture: peaceful, relaxing and **very** green.

Encompassing just 47 acres (19ha), the park is an important link in a chain of parks which stretches from Kensington to Westminster – the green lungs of central London. It's said that Charles II wanted to be able to walk from Hyde Park to St James's without leaving royal soil, so in the 1660s he acquired land between the two established parks, built a wall around it and called it Upper St James's Park. It only became known as Green Park after it was opened to the public in 1826.

The wedge-shaped park is bordered to the northwest by Piccadilly and to the south by Constitution Hill – the name may come from Charles's habit of taking his daily walk or 'constitutional' along this route. The park is bisected by the wide, tree-lined Broad Walk, but the most interesting route is the Queen's Walk, a private walkway built around 1730 for Queen Caroline, the wife of George II, which traces the edge of elegant St James's.

Though there's little doubt that Henry VIII once hunted deer on this land, the first recorded mention of the park was in 1554, when it was the location for Sir Thomas Wyatt's rebellion in protest against the marriage of Mary I to Philip II of Spain. Back then it was still meadowland and only became a formal park after Charles II obtained it in 1668; it was he who laid out the walkways and built features such as the icehouse (now long gone).

Although Green Park is now 'empty' save for its trees and some fascinating memorials (see below), during George II's reign (1727-1760) it was crammed with amusing features. These included the Queen's Library, a summer pavilion built for Queen Caroline by William Kent (1685-1748), and a reservoir called the Queen's Basin, which supplied water from the River Tyburn to St James's and Buckingham Palaces. The park became a fashionable place to see and be seen – and to settle differences. One notorious duel took place in 1730 between William Pulteney, 1st Earl of Bath, and John Hervey, 1st Earl of Bristol (both survived).

FOOD & DRINK

The Ritz: If you want to push the boat out, Green Park is next door to this iconic hotel renowned for its afternoon teas. Prices start from £42 and booking is essential (⌨ theritzlondon.com), but it's a once-in-a-lifetime experience.

Picnic: There are kiosks at Ritz Corner and Canada Gate serving coffee, ice cream and sandwiches, or you can stock up on goodies at the world-famous Fortnum & Mason (⌨ fortnumandmason.com) on Piccadilly.

Green Park was also the setting for lavish firework displays. Handel was commissioned to write *Music for the Royal Fireworks* to accompany a display in 1749 to celebrate the end of the War of Hanoverian Succession. The Temple of Peace, used to store fireworks, was hit by a rocket and went up in a ball of flame.

For all its royal connections, the park remained a remote spot well into the 18th century, and visitors risked robbery from highwaymen – Horace Walpole was one of many victims. In 1767, a slice of Green Park was appropriated to enlarge the garden of Buckingham House (later Palace). The next major change occurred in the 1820s, when John Nash was tasked with redesigning St James's Park and re-landscaped Green Park at the same time. Trees were planted – lime, chestnut and hawthorn, but mainly hardy London planes – and over time, the buildings were demolished and the lake filled in. By 1855, it was once again a vast green space, much as it had been in Charles II's time.

Bomber Command Memorial, Philip Jackson

Canada Ga

Today, the park is a popular venue for picnics, sunbathing and jogging, and commuters also use it as a short cut. There are no formal sports or playgrounds and no lake for wildlife, although there are common birds such as blackbirds, starlings and tits and, in winter, migrant birds such as redwing and fieldfare. And in spring there's a magnificent display of thousands of daffodils.

More recently, the park has become a place to remember people who served in the two world wars, and there are some important memorials:

♦ **The Canada Memorial**: Designed by Canadian sculptor Pierre Granche, this memorial was unveiled in 1994 as a tribute to the one million Canadians who served with British forces during the First and Second World Wars. It comprises two wedges of red granite, over which water flows, inset with bronze maple leaves. The memorial is close to the **Canada Gate**, which marks the entrance to the park from the Mall, an impressive screen of gilded wrought iron gates that were presented to London by Canada in 1908 to form part of the Queen Victoria memorial.

♦ **Commonwealth Memorial Gates**: At the top of Constitution Hill, four massive stone pillars and a memorial pavilion remember the 5m servicemen from the Indian subcontinent, Africa and the Caribbean who served in the two world wars.

♦ **RAF Bomber Command Memorial**: This is the UK's newest – and long overdue – war memorial, unveiled by the Queen in June 2012 to mark the sacrifice of 55,573 aircrew from Britain, Canada, Czechoslovakia, Poland and other Commonwealth countries, as well as civilians of all nations killed during air raids. It features a striking 9ft (2.7m) bronze sculpture by Philip Jackson of seven air crew returning from a bombing mission.

There are no formal flower beds in Green Park. This is reputedly due to instructions from Catherine of Braganza, wife of Charles II, who on discovering that the king had picked flowers in the park and given them to another woman, ordered that every single flower be uprooted and no more planted!

The Canada Memorial

Diana of the Treetops, EJ Clack

6 BUCKINGHAM PALACE GARDENS

Address: Buckingham Palace, SW1A 1AA (☏ 020-7766 7300, 🖥 royalcollection.
org.uk/visit/buckinghampalace).
Opening hours: Aug-Sep, 9.30am to 6.30pm (dates vary, so phone or check
website for details). State Rooms & Garden Highlights Tour (3½hrs), 9.30am,
1.15pm and 2pm.
Cost: £27.75 adults, £25.50 over 60s/students, £16.35 5-17s, under 5s free, £74
family. Note that the garden can only be visited as part of a tour.
Transport: Green Park or Hyde Park Corner tube or Victoria tube/rail.
Attractions & amenities: Palace State Rooms, café, shop, unsuitable for
wheelchairs but buggy available.

Behind Buckingham Palace is the largest private garden in London and also one of the most tantalising, especially when glimpsed from the top of a double-decker bus. Until recently, the only way to access the palace gardens was to be invited to one of the Queen's garden parties, but they can now be visited on a tour that also takes in the State Rooms.

 FOOD & DRINK

Garden Café: No visit to Buckingham Palace is complete without a stop at the Garden Café on the palace's West Terrace, which serves light refreshments, including tea, coffee, sandwiches and delicious pastries specially created for Buckingham Palace.

The gardens occupy a 42-acre (17ha) site with 2½mi (4km) of paths. The planting is varied and in parts exotic, with trees ranging from London's sturdy plane to a Chinese chestnut and Indian bean, as well as a silver lime planted to mark the Queen's Silver Jubilee in 1977. In the southwest corner there's a single surviving mulberry tree from a plantation created by James I, who tried (unsuccessfully) to breed silkworms.

The current layout dates back to John Nash's transformation of Buckingham Palace for George IV in the 1820s. The gardens were redesigned by William Townsend Aiton (1766-1849), director of Kew Gardens, who swept away the formal lines imposed by previous designers to create a romantic vista. He also added the famous lake which is noted for its variety of waterside plants and numerous water birds, which include a visiting flock of flamingos!

Described as 'a walled oasis in the middle of London', the garden is among the capital's 'greenest' and most environmentally friendly. It contains some 350 species of wildflower attracting moths, dragonflies and other insects, and over 40 bird species, including kingfishers, woodcocks and redwings. Since 2009 it has also supported four bee hives.

Visitors to the State Rooms get a glimpse of the garden as they stroll to the exit gate, but the 45-minute garden tour also takes in the beautiful herbaceous border (dug up to plant vegetables during the Second World War), the wisteria-clad summer house, the world-famous Rose Garden, and the tennis court, where George VI played Wimbledon champion Fred Perry in the '30s (no prizes for guessing who won!).

There's no seating in the garden but visitors are welcome to use walking sticks or folding stools with seat attachments (folding stools can also be borrowed). Visitors should note that the garden path is a mixture of gravel and sand, and quite long distances need to be covered. However, mobility scooters can be used in the gardens and a buggy is usually available to transport visitors with particular access requirements.

👁 DON'T MISS!

Among the works of art on display in the palace's garden is the famous **Waterloo Vase**. This huge Carrara marble urn was commissioned by Napoleon and presented (unfinished) to the Prince Regent (George IV) in 1815. At 15ft (5m) high and weighing 20 tons, it was too heavy for any of the floors in Windsor Castle, so ended up in the National Gallery. When the gallery insisted on giving it back in 1906, Edward VII installed it in the garden where it has remained ever since.

7 GARDEN OF ST JOHN'S LODGE

Address: Inner Circle, Regent's Park, NW1 4NX (✉ londongardensonline.org.uk or royalparks.org.uk).
Opening hours: Daily, 7am to dusk.
Cost: Free.
Transport: Baker Street or Regent's Park tube.
Amenities: Café and refreshments in **Regent's Park** (see page 24).

St John's Lodge was in private hands until 1916 – past owners included Lord Wellesley (1st Duke of Wellington), Sir Isaac Goldsmid and the Marquesses of Bute – when it saw service as a hospital for wounded soldiers. From 1937 to 1959 it housed London University's Institute of Archaeology, and later Bedford College. It's now leased by Prince Jefri Bolkiah of Brunei.

The garden of St John's Lodge is exquisite. It's the quintessential English garden tucked away down a pergola-draped path, providing sanctuary from the clamour of the city. It has glorious views of the imposing lodge, which was the first house to be built on Regent's Park in 1817-19, Designed by John Raffield for Charles Augustus Tulk MP, it was one of the great villas envisaged by John Nash in his 'jewel in the crown' plan to transform the park and surrounding area in the 1800s. Sadly, it was one of only a few villas that were actually built.

In 1892, a new garden 'fit for meditation' was designed by Robert Weir Schultz (1860-1951) for the 3rd Marquess of Bute. Schultz's design included formal areas, a fountain pond, a Doric temple, stone portico and partly sunken chapel, all reflecting Arts and Crafts ideas popular at the time, as well the revival of interest in classical themes.

The garden is completely separate from the lodge and has been open to the public since 1928, managed and maintained by the Royal Parks who look after Regent's Park. It was renovated and redesigned in 1994 by landscape architects Colvin & Moggridge to reflect the original plan and honour the 3rd Marquess of Bute. A new entrance walk was created to the east of the gatehouse and bungalow, with double gates to provide privacy for the house. The east-west scalloped hedge was replanted in yew, but the '20s flower beds were renewed due to popular demand – a variation from Schulz's original plan. The new planting established quickly, and today the gardens form an unexpected, luxuriant oasis.

As well as the planting, there's a metal arbour, reflecting the original

FOOD & DRINK

Garden Café in Regent's Park:
The original '60s park café has been refurbished and offers drinks, lunches and suppers in the lush surroundings of Queen Mary's Gardens in the Inner Circle. Open from 9am to 8pm (6pm in winter).

The Cow and Coffee Bean:
Farm-made dairy ice cream, real milk shakes, cream scones, sandwiches and treats on the Broad Walk at Chester Road.

stone portico, and a wooden covered seat, plus a number of new statues and urns. Among the fine statues are *Hylas and the Nymph* by Henry Pegram (1933), centre stage in a small round pond: a bronze of the nude Argonaut with a sensual mermaid seizing his legs to pull him to his doom. Another delightful bronze is by Charles L Hartwell (1932), depicting a semi-draped shepherdess holding a goat. Grade II listed, it was erected in honour of Harold and Gertrude Baillie Weaver by the National Council for Animal

Welfare, and the inscription reads: 'To all the Protectors of the Defenceless'.

In order to enjoy this haven of calm and beauty, you first have to find it! From the Inner Circle, proceed anti-clockwise past Chester Road on your right, and some 200yds (180m) further on you should find the (hidden) entrance gate to St John's Lodge Gardens – if you pass the lodge you've gone too far!

Shepherdess, CL Hartwell RA

8 WESTMINSTER ABBEY CLOISTERS & COLLEGE GARDEN

Address: 20 Dean's Yard, SW1P 3PA (☎ 020-7222 5152, 🖥 westminster-abbey.org).
Opening hours: Cloisters, daily, 8am to 6pm. College Garden, Tue-Thu (Apr to Sep, 10am to 6pm, Oct to Mar, 10am to 4pm).
Cost: Free.
Transport: Westminster or St James's Park tube.
Amenities: Restaurant, coffee kiosk

College Garden

The gardens surrounding Westminster Abbey are hidden, tranquil gems, in which it's still possible to imagine the great church as the haunt of monks and pilgrims, rather than busloads of tourists. They're a great place to escape the often crowded confines of the abbey – and you don't have to pay a Pope's ransom to enjoy them!

The gardens of Westminster Abbey are accessed via Dean's Yard (south of Victoria Street), a handsome square built on the site of the former monastery's farmyard. The broad lawns provide a centrepiece to the picturesque 'collegiate' architecture of Dean's Yard, in part designed by George Gilbert

Scott. It has a number of mature trees, including London planes, a red horse chestnut, a tulip tree and a sycamore.

 FOOD & DRINK

Cellarium Café and Terrace (🖥 cellariumcafe.com): Set in the monks' original larder, this historic café is open Mon-Fri, 9am to 6pm (9am to 4.30pm Sat, closed Sun). Fully licensed, it serves imaginative salads and tasty mains. Free access is provided via Dean's Yard.

There are four gardens within the Westminster Abbey complex: the three original gardens (the Great Cloister Garden or Garth, the Little

Cloister and College Garden) and St Catherine's Garden, which lies in the area of the ruined monastery and was created more recently. When open, St Catherine's Garden is approached by a door from the Little Cloister and you can see the truncated columns of the chapel which once stood here. It was an important place in the 12th and 13th centuries when bishops were consecrated here, including Hugh of Lincoln in 1186, but is now a calm and reflective place.

Each of the Abbey's gardens had a separate function: the Garth with its square of turf, bounded by Cloisters, provided the monks with somewhere to rest their eyes and minds as they walked around it, while the Little Cloister Garden – small but charming, with borders of scented plants and a fountain – was reserved for recuperation after illness (its inner arcade is thought to date from the 17th century).

> The Cloisters were the centre of monastic life, where the monks could enjoy some fresh air, sheltered from the rain and wind.

The largest and most important garden at the Abbey is the College Garden ('college' refers to the old meaning of the word: a community of clergy). A thousand years ago it was the infirmary garden of the monastery and is said to be the oldest garden in England under continuous cultivation; records refer to a special medicinal herbarium which was completed in 1306. The 'infirmarer', a senior monk, took care of sick and elderly members of the monastery, as well as administering a dispensary for local people. He directed the planting and cultivation of medicinal herbs; some of which, such as fennel and hyssop, are still grown today. While the original garden was principally an area in which to grow herbs, fruit and vegetables, it also provided convalescing monks with a place for relaxation and gentle exercise – and a final resting place, as part of the orchard was set aside as a cemetery.

The oldest surviving features visible today are the 14th-century stone precinct walls at the far end of the garden and along the left-hand side as you stand at the entrance gate, and the four weathered statues of the apostles carved in 1686 by Grinling Gibbons that were formerly in the Queen's Chapel in the Palace of Whitehall. The garden is dominated by five tall plane trees, planted in 1850; other trees of interest include quince, step-over apple trees (at the entrance) and a white mulberry near the fountain.

During July and August there are free lunchtime band concerts on Wednesdays, and children's workshops featuring drama, painting, puppet making, gardening, dressing up and music.

Westminster Abbey

9   MOUNT STREET GARDENS

Address: South Audley Street, Mayfair, W1K 3AH (☎ 020-7641 5264,
🖥 westminster.gov.uk > Parks and open spaces).
Opening hours: Daily, 8am to dusk.
Cost: Free.
Transport: Green Park or Bond Street tube.

Mount Street Gardens are a secret oasis in Mayfair and, although well frequented by locals and Americans working at the nearby US embassy, are relatively unknown. They are situated on the site of an early Georgian cemetery which served as the burial ground for St George's Hanover Square, one of the 50 New Churches commissioned for London in the early 18th century. The burial ground closed in 1854 and, like many urban cemeteries, was later converted into a public garden.

> During the Cold War it's said that Mount Street Gardens were a favourite haunt of KGB spies, who left secret notes in the slats of the benches.

The gardens were laid out in 1889 with plants, paths and a small fountain, and have changed little since, retaining their late 19th-century gate piers at the South Audley Street entrance. The bronze drinking fountain, at the east end of the gardens near the beautiful Farm Street Church, depicts a rearing horse and was designed in 1891 by Sir Ernest George (1839-1922) and Harold Peto (1854-1933).

Planting in the gardens includes mature London plane trees and a variety of smaller trees, shrubs and flower beds. The buildings which enclose the gardens create a microclimate which allows an Australian mimosa, a Canary Islands date palm and three dawn redwoods to flourish. Around 90 sponsored benches line the paths, many donated by employees of the US Embassy. One inscription reads: 'An American who did not find a park like this in New York City.'

The gardens are designated a Site of Importance for Nature Conservation and are home to a variety of bird species, depicted on a bird life interpretation panel. They were restored in 2005 through the efforts of local residents and have been awarded a Green Flag annually since 2007.

QUEEN MARY'S GARDENS   10

Address: Inner Circle, Regent's Park, NW1 4NU (☎ 0300-061 2300,
🖥 royalparks.org.uk/parks/the-regents-park).
Opening hours: Daily, 5am to sunset. Garden Café, 9am to 8pm (summer), 9am
to 6pm (winter).
Cost: Free.
Transport: Baker St or Regent's Park tube.
Attractions & amenities: Café, open-air theatre.

Queen Mary's Gardens – tucked away in the Inner Circle of Regent's Park – contain London's largest and best formal rose garden. It's a honey-pot for garden lovers (and bees) in spring and summer, when tens of thousands of plants are in bloom and the scent is intoxicating.

The gardens – named after the wife of George V – were laid out in 1932 on a site originally used as a plant nursery and later leased to the Royal Botanic Society. There are still some of the original pear trees which supplied fruit to the London market in the early 19th century.

Queen Mary's Gardens' famous rose garden contains over 400 different varieties of roses in separate and mixed beds, and a total of some 30,000 rose plants. In addition, there are around 30,000 other plants, including the national collection of delphiniums and 9,000 begonias, all set out in landscaped beds surrounded by a ring of pillars covered in climbers and ramblers. The planting was renewed by landscape architects, Colvin and Moggridge, in the '90s, and is arranged in a design which complements the circular site and adds a 'sense of mystery'.

It's a lovely garden to wander around before attending a performance at the open-air theatre, also within the Inner Circle (see **Regent's Park** on page 24 for more information). For refreshments, try the Garden Café, which serves teas, coffees, lunches and summer suppers in a modern version of the original '60s park café. It's the perfect spot to round off the perfect day.

The Inner Circle contains the beautiful Triton Fountain – at the northern end of the central walk – designed by William McMillan RA (1887-1977) and donated in 1950 in memory of the artist Sigismund Goetze (1866-1939) by his wife Constance.

11 PHOENIX GARDEN

Address: 21 Stacey Street, WC2H 8DG (✉ info@thephoenixgarden.org; 🖥 phoenixgarden.org).
Opening hours: Daily, 8.30am to dusk.
Cost: Free.
Transport: Tottenham Court Road, Leicester Square or Covent Garden tube.
Attractions & amenities: Pond, play area, volunteer opportunities.

This little oasis is the last remaining of Covent Garden's seven community gardens, and one of the West End's best kept secrets. Founded in 1984, it's maintained by volunteers and funded by donations. Tucked away behind the Phoenix Theatre – the entrance is in St Giles Passage – the award-winning garden sprang phoenix-like from the site of a row of Georgian houses which were tragically destroyed by a bomb in 1940.

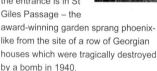

Phoenix Garden is located on the site of the old St Giles Leper Hospital (established by Queen Maud), which existed from 1117 to 1539.

The less-than-ideal urban growing conditions at the Phoenix Garden have proved no obstacle to a flourishing display of flowers, grasses, shrubs and trees, including rowan, willow, walnut and ginkgo. There's a rockery and fish pond, benches (with quirky inscriptions) and a play area – it's a living garden with a real heart and soul.

Innovation and environmentally-sound thinking go hand in hand – the retaining walls are made from recycled newspapers and the gabion dry stone wall is constructed from excavated bomb rubble. The garden is maintained using an innovative approach, with plants that grow reliably in dry conditions, look good year round and are of maximum benefit to wildlife. It's a haven for city wildlife, including five species of bee, butterflies and a variety of birds such as the blue and great tit, robin, wren, greenfinch, sparrow hawk, woodpecker and kestrel. It's also home to possibly the West End's only frogs, which inhabit its ponds along with colourful damselflies.

Phoenix Garden hosts regular community events such as an annual agricultural 'Country Show' which showcases locally grown plants and produce, Morris dancing and other traditional entertainments such as falconry displays.

PRIMROSE HILL   12

Address: Primrose Hill Road, NW3 (☎ 0300-061 2300, ⌨ royalparks.org.uk/
parks/the-regents-park or primrosehill.com).
Opening hours: Unlimited access.
Cost: Free.
Transport: Chalk Farm tube.
Attractions & amenities: Splendid views, refreshments, outdoor gym,
playground.

One of the most scenic spots in London, Primrose Hill (62 acres/25ha) is celebrated for its grassy slopes, stunning views and roll-call of famous residents. Occupying the northernmost section of Regent's Park, Primrose Hill has lent its name to the streets of Victorian terraces which surround it, which are among the most expensive and exclusive in north London, with an air of middle-class bohemian chic. In the 19th century it was a patch of rough farmland owned by the College of Eton, which became Crown property in 1841; the following year an Act of Parliament secured it as a public open space.

At 256ft (78m), Primrose Hill isn't particularly high, but elevated enough to provide wonderful views of central London to the southeast, and on a clear day you can gaze past London Zoo and its soaring aviary towards landmarks such as St Paul's Cathedral, the Gherkin, the BT Tower and the London Eye.

Primrose Hill isn't a park full of attractions. There's an outdoor gym, playground and a boules pitch in the area adjacent to Prince Albert Road, but other than that it's somewhere people come to walk dogs, fly kites, throw frisbees, picnic and relax.

The top of the hill has been exposed and treeless since the Middle Ages, but the lower slopes have mature trees including oak, horse chestnut, London planes, whitebeam and hawthorn. The park is criss-crossed with paths, benches and Victorian cast iron street lamps, which cast an atmospheric glow on murky winter evenings.

In 1678, MP and magistrate Edmund Berry Godfrey was found face down in a ditch on Primrose Hill, impaled on his own sword. He was thought to have been the victim of an anti-Catholic plot and three Catholics were executed for his murder, although they later turned out to be innocent.

13 ST JOHN'S WOOD CHURCH GROUNDS

> **Address:** Wellington Place, St John's Wood, NW8 7PF (☎ 020-7641 5271,
> 🖥 westminster.gov.uk > Parks and open spaces and stjohnswoodchurch.org.uk).
> **Opening hours:** Daily, 8am to dusk.
> **Cost:** Free.
> **Transport:** St John's Wood tube.
> **Attractions & amenities:** Nature reserve, picnic area, play areas.

The grounds of St John's Wood Church are one of London's most acclaimed gardens. They were among the first of Westminster City Council's gardens to be awarded a Green Flag and have won the award annually since 2004 – as well as being a regular winner of the London Squares and Gardens Competition in the 'Large Square Category'.

> The great and the good buried here include water-colourist John Sell Cotman (1782-1842), and Private Samuel Godley (1781-1832), who fought at the battle of Waterloo – look for markers on the west side of the grounds in the Glade. It's also the last resting place of Joanna Southcott (1750-1814), a religious fanatic who at the age of 64 persuaded her followers that she was about to give birth to the next Messiah!

St John's Wood was once part of the Great Forest of Middlesex and was owned from 1323 by the Knights of the Order of St John of Jerusalem. St John's Church, designed by Thomas Hardwick, was built in 1813, and both church and burial ground were consecrated the following year. The cemetery was used until 1855 – when there were thought to have been some 50,000 graves – and became a public garden in 1886.

The current grounds (5 acres/2ha) date from the early '50s when the gravestones were removed from the three main lawn areas. Trees include London plane, lime, white horse chestnut, Turkey oak, English oak, yew, and a tulip tree planted in memory of legendary cricket commentator Brian Johnston.

The much-admired garden is tucked between the western edge of Regent's Park and Lord's Cricket Ground, to the rear of St John's Church. The former burial ground now provides excellent facilities for the living, including formal gardens, lawns, a picnic area and a play zone. Part of it's designated a Local Nature Reserve and the whole is an oasis of calm in a busy corner of the capital.

VICTORIA EMBANKMENT GARDENS   14

Address: Victoria Embankment, WC2N 6PB (☎ 020-7641 5264, ☐ westminster.gov.uk > parks and open spaces).
Opening hours: Mon-Sat 7.30am to dusk, Sun and Bank Holidays 9am to dusk (dusk is between 4.30 and 9.30pm – see website for seasonal times).
Cost: Free.
Transport: Embankment or Temple tube.
Attractions & amenities: Lovely specimen trees, benches, sculptures, café, bandstand.

Victoria Embankment Gardens (11 acres/4.5ha) stretch along the north side of the Thames between Westminster and Blackfriars Bridge. A refuge for Londoners, they're the welcome by-product of a Victorian sanitation project. When Sir Joseph Bazalgette created London's sewerage system in the mid-19th century, he built a sewer along the river and used reclaimed land to create the Victoria Embankment and a series of gardens.

Floral cyclists

Built 1870-75 by Alexander McKenzie and George Vulliamy – a final section was added in front of the massive Ministry of Defence building in the '50s – Victoria Embankment Gardens are a delightful and varied space, lined with lawns and trees, and scattered with flower beds, monuments and memorials. They have been awarded a Green Flag annually since 2002.

Temple Gardens, adjacent to the Inns of Court, is a quiet corner shaded by plane trees and shrubs, with monuments to John Stuart Mill and Isambard Kingdom Brunel. The main section (once called the Adelphi Gardens) is noted for its outstanding displays of bedding. There's a café and a bandstand with deckchairs where concerts are held daily in summer. Statues include an elegant memorial to the Imperial Camel Corps and figures of Robert Burns (Scots poet) and Sir Arthur Sullivan (the composer who worked with Sir William Gilbert, who has a memorial near Embankment Pier).

Beyond Hungerford Bridge, Whitehall Garden returns to a formal layout of lawns and statues, but in the MoD section, just after Horse Guards Avenue, is the most fascinating relic of all: the remains of the old Whitehall Steps to the Thames, also known as 'Queen Mary Steps' – built for Mary II in 1691 by Sir Christopher Wren – together with the early 16th-century embankment wall. Discovered in 1939, these are the only remains of Whitehall Palace, the seat of Tudor monarchs.

Look out for the York House Water Gate (1626, Grade I listed), which is where the Duke of Buckingham would have alighted from his river craft in the 17th century. It's now more than 100m from the Thames.

15 VICTORIA TOWER GARDENS

Address: Millbank, SW1P 3SF (☎ 0300-061 2000, 🖳 royalparks.org.uk).
Opening hours: Daily, 7am to dusk.
Cost: Free
Transport: Westminster tube.
Amenities: Fountain, statuary.

Victoria Tower Gardens is a long strip of park in the shadow of Victoria Tower, at the south-western corner of the Palace of Westminster (Houses of Parliament). They extend south to Lambeth Bridge, sandwiched between Millbank and the Thames, and consist of a broad swathe of grass bordered by mature trees – mostly London planes – that's perfect for relaxing, reading or rehearsing a parliamentary speech (or sleeping off a heavy lunch).

Like Victoria Embankment Gardens to the north, the gardens grew out of the sewerage project masterminded by Sir Joseph Bazalgette on reclaimed land that was previously wharves and jetties. They were laid out in 1864-70 and extended around 1914.

Being so close to the heart of British politics, it's perhaps inevitable that the statues in the gardens have a political theme. The best known is a cast of Auguste Rodin's *The Burghers of Calais* (1889), installed here in 1915. It commemorates a pivotal moment during the Hundred Years' War when the French port of Calais was under siege by the English, and six of its leading citizens gave themselves up in an act of self-sacrifice to save their fellow townspeople (they were spared).

Another statue commemorates the suffragette Emmeline Pankhurst (1858-1928) who endured many spells of imprisonment to win women the right to vote (in 1918). Sculpted by A G Walker, it was erected just two years after her death.

Probably the most ornate drinking fountain in London, the Buxton Memorial Fountain is a grand Gothic confection which commemorates the emancipation of slaves in the British Empire in 1834. Commissioned by Charles Buxton MP and designed by Samuel Sanders Teulon (1812-1873) in 1865 – by coincidence, the same year that the US passed the 13th Amendment outlawing slavery – it originally stood in Parliament Square, but has been in the gardens since 1957.

Buxton Memorial Fountain & Palace of Westminster

BROWN HART GARDENS   16

Address: Brown Hart Gardens, W1K 6WP (☎ 020-7408 0988, ✉ londonweb@ grosvenor.com, 🖥 grosvenorlondon.com).
Opening hours: Undergoing renovation in 2013. Call or email to check the opening hours before visiting.
Cost: Free.
Transport: Bond Street tube.

This is one of the more unusual gardens in London: an Italian garden built above an electricity substation on the orders of a duke. Located between Duke Street and Balderton Street in Mayfair, it's a wonderful example of Edwardian Baroque and a great place to escape from the hustle of Oxford Street just to the north.

In 1902, the building of the Duke Street substation led to the removal of the communal garden which served residents of Brown Street and Hart Street. The Duke of Westminster insisted an alternative garden be provided, so when C Stanley Peach designed the new building, he included a pavilion and steps at either end leading to a 10,000ft² (929m²) paved garden above street level.

The Grade II listed structure, managed by Grosvenor Estates, is made from Portland stone and appears out of place among the red brick buildings which surround it. It's easy to see why it was once rumoured (incorrectly) to be Queen Victoria's elephant house!

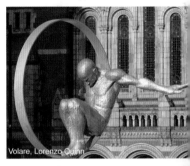
Volare, Lorenzo Quinn

BRUNEI GARDENS, SOAS   17

Address: School of Oriental and African Studies (SOAS), University of London, Thornhaugh Street, Russell Square, WC1H 0XG (☎ 020-7637 2388, 🖥 soas. ac.uk/visitors/roofgarden).
Opening hours: Tue-Sat, 10.30am to 5pm.
Cost: Free.
Transport: Russell Square or Goodge Street tube.
Attractions & amenities: Gallery, bookshop.

The Brunei Gallery at the School of Oriental and African Studies (SOAS) has a delightful roof garden which is open to visitors and students, and provides a tranquil area for study, relaxation and contemplation.

The Japanese-style garden was built during the Japan 2001 celebrations and was officially opened by its sponsor Mr Haruhisa Handa, an honorary fellow of the school, in November 2001. The garden is dedicated to forgiveness, which is the meaning of the Kanji character engraved on its granite water basin. The designer, Peter Swift, conceived the space as a place of quiet meditation, as well as a functional space for receptions and exhibitions – it also has a small stage used for musical events and tea ceremonies.

Planting includes climbing wisteria, which adds a splash of colour in spring, and lemon thyme used in a chequerboard pattern to provide texture and scent; but the main appeal of the garden is its contrasting mediums of gravel and granite, slate and sandstone, which give it a peaceful, Zen-like quality that complements its location.

18 NATURAL HISTORY MUSEUM WILDLIFE GARDEN

Address: Cromwell Road, SW7 5BD (☎ 020-7942 5011, 🖳 nhm.ac.uk/visit-us/whats-on/wildlife-garden-whatson).
Opening hours: 1st Apr to 31st Oct, 10am to 5pm, including Bank Holidays. Open at other times by appointment.
Cost: Free.
Transport: South Kensington tube.
Attractions & amenities: Museum, restaurant, café, shop.

The Natural History Museum Wildlife Garden is a real secret garden; few people know it exists and even fewer have visited it. Designed by Mark Loxton and Dennis Vickers in 1995, this 1 acre (0.4ha) space is the museum's first living exhibition, designed to show the potential for wildlife conservation in the inner city. It has a range of British lowland habitats, from fen and reed bed to heathland and woodland, and with over 2,000 plant and animal species, it has a delicacy that's rare in an urban open space.

Dragonflies, moorhens, butterflies, foxes, robins, marsh marigolds, primroses, lime, hornbeam and even grazing sheep are just some of the abundant wildlife that lives in or visits the garden. Birds include greenfinches, robins and a variety of tits, while squirrels invade the shed. The meadow attracts many insects, including the common blue butterfly and azure damselflies – there's also a Butterfly House – while tiny froglets migrate there in summer. Whatever time of the year, the garden is buzzing with life.

PADDINGTON GREEN & ST MARY'S CHURCHYARD   19

> **Address**: Harrow Road, W2 1LG (☎ 020-7641 5271, 🖥 westminster.gov.uk > Parks and open spaces).
> **Opening hours**: Daily, 8am to dusk.
> **Cost**: Free.
> **Transport**: Edgware Road tube.
> **Attractions & amenities:** Benches.

Paddington Green harks back to the days when Paddington was a fashionable village with a green, while St Mary's Churchyard is one of the many burial grounds-turned-parks for which London is famous. Together, they provided a calm green antidote to the traffic thundering past on Harrow Road and the Westway.

Paddington Green is the oldest part of Paddington and became a separate conservation area in 1988; it was once surrounded by large Georgian houses, of which only two remain. (The Schmidt Hammer Lassen-designed City of Westminster College now dominates one corner of the Green.) St Mary's was built in 1791 by John Plaw and its graveyard was converted into a public park in the late 1890s. Like the Green, it consists mainly of open lawns with scattered trees, including a fine weeping ash.

Points of interest include a white marble statue by Chevaliand of the actress Sarah Siddons (1755-1831), who lived in nearby Westbourne Grove and is buried in the churchyard. There are also monuments to sculptor Joseph Nollekens and lexicographer Peter Mark Roget (of *Roget's Thesaurus* fame).

PADDINGTON RECREATION GROUND   20

> **Address:** Randolph Avenue, Maida Vale, W9 1PD (☎ 020-7641 3642, 🖥 better.org.uk/leisure/paddington-recreation-ground).
> **Opening hours**: Daily, 7am to dusk.
> **Cost**: Free.
> **Transport**: Maida Vale tube.
> **Attractions & amenities:** Gardens, café, gymnasium, playground, bandstand, comprehensive sports facilities.

Despite its name and host of sports facilities, Paddington Recreation Ground is much more than simply a sports ground and offers something for everyone.

Westminster's largest park occupies a beautiful 27-acre (11ha) site in Maida Vale which has provided the local community with recreational facilities since 1860.

The landscaping in the southern part includes modern shrub borders to the circuit path and a large hedged rose garden in the southern angle created in memory of Boy Scouts 1939-45. The landscape in the north is dominated by all-weather surfaces and is separated from the southern part by a row of mature London plane trees.

The park's sport facilities include a gym, floodlit tennis courts, hockey and soccer pitches, a village green for cricket matches and a lawn bowls green in the summer months, while the outdoor gym and fitness trail allows work outs in the fresh air. There's also a basketball court and a new athletics track, plus a playground, bandstand and a café.

21   PADDINGTON STREET GARDENS

Address: Paddington Street, Marylebone, W1U 5QA (☎ 020-7641 5271, 🖥 westminster.gov.uk > Parks and open spaces).
Opening hours: Daily, 7am to dusk.
Cost: Free.
Transport: Baker Street tube.
Amenities: Playground, deckchairs, concerts.

Divided in two by Paddington Street, these Green Flag gardens make up the archetypal city park, providing a haven in heavily populated Marylebone. Most of the action takes place in the larger garden to the south, where in summer you can hire a deckchair and enjoy a concert, while a playground caters to younger users. As well as the ubiquitous London plane, there are many species of tree, including cherry, laburnum, hawthorn and a monkey puzzle, as well as shrubs, roses and seasonal bedding. The smaller, north garden provides a quieter space.

During the 18th century, Paddington Street Gardens were a burial ground for the old St Marylebone Parish Church (1733) and the site of the St Marylebone Workhouse. They didn't become a place of recreation until 1885. Most of the tombstones have been removed but the mausoleum of Susanna Fitzpatrick (who died in 1759, aged just 30) was left because of its fine design. A popular statue is that of the orderly boy (or street cleaner) by Milanese sculptor Donato Baraglia, installed in 1943.

ST ANNE'S CHURCHYARD 22

Address: Wardour Street, W1 (☎ 020-7641 5264, 🖥 westminster.gov.uk > Parks and open spaces).
Opening hours: Daily, 10am to dusk.
Cost: Free.
Transport: Piccadilly or Leicester Square tube.
Attractions & amenities: Art, children's toilet, no wheelchair access.

Once an overcrowded graveyard, this pocket park provides the perfect spot to escape the busy streets of Soho. A public garden since 1892 (and a Green Flag winner since 2007), it's well used by local residents and pupils from Soho School (who grow vegetables there). As well as a broad sweep of lawn, shrubs and seasonal bedding, it has 11 venerable London plane trees and a handsome line of espaliered limes. There's also a small 'toilet pod' which doubles as a mini museum.

The original church and churchyard date from 1686 and over time the churchyard was raised 6ft (1.8m) above street level to accommodate over 13,000 parishioners who were buried here. They include essayist William Hazlitt (1778-1830) and Theodore, King of Corsica (1694-1756), who is commemorated by a plaque on the tower. The early 19th-century Grade II* listed tower is all the remains of the older St Anne's, which took a direct hit during the London Blitz.

SPENCER HOUSE GARDEN 23

Address: 27 St James's Place, SW1A 1NR (☎ 020-7514 1958 or 020-7499 8620, 🖥 spencerhouse.co.uk).
Opening hours: Tours of Spencer House (1 hr) on Sun (except Jan and Aug), 10.30am to 5.45pm, by timed ticket, which can only be purchased in person from 10.30am. Occasional tours of the garden – phone or check website for details.
Cost: House: £12 adults, £10 concessions (students, seniors and under 16s). Children aged under ten aren't admitted.
Transport: Green Park tube.
Attractions & amenities: Mansion house tour.

Spencer House is one of London's finest examples of a Palladian mansion, a glorious palace overlooking Green Park. Built in 1756-66 for the Spencer family – ancestors of the late Princess Diana – it's a splendid example of 18th-century aristocratic taste.

Its garden is just as extravagant. Originally designed by Henry Holland for the second Earl Spencer in the 1790s, possibly in collaboration with

Lavinia, Countess Spencer, it was planted by July 1798 at the then vast cost of £1,500, and was one of the largest gardens in Piccadilly. Plans from 1799 reveal a design of long narrow shrubberies on three sides and a lawn containing a central oval path defining seven round beds.

In 1990, a ten-year restoration programme to return Spencer House to its original splendour was undertaken by RIT Capital Partners under the chairmanship of Lord Rothschild. This included the garden, which was reinstated with paths, lawn and perimeter beds using plants and shrubs appropriate to the late 18th and early 19th centuries.

The garden is open to the public on specific days during spring and summer and can be seen as part of a house tour.

24 GARDEN SQUARES

London is famous for its garden squares, which once provided outside space for the wealthy residents of townhouses, and now offer respite to workers and tourists. All the following squares are open to the public (times shown below) and have wheelchair access.

A: Berkeley Square Gardens (W1, 8am to dusk, Green Park tube) is a formal garden square laid out in the mid-18th century by the architect William Kent (1685-1748), designer of Devonshire House which once stood at the southern end of the square. It's an open, grassy rectangle which boasts some of Mayfair's oldest plane trees – planted in 1789 – as well as some interesting statues. Look out for Alexander Munro's elegant Fountain Nymph (1867, Grade II listed), in marked contrast to Lynn Chadwick's angular cast of a seated couple (1989). Famous ex-residents include the young Winston Churchill, Robert Clive of India and PG Wodehouse's fictional characters, Jeeves and Wooster.

B: Bessborough Gardens (SW1, 8am to dusk, Pimlico tube) provide a quiet refuge just off Vauxhall Bridge Road with planted borders and a central lawn, screened from the traffic by mature trees. The gardens were laid out in the 1840s as part of a development by builder Thomas Cubitt, but the houses which now border two sides of the gardens are a modern pastiche of the stucco originals, which were demolished in the '80s. The centrepiece is the Queen Mother's Commemorative Fountain by Sir Peter Shepheard (1913-2002), which incorporates a cast of one of George Vulliamy's dolphin lamp standard bases from the Embankment.

C: Cavendish Square Gardens (W1, 8am to dusk, Oxford Circus tube) to the north of bustling Oxford Street is a quiet oasis of mature trees, shrubs and flower beds enclosed by a perimeter hedge. Originally a sheep meadow, it was developed into a garden by Charles Bridgeman in

Cavendish Square gardens

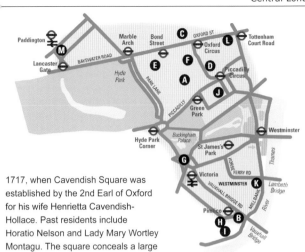

1717, when Cavendish Square was established by the 2nd Earl of Oxford for his wife Henrietta Cavendish-Hollace. Past residents include Horatio Nelson and Lady Mary Wortley Montagu. The square conceals a large underground car park and features a raised grassy mound enjoyed by sun worshippers.

D: Golden Square Garden (W1, 8am to dusk, Piccadilly Circus tube) is tucked away in Soho, close to Regent Street, and dates back to the 1670s when it's thought to have been planned by Sir Christopher Wren. The garden has been remodelled several times, most recently in the '50s, and consists of bedding displays and shrub planting with perimeter rose beds and grass verges, and four mature Hornbeam trees marking the east and west entrances. At the centre is one of only two statues of George II in London. Grade II listed, it's by John Nost the Elder and dates from around 1720, when it was fashioned for the Duke of Chandos. Interesting modern sculptures are also often displayed.

E: Grosvenor Square Garden (W1, 8am to dusk, Bond Street tube) in Mayfair is virtually a park, set within the second-largest square in London. It's dominated by Eero Saarinen's monolithic US Embassy building, and has a wide sweep of lawns, mature trees, plus some significant statues and memorials. A key feature is a statue of President Roosevelt by Sir William Reid Dick (1948, Grade II listed) and there are also statues of Eisenhower and Ronald Reagan. The square was licensed for development by Sir Richard Grosvenor in 1710 and became a highly desirable place to live. It was opened to the public in 1948 following a redesign, which saw its evergreens replaced by London planes and cherry trees.

👁 DON'T MISS!

Grosvenor Square Garden

The memorial to Britons who died in the September 11 attacks on the World Trade Centre and Pentagon in 2001. Consisting of a small garden enclosing a pavilion and pergola inscribed with the names of the victims and the words 'Grief is the price we pay for love', it features plants which are at their best in September.

F: Hanover Square Garden (W1, 8am to dusk, Oxford Circus tube) is one of the oldest garden squares in London, set in Mayfair just south of Oxford Street. The square was laid out in 1717 and named after the new king, George I, who was the Elector of Hanover. The design has changed with the fashions over three centuries and now features diagonal pathways, a pond with a fountain and an elegant bronze of William Pitt the Younger by Sir Francis Legatt Chantrey (1781-1841), which famously survived an attempt by Reform Bill agitators to pull it down at its unveiling in 1831.

G: Lower & Upper Grosvenor Gardens (SW1, Upper Gardens 8am to dusk, Lower Gardens 10am to dusk, Victoria tube/rail) are a pair of triangular gardens near Victoria Station with ornamental bedding and shrubs, a swathe of lawn and some interesting monuments. The more southerly lower garden was remodelled in 1952 as a memorial to Anglo-French understanding, with a central bed in the form of a *fleur-de-lys*, topiary and two lodges studded with shells and molluscs imported from France. An equestrian statue of First World War hero Marshall Foch stands at the entrance. Upper Grosvenor Garden opened to the public for the first time in 2000 and features a stunning life-size sculpture of a lioness chasing a kudu by Jonathan Kenworthy.

H: St George's Square Gardens (SW1, 8am to dusk, Pimlico tube) date from 1839 and were designed by master builder Thomas Cubitt, whose elegant stucco houses define the image of Pimlico. The square was a highly desirable place to live, as it was London's only residential square open on one side to the River Thames, and until 1874 had its own pier for boats and steamers. The gardens retain their formal 19th-century character with barley sugar edging to paths and shrubberies, and an ornamental fountain in the centre surrounded by flower beds. Mature trees line the perimeter and, at the north end, the church of St Saviour (1864) shelters the square from busy Lupus Street.

I: Pimlico Garden

At the southern end of St George's Square is Pimlico Garden, overlooking the Thames. It has a stone statue depicting William Huskisson, a 19th-century MP who has the unfortunate distinction of being the first person to be run over and killed by a railway engine – George Stephenson's locomotive engine Rocket, no less – in 1830.

Lioness chasing a Lesser Kudu, Jonathan Kenworth (Upper Grosvenor Gardens)

J: St James's Square (SW1, Mon to Fri 10am to 4.30pm, Green Park tube) is the only garden square in the exclusive St James's district. It was first enclosed in the 1660s and has undergone several designs, notably by Charles Bridgeman in the 18th century. The Grade I listed equestrian statue of William III by John Bacon (1777-1859) was added in 1807. The privately-owned square was gradually opened to the public from 1933 and retains an air of exclusivity, ringed by mature trees and iron railings. At the northernmost corner there's a memorial to WPC Yvonne Fletcher, shot during the 1984 Libyan Embassy Siege.

K: St John's Gardens (SW1, 8am to dusk, St James's Park tube) off Horseferry Road is a tranquil spot with a gruesome history. It was once a burial ground for St John's Smith Square and had a reputation for being the cheapest place in London to inter a body; it became one of the capital's most overcrowded cemeteries and a magnet for body snatchers. Closed to burials in 1853, it re-opened as a public garden in 1885, and is an attractive, shady spot with some interesting trees – gingko, specimen maple and London plane – and a central fountain. Many old gravestones are stacked against the perimeter of the garden and a few striking monuments have been left as features.

L: Soho Square Garden (W1, 8am to dusk, Tottenham Court Road tube) was laid out in the late 17th century and was originally called King's Square, after Charles II whose statue (1681, Caius Gabriel Cibber) stands at the centre. The garden was first opened to the public in 1954 and is one of the busiest in Westminster. It won its first Green Flag award in 2011 and during the summer hosts free, open-air concerts.

Soho Square Garden

An unusual attraction is the Grade II listed two-storey, half-timbered 'gardener's hut' – part tool-shed, part arbour – which has been described as 'an octagonal market cross building in the Tudorbethan style'.

M: Talbot Square Gardens (W2, 8am to dusk, Lancaster Gate or Paddington tube) is a small but delightful London square bordering Sussex Gardens, south of Paddington Station, which was opened to the public in 1996. Fully refurbished in 2009, it's dominated by two magnificent London planes, one at each end, while its focal point is a weeping ash with a circular bench around it.

Talbot Square Gardens

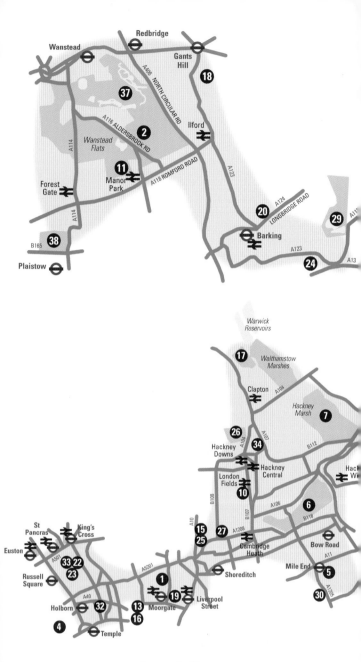

See overleaf for more maps

CHAPTER 2

CITY & EAST LONDON

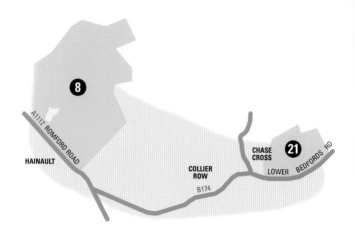

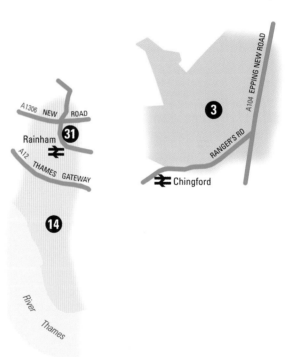

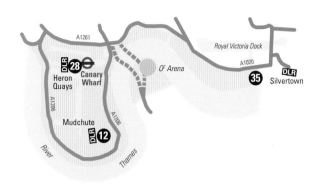

A1261
DLR 28 ⊖ Canary Wharf
Heron Quays
A1206
Mudchute
A1206
DLR 12
River
Thames

Royal Victoria Dock
A1020
35 DLR Silvertown
O² Arena

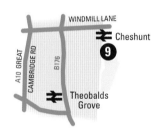

WINDMILL LANE
A10 GREAT CAMBRIDGE RD
B176
⇌ Cheshunt
9
⇌ Theobalds Grove

Chadwell Heath ⇌
A1083 GREEN LANE
36
A124 WOOD LANE

See previous page for key and more maps

1 BUNHILL FIELDS

Address: 38 City Road, EC1Y 1AU (☎ 020-7374 4127, 🖥 cityoflondon.gov.uk/things-to-do/green-spaces/city-gardens).
Opening hours: Oct-Mar, weekdays 7.30am to 4pm; weekends and Bank Holidays, 9.30am to 4pm. Apr-Sep, weekdays 7.30am to 7pm; weekends and Bank Holidays, 9.30am to 7pm. Guided walks 12.30pm on Wed, Apr-Oct.
Cost: Free. Guided walks £5.
Transport: Old Street tube.

Bunhill Fields (3.7 acres/1.5ha) is a tranquil, verdant cemetery in Islington, which is intriguingly in stark contrast with the busy roads and modern office blocks that surround it. A site of some historical and religious significance, Bunhill Fields has recently been granted Grade I listed status, while many of its monuments are Grade II listed.

The name comes from 'Bone Hill' and the area was associated with burials from Saxon times, perhaps much earlier. It was never consecrated ground and was therefore used for centuries to bury non-conformists (those who refused to conform to the rules of the established church), dissenters and others who weren't acceptable to or part of the Church of England.

NEAR BY LIE THE REMAINS OF
THE POET-PAINTER
WILLIAM BLAKE
1757 — 1827
AND OF HIS WIFE
CATHERINE SOPHIA

🔍 HIDDEN CORNER

Just west of Bunhill Fields in Banner Street are the remains of another unusual cemetery. Bunhill Quaker Gardens occupy a small fragment of a Quaker burial ground that was the first freehold property owned in London by the Quakers or Society of Friends. It was purchased in 1661 and used until 1855 – some 12,000 Friends were buried here, including the Society's founder George Fox (1624-1691). Now a public garden, presided over by a giant old plane tree, it receives visitors from over the world.

The site was part of the ancient manor of Finsbury, dating from 1104.

It was enclosed by the Corporation of London in 1665 as a burial ground for plague victims and was in use until 1854, by which time, like many London graveyards, it was full to overflowing – estimates suggest there were some 120,000 bodies piled on top of each other in graves, with the uppermost covered by just a few inches of soil!

Many of the 2,500 plus graves are packed closely together, giving a good idea of how inner London cemeteries used to look (as opposed to the more spacious ones created in the suburbs). Many of the old monuments remain, the earliest still visible dating from 1666. Of particular note are monuments to John Bunyan, author of *The Pilgrim's*

Tomb of John Bunyan

Progress, and Dr Isaac Watts, whose hymns are popular worldwide.

Other famous interments include William Blake, painter, poet and mystic; Daniel Defoe, author of *Robinson Crusoe*; Eleanor Coade, inventor of the artificial 'Coade' Stone; Susanna Wesley, mother of John Wesley, founder of Methodism; and various relatives of Oliver Cromwell.

 FOOD & DRINK

Shoreditch Grind: Coffee house by day, cocktail bar by night, with a tempting food menu, this café at 213 Old Street is one of a number of excellent coffee stops in the area.

Picnic: Bunhill Fields is a serene setting in which to eat your cheese & pickle sandwiches.

In 1868 the cemetery was converted into public gardens with new walls, paths and trees – described by Augustus Hare in 1878 as 'a green oasis in one of the blackest parts of London' – further restoration took place after the Second World War. Today, Bunhill Fields covers 10 acres (4ha), around half of which is parkland, and provides a refuge for nature in a built-up part of the City. There are around 130 trees, including Norway maple, sycamore, chestnut, lime, oak, fig and mulberry, as well as the ubiquitous London planes. It's worth visiting in spring when snowdrops, crocuses, daffodils and hyacinths provide swathes of scent and colour.

2 CITY OF LONDON CEMETERY

Address: Aldersbrook Road, Manor Park, E12 5DQ (☎ 020-8530 2151, 🖥 cityoflondon.gov.uk/things-to-do/green-spaces/cemetery-and-crematorium).
Opening hours: Daily: winter, 9am to 5pm (Christmas and Boxing Day, 3pm); summer, weekdays, 9am to 7pm, weekends, 9am to 5pm. Walking tours, 10am to noon on selected days in spring and summer (telephone to check dates). No dogs allowed.
Cost: Free.
Transport: Manor Park railway or East Ham or Wanstead tube and 101 bus.
Attractions & amenities: Crematorium, columbarium, formal gardens, nature area, tea room, wheelchairs and mobility scooters for hire.

The City of London Cemetery and Crematorium (Grade I listed) is probably London's most beautiful cemetery, owned and managed by the City of London Corporation. Once part of Epping Forest, it was purchased by the City's Commissioners of Sewers and designed by William Haywood (1821-1894 – his ashes are housed in a monument near his magnificent entrance gates). Opened in 1856, the 200-acre (81ha) site blends picturesque parkland with beautiful formal gardens, tree-lined avenues, striking monuments and an interesting local heritage.

The cemetery is one of the largest municipal cemeteries in Europe – at least 500,000 people have been interred here – and is non-denominational, so that anyone can be buried here irrespective of faith. Several chapels remain, including the Anglican chapel with its 61ft (19m) spire and an unusual round Dissenter's chapel designed by Haywood. The original crematorium opened in 1904 and was one of the first to be built in Britain. It's now a chapel – a 'new' crematorium has been in use since 1971 – and there's also a columbarium with niches for the storage of cremated remains. The cemetery was one of only a few in London to contain catacombs, although they proved unpopular and were partly converted into columbarium space.

By the mid-19th century, there were almost 90 churches crammed into the City's Square Mile, many of which were demolished under radical Victorian building schemes. The remains of people interred in the churchyards were transferred to the City of London Cemetery – from churches as diverse as St Mary Aldermanbury, St Dionis Backchurch and St Mary Somerset – as were those from churches destroyed as a result of bombing during the Blitz.

As well as its architectural heritage, the cemetery is rich in ecology, geology, horticulture and history, and was the first to be awarded the prestigious Green Flag award in 2000. It contains over 3,500 trees, a woodland area, shrubberies – the rhododendrons are magnificent in late spring – water features, ponds and a nature area, which is home to a wide variety of birds, insects and mammals (including squirrels, terrapins, frogs, bats, hedgehogs and moles). In 1937, a garden of rest was created, followed by a series of glorious memorial gardens, which now extend to 32 acres (13ha) containing some 20,000 rose bushes.

There are an estimated 150,000 gravesites and it's easy to while away a day exploring the graves of well-known 'residents'. These include Elizabeth Ann Everest, nanny to Winston Churchill; philosopher and inventor Sir Robert Hooke; actress Dame Anna Neagle; two Lord Mayors of London; and George Binks, the inventor of wire ropes. Two of the most poignant graves belong to victims of Jack the Ripper – Mary Ann Nichols and Catherine Eddowes.

 HIDDEN CORNER

One of the best ways to explore the lesser-known corners of the cemetery is on a walking tour (see Info Box). Highlights include a glimpse of 150 years of the Burial and Cremation registers; insights into striking mausoleums and memorials; famous tombs and graves; exploration of some of the Grade II listed chapels and catacombs; and fascinating stories of the siege of Sidney Street and of Edith Thompson, who was one of the last women hanged in the 20th century. She was found guilty of the murder of her husband Percy, who's also buried here (but not in a shared grave!).

3 EPPING FOREST

Address: Rangers Road, Chingford, E4 7QH (☎ 020-7332 1911, 💻 cityoflondon.gov.uk > Green spaces).

Opening hours: Unrestricted access (mostly). The main visitor centre (address above), daily, 10am to 5pm.

Cost: Free.

Transport: Epping or Loughton tube to the north, Leytonstone, Snaresbrook or Wanstead tube to the south,

Attractions & amenities: Restaurant, refreshments, visitor centres, some easy access tracks for wheelchair users.

Epping Forest comprises a long chain of woodland, grass and heathland, stretching 12 miles (19km) from Epping in Essex to Manor Park in East London via Chingford, Loughton, Woodford and Wanstead (including Wanstead Flats). It covers over 6,000 acres (2,400ha), making it the capital's largest green space, and is a surviving remnant of the ancient woodland which cloaked much of Britain in Neolithic times.

In the 12th century, Epping – then ten times the size it is today – was made a royal forest, meaning that commoners could graze livestock and gather wood, but only the king could

Adjacent to Epping Forest Gateway, Queen Elizabeth I's Hunting Lodge is a rare example of a 'hunt standing' still surrounded by its medieval forest. It was built for Henry VIII in 1543 and intended as a grandstand from which guests could view the royal hunt and even shoot deer with crossbows from the upper floors! It was renovated in 1589 for Elizabeth I and now hosts displays revealing how the Tudors ate, dressed and entertained.

hunt deer. From the 17th century onwards the forest was in danger of being carved up by landowners into enclosures, but protests lead to an Act of

Parliament in 1878 which placed it in the care of the City of London Corporation and preserved it in perpetuity for the enjoyment of all. When Queen Victoria visited in 1882 she dubbed it the 'People's Forest', and it has remained so to this day.

Even though it's crisscrossed by major roads, Epping Forest still feels like a secret place. Now designated a Site of Special Scientific Interest, its venerable age and range of habitats make it a haven for everything from insects and fungi to birds and animals, including fallow and Muntjac deer. Major tree and shrub species include oak, beech and hornbeam, silver birch and holly, butcher's-broom and drooping sedge.

One interesting aspect of the forest is its density of tree cover. The trees haven't been pollarded (pruned) since the 1870s and have formed thick branches which, in places, cut out the light; strolling here it's easy to imagine how the early hunter gatherers must have felt walking through one of the ancient forests of Europe.

The forest also consists of wide swathes of grass and heathland, now grazed by English Longhorn cattle to keep the trees from encroaching into the open spaces. There are over 100 ponds, although few are natural: most originated as cattle ponds, through land drainage, or as a result of wartime rockets and bombs!

There are several 'gateways' to the forest, offering information, guides, refreshments and facilities. The newest is in Chingford, also called the View, and there are centres at High Beach and in **Wanstead Park** (see page 98).

Epping Forest is popular with walkers, mountain bikers, cyclists and horse riders, among others. There are several designated walking trails (see website) and walks are organised by the City of London and the Friends of Epping Forest (friendsofeppingforest.org.uk). An important event for ramblers is the traditional Epping Forest Centenary Walk (third Sunday in September), which commemorates the preservation of the forest as a public space.

FOOD & DRINK

Butler's Retreat: This refurbished 19th-century barn in Chingford is the last remaining working 'retreat' for visitors to the forest. Open from 9am to 5pm on weekdays and 8am to 5pm at weekends, it has a wide-ranging menu, include mezze and tapas, and hosts hog roasts in summer.

High Beach tea huts and the **kiosk in Wanstead Park** offer drinks and snacks to augment picnics, and there are also some excellent pubs.

4 INNER & MIDDLE TEMPLE GARDENS

Address: Inner Temple, EC4Y 7HL (☎ 020-7797 8243, 💻 innertemple.org.uk > About > The Inner Temple Garden) and Middle Temple Lane, EC4Y 9AT (☎ 020-7427 4820, 💻 middletemplehall.org.uk/gardens.html).
Opening hours: Summer (Easter to Sep), 12.30 to 3pm and on special 'open' days (see website or call to confirm).
Cost: Free.
Transport: Temple tube.
Attractions & amenities: Middle Temple Hall, Temple Church, restaurant.

You don't need to be a member of the legal professional to enjoy the glorious gardens of the Inner and Middle Temple, two of the City's famous Inns of Court. Overlooking the River Thames, these gardens with their sweeping lawns, lavish floral displays and elegant courtyards, are thought to date back to the 12th century when the Knights Templar first arrived, although they've been reworked and enlarged over the last 900 years.

One of Britain's best-loved flower shows has its roots at the Inner Temple. The garden was the venue for the Royal Horticultural Society's Great Spring Show from 1888 to 1911 until, following the event's increasing popularity, and complaints by some of the resident lawyers, it was moved to the Royal Hospital Chelsea – now better known as the Chelsea Flower Show – where it remains to this day.

The Inner and Middle Temple have been leased to law students since the 13th century and are now mainly occupied by barristers' offices, although they're also home to the grand Temple Church (dating from 1185) and Middle Temple Hall, built between 1562 and 1573 and probably the finest example of an Elizabethan hall in the UK. Although the Temples have operated independently since the mid-15th century, the gardens still complement one another.

The Great Garden of the Inner Temple has extensive lawns with scattered trees, including catalpa, ailanthus, thorn, flowering cherry, sorbus, cedar, magnolia and gingko. Fruit trees, recalling the medieval orchards once planted here, include a black mulberry, fruiting walnut and medlar. Seasonal planting ensures that the borders are a riot of colour from spring to autumn, and there's also a peony garden and a woodland garden, as well as an area of Mediterranean planting.

The Temple is particularly well known for its roses, which are said to have inspired Shakespeare – he used it as the setting for the meeting between Richard Plantagenet and John

Beaufort, which sparked the Wars of the Roses in *Henry VI Part I*.

The Middle Temple Garden still looks much as it did in the 1870s when Victoria Embankment was created, doubling the garden's size. In the southern half of the lawn is a circular flower bed with a sundial from 1719 at its centre, and a statue of a boy holding a book, erected in 1930 in memory of the children's author Charles Lamb (1775-1834). The northern part of the garden (below Middle Temple Hall) has terraced bedding displays – look for a small bed containing the Roses of York and Lancaster.

Middle Temple has a number of courtyards, including Elm Court, Brick Court and Fountain Court. The latter reputedly has the oldest permanent fountain in London (1681) and is where Ruth Pinch met John Westlock in Dickens' *Martin Chuzzlewit*.

Both gardens attract plenty of wildlife, from bees and butterflies in the borders, to nesting birds such as robins, coal tits and blue tits. A sparrowhawk occasionally visits from its eyrie in the Oxo Tower over the river, and a heron often perches beside the pond.

 FOOD & DRINK

Middle Temple Hall: You can enjoy lunch in this magnificent building, which has a double hammer beam roof carved from the oaks of Windsor Forest, and a 29ft (8.8m) bench table believed to have been a gift from Elizabeth I. Open weekdays between 12.30 and 2pm, the menu features an extensive cold table, a selection of hot dishes and a carvery (bookings, ☎ 020-7427 4820, ✉ events@ middletemple.org.uk).

5 TOWER HAMLETS CEMETERY PARK

Address: Southern Grove, E3 4PX (☎ 07904-186 981, weekdays only,
🖳 towerhamletscemetery.org).
Opening hours: Daily, 8am to dusk. Guided tours (2 hours) at 2pm on the third
Sun of most months.
Cost: Free.
Transport: Mile End or Bow Road tube.
Attractions & amenities: Nature reserve.

public graves, i.e. communal graves for those who couldn't afford a funeral and their own plot.

> Public graves were an efficient if unsentimental way of disposing of 'paupers'. People entirely unrelated to each other would be buried in the same grave within the space of a few weeks, and there were stories of graves 40 feet (12m) deep containing up to 30 bodies!

Tower Hamlets Cemetery Park (known locally as Bow Cemetery) is a historic 19th-century burial ground which was transformed into a public park in 1990. It sits in the shadow of high-rise blocks just south of Mile End Road in one of the most deprived boroughs in London; yet behind its high brick walls is an unexpected woodland idyll where wildlife thrives among the old headstones.

Opened in 1841, Tower Hamlets (27 acres/11ha) was the last of the 'Magnificent Seven' cemeteries created in the 1830s and 1840s to solve London's chronic shortage of burial grounds; these included the famous cemeteries at Highgate and Kensal Green, as well as Abney Park, Brompton, Nunhead and West Norwood. Popular with East End folk, it was by far the most working class of the seven cemeteries: by the 1880s, some 80 per cent of burials were in

However, not everyone buried here was a pauper. Explore the park and you'll find memorials to politician Will Crooks (1852-1921), MP for Poplar and Woolwich; singer Alexander Hurley (1871-1913) who was married to music hall star Marie Lloyd; and John 'White Hat' Willis, the original owner of the Cutty Sark.

By the late 19th century, almost 250,000 burials had taken place, but the cemetery was sadly neglected in the early part of the 20th century and suffered further damage during the Blitz. It was eventually purchased by the Greater London Council in 1966 and closed for burials. Two decades later, ownership passed to the borough of Tower Hamlets, and in 1990 the Friends of the Tower Hamlets Cemetery Park were created. The cemetery became Tower Hamlets' first local nature reserve in 2001, and is managed and maintained by the Friends who organise walks and other

 FOOD & DRINK

Burdett Road: West of the Cemetery Park and facing Mile End Park, Burdett Road has a selection of cafés and takeaways, including a Lebanese restaurant, and plenty of shops where you can buy the basics for a picnic.

activities (and are always keen to recruit new volunteers!).

The park is largely mature woodland and meadow, with an outstanding variety of wild plants, flowers and animals. The years of neglect encouraged great ecological diversity; over 100 species of birds have been recorded as well as pipistrelle bats, rare butterflies and foxes. Parts of the park are managed wilderness, while others, particularly the two pond areas, are used as an outdoor classroom for local school children.

The high brick walls surrounding the cemetery are Grade II listed, as are 16 individual grave memorials – there are some fascinating memorial stones,

particularly of angels. Today, the park is a wonderful, if slightly spooky, green space, and has been designated a conservation area, a Local Nature Reserve and a site of Metropolitan Importance for Nature Conservation.

6   VICTORIA PARK

Address: Grove Road, Bow, E3 5SN (☎ 020-7364 2494, 🖥 towerhamlets.gov.
uk > Parks).
Opening hours: Daily, 7am to dusk.
Cost: Free.
Transport: Mile End tube.
Attractions & amenities: Lake, café, animal park, sports and fitness facilities,
playgrounds, designated walks.

©AdamBishop

Victoria Park – known colloquially as 'Vicky Park' – is a beautiful space covering 218 acres (86ha) bordering parts of Bethnal Green, Hackney and Bow (situated entirely within the borough of Tower Hamlets, which manages the park). Today it's a key link in a green corridor stretching from the Thames at Limehouse, along the Regents Canal and through Mile End Park.

Opened in 1845, Victoria Park is the oldest public park (Grade II listed) in Britain built specifically for the public – hence its nickname of the People's Park. It remains at the heart of East London life and has long been a centre for political meetings and rallies. It once had several Speakers' Corners, hosting socialist soapbox stars such

as William Morris and Annie Besant. It later became the venue for politically-oriented rock concerts, including those staged by Rock Against Racism and the Anti-Nazi League in the '70s and '80s.

 FOOD & DRINK

The Pavilion Café: Situated in the domed pavilion on the lake near Crown Gate West, and serving excellent all-day breakfasts, the Pavilion is rated one of London's best park cafés by *Time Out* magazine. Open daily from 8am to 5pm in summer and from 8.30am to 4pm in winter.

The need for a park in the East End of London became apparent when

Drinking fountain

the oldest model boat club in the world – as well as sponsored activities, festivals and concerts throughout the year. It's great for children and has herds of deer and goats, a programme of summer events, plus play parks and a paddling pool.

In 2011 the park underwent a £12m refurbishment, including the creation of a Chinese pagoda in the West Lake, a new community facility, and two new play areas. It's regularly voted London's favourite park and in 2012 won the People's Choice award for London's most popular Green Flag open space.

The park contains a number of unusual features, including a pair of stone alcoves from the old London Bridge (demolished in 1831), Grade II listed, which once provided protection for pedestrians crossing the bridge and now serve as historic and elegant park 'benches'. There's also an elaborate drinking fountain erected in 1862 by Baroness Angela Burdett Coutts (1814-1906). A major philanthropist, she was disinherited by her family for running off with (and marrying) her 29-year-old American secretary at the age of 67!

the population grew rapidly in the early 19th century due to the development of the docks and industry. This resulted in overcrowded housing, leading to poor health and low life expectancy. The first official acknowledgment of the situation came in the 1839 annual report of the Registrar General of Births, Deaths and Marriages, which showed a mortality rate far higher than in the rest of London.

Victoria Park was designed by James Pennethorne, a student of John Nash, and is a stunning example of a formal London park, reminiscent of Nash's Regent's Park. Although created as a place for people to breathe clean air, it also became a centre of horticultural excellence and still boasts some delightful open parkland, wide carriageways, lakes, leisure gardens and ornate bridges over canals. A Green Flag park since 2011, it contains a wide variety of shrubs and trees, including copper beech and tulip, which can be explored on one of three 'tree walks' (see website).

It's also an important leisure hub for local people and hosts a wide range of formal and informal sports – including soccer, cricket, athletics, fishing, and

7 HACKNEY MARSHES

Address: Homerton Road, E9 5PF (☎ 020- 8986 7955, 🖳 hackney.gov.uk/hackney-marshes.htm).
Opening hours: Unrestricted access.
Cost: Free.
Transport: Hackney Wick or Homerton rail, or Leyton tube.
Attractions & amenities: Café, sports facilities, partial wheelchair access.

A wide-open tract of grassland encircled by the Old River Lea and the Hackney Cut, Hackney Marshes is a favourite spot for walkers, cyclists and, especially, amateur footballers. This is the spiritual home of Sunday league football, with over 70 matches played weekly by local league teams.

Covering 337 acres (136ha), the Marshes were once true marshland, regularly flooded by the waters of the Lea, but were drained from medieval times. They were preserved for public use in 1890, and although some land has been lost to housing and other developments (and more recently to the Olympic Park), they provide an essential space for recreation, boasting over 80 soccer, rugby and cricket pitches. A multi-million pound development plan implemented prior to the 2012 Games led to improved pitches, footpaths, cycle ways and community facilities

The Marshes are also an important area for nature and ecology, with a bird hide and tree nursery, and received a Green Flag in 2011. Just below Lea Bridge Road, a nature reserve occupies the former Middlesex Filter beds, while to the south is Wick Woodland, planted in the '90s with ash and native black poplar trees. Hackney Marshes User Group has some excellent maps, as well as self-guided walks, on their website (🖳 sustainablehackney.org.uk/hmug).

Opened in 2010, the Hackney Marshes Centre provides education and meeting rooms, changing facilities, and has a café/bar with a viewing terrace.

> Hackney Marshes had a dubious reputation in the 18th century when it was reputedly home to a number of 'low public houses' which attracted criminals, including infamous highwayman Dick Turpin.

HAINAULT FOREST COUNTRY PARK 8

> **Address:** Foxburrows Road, Chigwell, IG7 4QN (☎020-8500 7353,
> 🖥 redbridge.gov.uk > Parks and open spaces and hainaultforest.co.uk).
> **Opening hours:** Daily, 7am to 7pm (4.30pm in winter). Farm/zoo, daily, 9am to 5pm (3pm in winter).
> **Cost:** Free.
> **Transport:** Hainault tube or Romford rail, then 247 bus.
> **Attractions & amenities:** Fishing lake, rare breeds farm/zoo, visitor centre, golf, nature trail, refreshments, play areas, limited wheelchair access.

One of the remnants of the ancient Forest of Essex has been preserved in this lovely country park, which straddles the borders of London and Essex. With 336 acres (136ha) of woodland and pasture, and designated a Site of Special Scientific Interest, it has plenty to keep the whole family entertained.

Hainault Forest is an important example of old wood pasture and reflects the way the use of the land was shared in bygone times: for grazing animals and harvesting wood. By the 19th century it was being carved up into building plots, until conservationist Edward North Buxton (1840-1924) led a campaign to preserve part of it. Some 800 acres (324ha) were purchased by the London County Council and opened to the public in 1906.

Today, the park includes the Hainault Forest Golf Club, as well as a rare-breeds farm which has Highland cattle, Jacob sheep, Oxford Forest pigs, plus goats, rabbits, geese, ducks and an irresistible family of meerkats. The forest contains a wide range of trees, including ash, black poplar, lime, English oak, hornbeam, horse chestnut and silver birch, which in turn support a range of wildlife, from owls and bats to an abundance of insects, mosses and fungi. There's also a wildlife garden which attracts bees, damselflies and butterflies, and also provides a home for newts and toads

The park's other attractions include adventure play areas and a fishing lake, and there are also special events such as guided walks and conservation activities. The park's café (9.30am-4pm) serves hot drinks, sandwiches and snacks.

 HIDDEN CORNER

Visit between April and June to seek out dense carpets of bluebells within the woods. In addition to creating a stunning display of colour and scent, these special flowers confirm Hainault's status as venerable old woodland.

9 LEE VALLEY REGIONAL PARK

Address: Office, Myddelton House, Bulls Cross, Enfield, EN2 9HG (☎ 08456-770 600, 🖥 visitleevalley.org.uk).
Opening hours: Unrestricted access.
Cost: Free.
Transport: East India DLR (for the southern end of the park).
Attractions & amenities: Nature reserves, sports facilities, cafés.

The Lee Valley Regional Park Authority owns 35 per cent of the Olympic Park – including its beautiful wildflower meadows – which was developed on part of the Lee Valley Park, and manages four venues created for the London 2012 Games, including the London Velopark and the hockey and tennis centres situated in the Olympic Park.

The award-winning Lee Valley Regional (Country) Park is a linear park stretching for 26 miles (42km) along the banks of the River Lee, from Ware in Hertfordshire to the East India Dock Basin on the Thames. The 10,000-acre (4,047ha) park comprises a diverse and unique blend of rural and urban areas; green spaces, heritage sites, country parks, public and private gardens, nature reserves, waterways, lakes and riverside trails – all linked by paths, walkways and cycle tracks.

You can download maps from the website showing access points and highlights of each section of the park, as well as information leaflets covering the wide range of sports available, from horse riding to white-water rafting.

The park's countryside teems with wildlife and many areas are designated as Sites of Special Scientific Interest (SSSIs) and a Special Protection Area (SPA). It's a haven for flora and fauna throughout the year, from orchids to sparrowhawks, dragonflies to otters, water voles to wildfowl. It's also one of the best places in the country to see water birds, including bitterns, goosanders, common terns, reed warblers and kingfishers.

The Lea River Park project in the Lower Lea Valley in East London forms the southern end of the park (a Lea within the Lee!), the backbone of which is the 'Fatwalk', a 3.7 mile (6km) path connecting the Olympic Park to the Thames.

London 2012 Olympics, White Water Centre

LONDON FIELDS 10

> **Address:** London Fields Westside, E8 3EU (☎ 020-8356 8428/9, 🖥 hackney.gov.uk/london-fields.htm and londonfieldsusergroup.org.uk).
> **Opening hours:** Unrestricted access. Lido, summer, weekdays 6.30am to 8pm, weekends 8am to 7pm; winter, weekdays 7.45am to 4pm, weekends 8am to 4pm. See website for more details.
> **Cost:** Free. Lido: non-members, £4.50 adults, £2.70 juniors (15 and under).
> **Transport:** London Fields rail.
> **Attractions & amenities**: Lido, café, sports facilities, play area.

L ondon Fields (31 acres/12.5ha) is one of East London's most popular green spaces, winner of several Green Flag awards. First recorded in 1540, it was on the main footpath from the village of Hackney to the City and was a grazing stop for cattle drovers en route to Smithfield Market. Hackney was a favourite of wealthy Londoners from the Middle Ages until the 19th century, due to its proximity to the court and the city; in 1756 Hackney was declared to excel all other villages in the kingdom in the opulence of its inhabitants!

A public park since 1872, London Fields is a pleasant green space with extensive grassy areas and many beautiful trees (notably London planes). It's a great place to play sports, swim, enjoy a picnic or just relax. Facilities include a much-used cricket pitch, soccer pitches, a BMX track, tennis courts and two children's play areas with a paddling pool (May to September).

London Fields Lido

The London Fields Lido (☎ 020-7254 9038, 🖥 better.org.uk/areas/hackney/centres/london-fields-lido) is one of only ten remaining from the original 68 lidos in Greater London. It opened in 1932 and closed in 1988, but was reopened in 2006 following a determined local campaign. It's been rebuilt to modern standards and is the only heated, outdoor, Olympic-size swimming pool in London. The lido café caters to park visitors.

 FOOD & DRINK

Pub on the Park (☎ 020-7923 3398): This popular watering hole on Martello Street, overlooking the park, is a family-friendly pub serving tasty pub grub. A cycle path runs from the pub, through the park, to…
　Broadway Market (🖥 broadwaymarket.co.uk): A mouth-watering food market on Saturdays (9am to 5pm). This area has other eateries and interesting shops open throughout the week.

11 MANOR PARK CEMETERY

Address: Sebert Road, Forest Gate, E7 0NP (☎ 020-8534 1486, 🖳 mpark.co.uk).
Opening hours: Weekdays, 9am to 7pm (5pm, Oct-Mar), weekends and Bank Holidays, 10am to 6pm (4pm, Oct-Mar).
Cost: Free.
Transport: Manor Park rail.

Just south of Wanstead Flats and close to the City of London Cemetery – with which it shouldn't be confused – this is the archetypal London cemetery with glorious headstones (including some wonderful Victorian angels) and an atmosphere of quiet timelessness.

Opened in 1874, Manor Park Cemetery (42 acres/17ha) has two areas of woodland (remnants of the old Hamfrith Wood) and many noble old trees: mature limes line the boundaries and an avenue of horse chestnuts follows the old path through the middle, with other trees scattered throughout, including cedars and conifers. The original chapel, built in 1877, was largely destroyed by bombing in 1944, apart from its spire, which still remains. There are also a war memorial, remembrance area and an extensive Garden of Remembrance featuring rose beds surrounding a central pavilion with a small fountain.

Historic graves include that of John Travers Cornwell VC, who died from his wounds in 1916 at the age of just 16; he's the youngest recipient of the Victoria Cross, awarded for remaining at his post in the Battle of Jutland during the First World War. Also buried here is Mary Orchard (1830-1906), who was nanny for over 40 years to the children of Queen Victoria's daughter Princess Alice (and also the ill-fated Alix, last Tsarina of Russia).

🔍 HIDDEN CORNER

Worth seeking out, if somewhat out of keeping with its sombre location, is the memorial to Steve Marsh, a car fanatic who died in 2009. His 'tomb' is an astonishingly realistic BMW convertible, complete with personalised number plate. Carved from solid granite it weighs a ton and had to be lowered onto the grave by crane.

In Memoriam
FIRST CLASS BOY JOHN TRAVERS
CORNWELL. V.C.
BORN 8th JANUARY 1900
DIED OF WOUNDS RECEIVED AT
THE BATTLE OF JUTLAND
2nd JUNE 1916.

THIS STONE WAS ERECTED
BY SCHOLARS AND EX-SCHOLARS
OF SCHOOLS IN EAST HAM.

"It is not wealth or ancestry
but honourable conduct and a noble
disposition that make men great"

MUDCHUTE PARK & FARM 12

> **Address:** Pier Street, Isle of Dogs, E14 3HP (☎ 020-7515 5901, 🖥 mudchute.org).
> **Opening hours:** Unrestricted access. Farm & pets corner, daily, 9am to 5pm (4pm in winter).
> **Cost:** Free, but a donation is appreciated if you visit the farm.
> **Transport:** Crossharbour, Mudchute and Island Gardens DLR.
> **Attractions & amenities:** Pets corner, equestrian centre, children's play area (in Millwall Park), car park, some wheelchair access (not all paths are paved).

Mudchute Park and Farm is a slice of country life in the shadow of one of the UK's financial hubs. Just to the south of Canary Wharf on the Isle of Dogs, Mudchute is London's largest city farm (32 acres/13ha), with over 200 animals and fowl. Its inelegant name comes from the fact that it was the dumping ground for Thames mud during the excavation of Millwall Dock in the 1860s, creating an area of fertile, hilly land. A natural wilderness for decades, in 1974 the site was saved from development by the Mudchute Association, formed in 1977 to preserve the area as a 'people's park' and educational facility.

🍴 FOOD & DRINK 🍸

Mudchute Kitchen: Run by Frizzante, the Kitchen serves freshly-cooked dishes using seasonal ingredients from farms in Kent, with an emphasis on breakfasts, brunches and Italian classics. Open Tue-Fri, 9.30am to 3.30pm, Sat-Sun, 9.30am to 4pm in summer and from 10.30am in winter. Closed Mondays.

The farm has an impressive range of animals, including cows (the Irish Moiled, a hornless breed), pigs (Gloucestershire Old Spot and Tamworth), sheep (Oxford Down and White Faced Woodland), goats (Anglo-Nubian and Pygmy), donkeys and llamas, while there are small animals in the pets corner, such as ferrets, giant rabbits and guinea pigs. Aviary birds include Chinese painted quail, diamond doves, golden pheasant, Java sparrows and zebra finches, while chicken breeds include Brahma, Light Sussex, Rhode Island Red and White-crested Black Polish. There's also a variety of ducks, geese and turkeys.

As well as providing a realistic image of a working farm, Mudchute includes a wide range of wildlife habitats, from wetlands and woodlands to open meadows and field margins. The nearby equestrian centre has around 25 horses and ponies, and provides lessons to adults and children.

13 POSTMANS PARK

Address: King Edward Street, EC1A 4AS (☎ 020-7606 3030, 🖥 cityoflondon.gov.
uk > Green spaces > City Gardens).
Opening hours: Daily, 8am to dusk.
Cost: Free.
Transport: St Paul's tube.

LEIGH PITT,
REPROGRAPHIC OPERATOR,
AGED 30, SAVED A DROWNING
BOY FROM THE CANAL AT
THAMESMEAD, BUT SADLY
WAS UNABLE TO SAVE
HIMSELF · JUNE · 7 · 2007

A short distance north of St Paul's Cathedral is the intriguingly titled Postman's Park – its name reflects its popularity with workers from the nearby old Post Office HQ. It occupies three old burial grounds, including that of St Botolph's Aldersgate, and has been a public garden since 1880, but is best known for its monument to human courage.

The Memorial to Heroic Self Sacrifice was the brainchild of George Frederic Watts (1817-1904), a Victorian painter, sculptor and philanthropist, who wanted to commemorate ordinary people who died saving the lives of others. It comprises a series of plaques on a wall beneath a loggia; parts of the memorial are Grade II listed and the plaques feature Arts and Crafts lettering and Art Nouveau borders.

Watts planned to include up to 120 plaques, but just four had been installed by the time of the opening ceremony in 1900. When Watts died in 1904, his wife Mary took over the project, and by the time of her death in 1938 there were 52 plaques telling tales of selfless sacrifice – rescuing people from burning buildings, sinking ships and runaway horses. Reading them is an inspiring and humbling experience.

A new plaque was added in 2009 (by the Diocese of London) to honour Leigh Pitt, who died in 2007 rescuing a boy from a canal in Thamesmead, and it's to be hoped there will be more in the future.

The garden also features a sundial surrounded by bright flower beds and a gently trickling fountain. Plants of particular interest are a large banana and a dove tree.

In the 2004 film, *Closer*, Natalie Portman's character bases her false identity on Alice Ayres, whose plaque she reads in Postman's Park. The real Miss Ayres was a labourer's daughter who died saving three children from a burning house in Borough in 1885.

RAINHAM MARSHES RSPB NATURE RESERVE

14

Address: New Tank Hill Road, Purfleet, RM19 1SZ (☎ 01708-899840, 🖥 rspb.org.uk/reserves/guide/r/rainhammarshes).

Opening hours: 1st Nov to 31st Mar, 9.30am to 4.30pm; 1st Apr to 31st Oct, 9.30am to 5pm. Closed 25-26th Dec.

Cost: Non-RSPB members, £3 adults, £1.50 children, £9 families (two adults and up to four children). Free to RSPB members and local residents.

Transport: Purfleet railway, but best reached by car. Car park 'voluntary' £1 donation.

Attractions & amenities: Visitor centre, café, shop, adventure play area, some wheelchair access.

Rare birds paying a flying visit to the reserve are afforded almost rock-star status. In December 2005, over 1,700 people flocked to Rainham Marshes in the hope of glimpsing the sociable lapwing, an exceptional visitor to Western Europe.

Rainham Marshes RSPB (Royal Society for the Protection of Birds) Nature Reserve is a wetland on the upper Thames Estuary, formerly used as a firing range by the Ministry of Defence. One of the few ancient medieval landscapes remaining in the London area, this flat, windswept marshland was closed to the public for over a century until being acquired by the RSPB and opening in 2006.

Today, Rainham Marshes hosts a wide variety of wetland plants and is teeming with wildlife, from birds and mammals (it has one of Britain's largest water vole populations) to insects and reptiles. But the main stars are the birds. Among the leading attractions are avocet, lapwing, little egret, peregrine and ringed plover, and each season brings a different experience. In spring, the air is filled with birdsong as birds compete to establish territories and attract a mate, while in summer you can see fledglings making their first tentative flights. Autumn brings large movements of migrating birds, while in winter flocks gather to feed or fly at dusk, and form large roosts to keep warm.

The reserve has an innovative visitor centre, with huge windows overlooking the marshes, and hides affording great views. It organises regular events for birdwatchers, including guided birding walks (Wednesdays), dawn chorus walks and a bird-watching club for children. If birds aren't your thing, there are 2.5mi (4km) of trails which are pushchair/wheelchair friendly, and a cycle route linking Purfleet and Rainham runs alongside the reserve.

15 ST MARY'S SECRET GARDEN

Address: 50 Pearson Street, E2 8EL (☎ 020-7739 2965,
🖳 stmaryssecretgarden.org.uk).
Opening hours: Weekdays 9am to 5pm. Closed weekends. Tours arranged.
Cost: Free.
Transport: Hoxton rail.
Attractions & amenities: Plant sales, courses.

St Mary's Secret Garden is named after St Mary's Haggerston, built by John Nash in 1827 but destroyed in the Second World War. Its ruins made way for prefab houses and when they were demolished in the '70s, the site was designated a community space. However, it was once an area of genteel Georgian houses and an old street lamp in the garden recalls grander times.

First established in the '90s, the garden has been named St Mary's Secret Garden since 2003. It's a small sanctuary – just 0.7acre/0.28ha – divided into four areas: a patch of natural woodland with a pond, a food growing area, a sensory garden and herbaceous borders. It also has a classroom and large greenhouse.

Organic principles are used to encourage wildlife and biodiversity, with the emphasis on social and therapeutic gardening. St Mary's offers horticultural therapy for people with mental health issues, terminal illnesses, learning and physical disabilities, and other health problems, while placements, volunteering and training opportunities are provided for Hackney's diverse community.

St Mary's has received a number of accolades. It was awarded its first Green Flag in 2010 and voted Hackney in Bloom's 'best community project (professional)' in 2012. It has also been selected as one of London's top ten culture secrets (*The Guardian* newspaper) and one of its top 'secret' gardens (*The Times*).

St Mary's organises a wide range of projects including accredited horticultural education (basic gardening courses, herbal workshops, etc.); work experience for students and school children; community events such as an annual flower show; and plant, fruit and vegetable sales. It's very much a community garden, but visitors are welcome and it's a beautiful spot to enjoy a few minutes' peace and quiet.

ST PAUL'S CATHEDRAL CHURCHYARD & FESTIVAL GARDENS

16

Address: St Paul's Churchyard, EC4M 8AD (☎ 020-7374 4127, 🖥 cityoflondon. gov.uk > Green spaces > City Gardens).
Opening hours: St Paul's Cathedral churchyard gardens, daily, 6am to dusk. Festival Gardens, unrestricted access.
Cost: Free.
Transport: St Paul's tube.
Attractions & amenities: Cathedral (tickets cost £15 adults, £6 children), restaurant, café, information centre.

Sir Christopher Wren's imposing cathedral is encircled by its lovely churchyard gardens (around 2.5 acres/1ha), which were laid out in the 1870s on the old burial grounds of St Paul's and neighbouring churches. They were designed by Edward Milner (who also worked on the gardens at Crystal Palace) and are noted for their noble trees: ginkgo, maple, lime, ash, mulberry and eucalyptus, as well as some of the oldest plane trees in London and the City's only giant fir. More modern additions include a rose garden planted near the south gate in 1976.

 FOOD & DRINK

Restaurant at St Paul's: Typically British fare, including shepherd's pie and cream teas, served in the cathedral crypt. Open daily for lunch from noon to 3pm; afternoon tea Mon-Sat 2.30 to 4pm. The adjacent café opens from 9am (10am Sun). Free access.
Paternoster Square: Plenty of places to grab some picnic fare, from gourmet salad bar chain Chop'd to French bakery Paul.

There are several monuments, including a reproduction of Francis Bird's statue of Queen Anne – the reigning monarch when the cathedral was completed in 1712 – and a granite memorial to 'the people of London 1939-1945' who were less fortunate than the cathedral in avoiding destruction during the Blitz.

South of the churchyard is Carter Lane Garden, which houses an information kiosk; while to the south east are the award-winning Festival Gardens, which were the Corporation of London's contribution to the Festival of Britain in 1951. They consist of a lawn with a wall fountain, donated by the Worshipful Company of Gardeners, a raised terrace and a number of trees. Between the two, the former coach park has been transformed into a swathe of green and contains over 200 lavenders planted by the St Paul's Choir school. All are great places from which to admire the iconic cathedral.

Young Lovers, George Ehrlich

17 SPRINGFIELD PARK

Address: Springfield, Hackney, E5 9EF (☎ 020-8356 8428/9, 💻 hackney.gov.uk/springfield-park.htm).
Opening hours: Daily, 7.30am to 9.30pm in summer (4.30pm in winter); café, 10am to 6pm summer (4pm winter).
Cost: Free.
Transport: Clapton rail.
Attractions & amenities: Two cafés, river walk, bandstand, playground, sports facilities.

Delightfully situated alongside the River Lee, Springfield Park in Upper Clapton was created from the grounds of three private houses, only one of which, the White House, remains (it now houses a café). The 38-acre (15ha) park opened in 1905 and was designed by JJ Sexby, whose

scheme included a pond with an island and lawns scattered with trees.

A regular Green Flag winner, Springfield Park was London's first Regionally Important Geological Site. During the Ice Age, a much larger River Lee wore a channel through the park's London clay and deposited a floodplain of sand and gravel. Today, rain flowing down towards the river pops up as temporary springs – hence the name. The views across the verdant green lawns, towards Walthamstow Marshes, are spectacular.

Its diverse habitats and proximity to the Lee Valley's green corridor make the park particularly attractive to wildlife. Its visitors number over 50 bird species, including kingfishers, owls and woodpeckers, as well as pipistrelle and noctule bats. There's also a remarkable Victorian collection of shrubs and trees, including

foxglove, tulip, swamp cypress, holm oak and walnut.

It's also a centre for sport. There are tennis courts and a cricket pitch, and the park is adjacent to the Lea Rowing Club and Springhill Sports Ground, used by Hackney Rugby Club. On the other side of the river is Springfield Marina, a large basin for narrow boats.

 FOOD & DRINK

Spark Café: Eat on the tea lawns overlooking the park or in the old White House, a Grade II listed Georgian mansion, where you can also enjoy local art (💻 springfieldparkcafe.co.uk).
Riverside Café: Pleasant café overlooking the Lee by the rowing club; recommended for its English breakfast, omelettes and baguettes.

VALENTINES PARK   18

Address: Cranbrook Road, Ilford, IG1 4XA (☎ 020-8708 3141, ▯ redbridge.gov.
uk > Leisure and events > Valentines Mansion and Park and valentines.org.uk).
Opening hours: Daily, 8am to dusk. See website for house opening times.
Cost: Free. Guided tours of house and garden, £4.50.
Transport: Gants Hill tube.
Attractions & amenities: Mansion, café, bandstand, boating lake, children's play
areas, sports facilities.

Tucked between Gants Hill and Ilford, Valentines Park (125 acres/50ha) comprises a splendid estate with a William III country house (Grade II* listed) and glorious gardens, which are Grade II listed and on the English Heritage Register of Parks & Gardens of Special Interest.

Valentines Mansion was built in 1696-7, when the estate was owned by Lady Elizabeth Tillotson, widow of the Archbishop of Canterbury. In 1724 it was purchased by City speculator Robert Surman, who created the walled gardens, dovecote and grottoes. Successive owners added to the house and gardens, until the estate passed to Ilford Council in 1907.

The gardens (and house) were extensively restored between 2006 and 2009 with a grant from the Heritage Lottery Fund, and now form a delightful series of 'rooms', displaying over two centuries of garden design. Many features from the 18th-century layout remain, including the rectangular canal (Long Water) with its rockwork grotto, an exceptional walled garden, plus a dovecote, sundial and ha-ha. There's also a historic kitchen garden, a Victorian rose garden, a boating lake, and a dry garden planted in 2012 to celebrate the Queen's Diamond Jubilee.

The park has extensive lawns and trees – including a 300-year-old maple – as well as areas of wilderness. Sports facilities include a basketball court, cricket pitch and outdoor gym, and the Gardener's Cottage café (10am to 6pm).

👁 DON'T MISS!

Allow time to explore Valentine's Mansion (☎ 020-8708 8100, ▯ valentinesmansion.com), which includes a recreated Victorian kitchen and Georgian rooms among its attractions, and runs a host of events, from art exhibitions to dressing up games.

Valentines Park is well supported by locals and in 2012 came sixth in the People's Choice awards (see ▯ greenflag.keepbritaintidy.org), an online ballot that includes all the UK's Green Flag parks (almost 1,500!). It regularly hosts public events, from farmer's markets to concerts, as well as the Redbridge Town Show.

19 BARBICAN GARDENS

Address: Silk Street, London Wall, EC2Y 8DS (☎ 020-7638 4141, ⌨ barbican.org.uk).
Opening hours: Centre, Mon-Sat, 9am to 11pm; Sun and Bank Holidays, noon to 11pm. Conservatory, noon to 5pm most Sun. See website for information about tours.
Cost: Free. Tours: £8 adults, £6 concessions.
Transport: Barbican tube.
Attractions & amenities: Tours, lake/ponds, conservatory, arts centre/gallery, library, restaurants and bars.

The Barbican Estate (Grade II listed) is a splendid example of British Brutalist architecture – love it or hate it! – built in the '60s and '70s by the Corporation of London on a 40-acre (16ha) site. The estate's relentless concrete structures are softened by oases of lawn, flowerbeds and water, linked by a network of walkways. Visitors to the Barbican Arts Centre can enjoy the lake and its neighbouring terrace and gardens, with waterside seating and panoramic views (and a restaurant). The lake also incorporates fountains, a cascade and red brick 'islands', while the roof of the Arts Centre has an alpine garden with sculptures and a pergola.

You can access a lovely 'secret' corner of the Barbican from St Giles' Church (off Fore Street), where steps lead to a small bridge over a canal and into a secluded communal garden, which incorporates excavated footings of the old Roman city wall. The Barbican Centre also contains London's second-largest conservatory, a tropical oasis that's home to over 2,000 species of plants and trees, plus an aviary housing finches and ponds full of exotic fish.

20 BARKING PARK

Address: Longbridge Road, Barking, IG11 8TA (☎ 020-8227 5289, ⌨ lbbd.gov.uk/LeisureArtsAndLibraries/BarkingPark/Pages/Findus.aspx).
Opening hours: Daily, 7.30am to dusk.
Cost: Free.
Transport: Barking tube.
Attractions & amenities: Miniature railway, boating lake, sports facilities, visitor centre, café, playgrounds.

First opened in 1898, Barking Park (72 acres/29ha) is a classic Victorian park. Its centrepiece is its lake, which is almost half a mile (1km) in length and a favourite place for boating – in the '50s people took trips here on a converted Mississippi paddle steamer – while its three islands provide nesting sites for mallards, moorhens and coots.

Since 2006, the park has been undergoing a transformation with Heritage Lottery Funding. A depot has become a new visitor centre and café, while the old lido is now a 'splash park' and sports pavilion. Natural additions include new ornamental shrubberies, and wildflower meadows to attract birds and insects.

A unique attraction is the Barking Park Light Railway, a miniature passenger railway which opened in the early '50s. It closed in 2005 but was revived in 2008 by a father and son team who purchased the line and added new trains, and new 7¼in (184mm) gauge track, with wheelchair-friendly access. The new train service operates regularly in summer – in 2012 it carried an Olympic torchbearer – and has its own website (🖳 bplr.co.uk).

BEDFORDS PARK 21

Address: Broxhill Road, Havering-atte-Bower, Romford, RM4 1QH (☎ 01708-748646, 🖳 essexwt.org.uk/visitor_centres__nature_reserves/bedfords_park).
Opening hours: Daily, 9am to sunset. Visitor centre, Tue-Sun, 9am to 5pm (4pm in winter) and Mon during school holidays.
Cost: Free.
Transport: Romford rail then 375 bus.
Attractions & amenities: Visitor centre, refreshments, shop, deer, trails, limited wheelchair access to park, car park.

Nestling between Havering-atte-Bower and Harold Hill, Bedfords Park was once a private estate with a manor house – its history dates back to 1212, when King John gave the land to William D'Aubigny for the annual rent of one sparrowhawk – but since 2003 it has been home to one of the Essex Wildlife Trust's visitor centres.

The 215-acre (87ha) site blends grassland and woodland, hedgerows and water, to provide a rich habitat for flora and fauna, including bluebells and wood anemones, pepper-saxifrage and sneezewort, nuthatches and woodpeckers, hairy dragonflies and wasp spiders, newts and grass snakes, weasels and wild deer. The park also has a captive herd of red deer, harking back to the days when it was a royal hunting ground. Many of the trees were planted in the 18th century, including monkey puzzle, cedar of Lebanon and wellingtonia – a relative of America's giant sequoia.

The visitor centre has an observation area, with views towards the Thames and London, and an education room where (in summer) you can watch honey bees coming and going at their beehive. Refreshments are also available for humans.

22 CALTHORPE PROJECT COMMUNITY GARDEN

> **Address:** 258-274 Gray's Inn Road, WC1X 8LH (☎ 020-7837 8019,
> 🖥 calthorpeproject.org.uk).
> **Opening hours:** Daily, 10am to 6pm in summer, 9am to 5pm in winter.
> **Cost:** Free.
> **Transport:** King's Cross tube/rail.
> **Attractions & amenities:** Café, playroom, five-a-side football, training courses.

The Calthorpe Project is a 1.2-acre (0.5ha) organic community garden that opened in 1984 on a site scheduled for office development; after fierce local opposition it was purchased for the community by Camden Borough Council (who also fund the project). However, it's much more than just a garden, as the website states: 'An inner city oasis – a community garden and centre where people grow and learn together, taking care of each other and the environment.'

The strength of the project comes from its management by community members and its sensitivity to local needs. The garden encompasses a broad range of facilities, including quiet areas, water features, seating, flower beds, glasshouses, swamp, under-5s area, wild garden, community composting area, Bangladeshi women's plots, family plots, outdoor AstroTurf futsal (five-a-side football) pitch, a Walter Segal self-build community building and a café (phew!). There's also a food-growing area with raised beds and a large polytunnel for use by local people, schools and community groups.

The garden is an accredited training centre, offering courses in basic construction skills and gardening.

23 CORAM'S FIELDS

> **Address:** 93 Guilford Street, WC1N 1DN (☎ 020-7837 6138, 🖥 coramsfields.org).
> **Opening hours:** Daily, 9am to 7pm (closes at dusk in winter).
> **Cost:** Free.
> **Transport:** Russell Square tube.
> **Attractions & amenities:** Play areas, sports facilities and pitch hire, city farm, café, children's and disabled toilets.

London's first public children's playground, Coram's Fields pays tribute to Captain Thomas Coram (ca. 1668-1751), a seaman turned philanthropist who created the London Foundling Hospital in 1739 to look after unwanted and abandoned children (said to be the world's first incorporated charity). When the hospital was relocated in the '20s, campaigning and fundraising

by local residents, and a donation from the Harmsworth newspaper magnates, led to the creation of the current park.

Open since 1936 and run as a charity, Coram's Fields occupies 7 acres (2.8ha) in Bloomsbury, close to Great Ormond Street Hospital and the Foundling Museum (🖳 foundlingmuseum.org.uk). It includes fragments of the original hospital building, which are Grade II listed, but its main attractions are focused on the young and include a playground, sand pits, a duck pond, a pets corner, café (Mar-Nov) and nursery, as well as sports facilities, coaching and play/youth schemes.

Adults – defined as anyone over the age of 16 – are only permitted entry to Coram's Fields when accompanied by a child aged under 16.

EASTBURY MANOR HOUSE GARDENS   24

Address: Eastbury Square, Barking, London IG11 9SN (☎ 020-8724 1000 or 020-8227 5216, 🖳 lbbd.gov.uk/eastbury and nationaltrust.org.uk/eastbury-manor-house).
Opening hours: Mar-Oct, Mon-Thu and first and second Sat of the month, 10am to 4pm; limited hours apply in winter (see website for details). House closed Jan and Bank Holiday Mons.
Cost: £4 adults, £2 concessions and children, £8 families. Discounts for borough residents; National Trust members free. Access to part of the gardens is free.
Transport: Upney tube or Barking rail.
Attractions & amenities: Manor house, walled gardens, tea room, shop.

Eastbury Manor is an impressive Tudor property, little altered since it was built in the 1570s, set in gardens in the centre of a '20s housing estate in Barking – the last place you'd expect to find a wealthy Elizabethan merchant's manor house!

The H-shaped house was built by Clement Sisley, who demonstrated his affluence by using brick – an expensive commodity in Tudor times. It was purchased by the National Trust in 1918 and is managed by the London borough of Barking and Dagenham.

The gardens date from the early 18th century and comprise two walled gardens – the one to the west is visible from the road, while the eastern garden is enclosed by high brick walls dating from the 1700s and, like the house, Grade I listed – as well as plots to the north and west of the house and a

small orchard to the south. The eastern walled garden has niches in its walls which were probably bee boles: an early kind of beehive. It can only be viewed as part of a tour but it's well worth the cost to view this beautifully restored building and gardens.

25   GEFFRYE MUSEUM & GARDENS

Address: Kingsland Road, Hackney, London E2 8EA (☎ 020-7739 9893, 🖥 geffrye-museum.org.uk).

Opening hours: Tue-Sat, 10am to 5pm; Sun and Bank Holiday Mon, noon to 5pm; closed Good Friday, Christmas Eve, Christmas Day, Boxing Day and New Year's Day. The gardens are open during museum hours, but closed Nov-Mar.

Cost: Museum and gardens free (£2.50 adults to see restored almshouses).

Transport: Hoxton rail.

Attractions & amenities: Museum, café, shop, some museum wheelchair restrictions.

A delightful discovery in the backstreets of Hackney, the Geffrye Museum traces the changing style of domestic interiors from 1600 to the late 20th century, while its tranquil gardens reveal how English town gardens evolved over the same period.

The museum is housed in a group of almshouses (Grade I listed) – built in 1715 at the bequest of Sir Robert

Geffrye (1613-1703), former Lord Mayor of London and Master of the Ironmongers' Company – and comprises a series of fascinating rooms dating from 1630 to 1998. A sequence of outdoor 'rooms' was added in the '90s, portraying garden design, layout and planting from the 17th to 20th centuries. The 17th century garden is a functional space, providing food and medicines, but from the 18th century onwards the emphasis switched to recreation and entertainment and, increasingly, displays of personal 'taste'. There's also a walled herb garden, with over 170 types of herb, and an Ironmongers Graveyard where Sir Robert is buried.

The excellent website provides virtual tours and 360 degree panoramas, which make you want to visit and see more.

26   HACKNEY DOWNS

Address: Downs Park Road, Hackney, E5 8NP (☎ 020-8356 8428/9, 🖥 hackney. gov.uk/hackney-downs.htm).

Opening hours: Unrestricted access.

Cost: Free.

Transport: Hackney Downs rail.

Attractions & amenities: Sports facilities, children's play area.

Hackney Downs is an open space in Lower Clapton, which was originally common land and is now

the quintessential urban park. It was one of many 'commons' preserved as parkland in the 1860s – others included

Hampstead Health and Wimbledon Common – and opened as a public park in 1884.

The Downs was laid out with a pattern of radiating paths, surrounded by plane, lime and ash trees. There was little formal planting, and it remains a laid-back park, dedicated to sport and recreation rather than horticulture, although it has been awarded a Green Flag and in 2012 took part in the 'Mad About Meadows' project led by London in Bloom and inspired by the Olympic Park wildflower meadows. A new urban meadow was planted, and its rainbow of wildflowers attracts bees, butterflies and other insects in summer.

Major works have also provided new sports and play facilities – including tennis courts, a multi-use games area and various sports pitches – and Hackney Council hopes to open a café at some point.

HAGGERSTON PARK | 27

Address: Audrey Street, off Goldsmith's Row, E2 8QH (☎ 020-8356 8428/9, 🖳 hackney.gov.uk/haggerston-park.htm and haggerstonpark.org.uk).
Opening hours: Daily, 7.30 to dusk. Hackney City Farm, 10am to 4.30pm.
Cost: Free. Donations appreciated at the farm.
Transport: Hoxton rail.
Attractions & amenities: City farm, BMX track, sports facilities, nature reserve, children's play area, café (in the farm).

One of the few landscaped parks in Hackney, Haggerston Park (26 acres/10.5ha) has a range of attractions, including a nature reserve and a city farm. The park dates from 1956 when it was laid out on the site of the old Shoreditch gasworks, and still features some '50s structures, such as the long pergola walk on its north side. It was extended south in the '80s to provide room for a playground and Hackney City Farm (🖳 hackneycityfarm.co.uk), which is home to poultry, sheep, goats, pigs, calves and donkeys, and also runs crafts workshops and has a café.

Ecology is important in Haggerston Park, which has a small but flourishing nature reserve, complete with a pond, while in 2013, a community orchard/market garden was being developed. There are also ample sports options, including a BMX bike track.

One of the park's more bizarre claims to fame is that Michael Jackson landed there in a helicopter in 1992, together with Mickey Mouse, to visit children at a nearby hospital.

28 JUBILEE PARK, CANARY WHARF

Address: Canary Wharf, E14 5AB (☎ 020-7418 2000, 🖥 canarywharf.com).
Opening hours: Unrestricted access.
Cost: Free.
Transport: Canary Wharf tube.
Attractions & amenities: Arts exhibits.

A roof garden built on top of a tube station among the towering skyscrapers of Canary Wharf, Jubilee Park provides a tranquil place for workers and shoppers to relax, and also hosts outdoor exhibitions and events.

Designed by Belgian architects Jacques and Peter Wirtz, its main feature is a sinuous raised water channel with fountains, contained by stone walls and surrounded by grassy knolls on which to catch the sun. Planting includes ornamental grasses and dogwood, while the park has around 250 semi-mature trees, including swamp cypress, spring-flowering cherry, evergreen oaks and over 200 dawn redwood trees (an unusual choice in a city park).

The park is also worth checking out for its public art installations, which in 2012 included a selection of works by abstract sculptor Sir Anthony Caro, and life-size portraits of some of Britain's best sporting champions by East London painter Teresa Wirtz.

29 MAYESBROOK PARK

Address: Lodge Avenue, Dagenham, RM8 2HY (☎ 020-8227 2332, 🖥 lbbd.gov.uk > Parks and countryside).
Opening hours: Unrestricted access.
Cost: Free.
Transport: Upney tube.
Attractions & amenities: Nature reserve, sports facilities, children's play areas.

Described as Britain's first climate change park, Mayesbrook Park in Dagenham has been undergoing restoration, begun in 2011, to turn it into a wetland park which can better cope with long-term changes in the weather, such as heavy rainfall and drought. Ecological planting includes more trees to provide shade and filter pollution, making it a natural haven on hot days.

The Mayes Brook, which runs through the park and gives it its name, has been cleaned up and released from its narrow channel to meander through the landscape. Its gravel banks attract wildlife, as do two large lakes in the south of the park which are a magnet for waterfowl, such as mute swan, tufted duck and shoveler.

Created in the '30s to provide open space for residents of nearby housing estates, Mayesbrook Park also has plenty of attractions for sporting types, including sports pitches, basketball courts and an outdoor gym.

MILE END PARK   30

Address: Burdett Road, E3 4TN (☎ 020-7364 4147 or 020-7364 2494, ⌨ towerhamlets.gov.uk > Parks and open spaces).
Opening hours: Unrestricted access.
Cost: Free.
Transport: Mile End tube.
Attractions & amenities: Café, pub, arts pavilion, sports facilities, children's play areas, audio guides and maps for disabled visitors.

This award-winning linear park, adjacent to the Regents Canal, stretches for 2.5 miles (4km) from Victoria Park south towards Limehouse Basin. It's actually a series of parks, devoted to themes such as art, ecology and sport, linked by grassy spaces, water features and even a 'green' bridge over busy Mile End Road.

The 90-acre (36ha) park was first planned in the '40s, but was only begun at the end of the millennium, and its on-going development mirrors the regeneration of East London. It's particularly worth visiting for its ecology park which attracts all manner of flora and fauna – a rare orchid was found there in 2005 – and its terraced garden, a quiet oasis of calm centred on a water cascade.

Sports facilities include the Mile End Stadium and one of the UK's best climbing walls, while youngsters are well catered for with a children's park and an adventure park. The arts park displays art both indoors and outside and has a pleasant café, and there's even a pub tucked away in the ecology park.

31 RAINHAM HALL GARDEN

Address: The Broadway, Rainham, Havering, RM13 9YN (☎ 020-8303 6359, 🖥 nationaltrust.org.uk/main/w-rainhamhall).
Opening hours: Sat and Bank Holiday Mon, Apr-May, 2-5pm, plus Rainham May Fair.
Cost: £2.80 adults, £1.60 children, £7.20 families. Free to National Trust members and to all on a few days a year.
Transport: Rainham rail.
Attractions & amenities: Historic house.

In the centre of Rainham village is Rainham Hall, a rare and original merchant's house, built in 1729 in the Dutch style for master mariner and merchant Captain John Harle. It's set in a 2-acre (0.8ha) plot which includes a charming garden and orchard, and the whole is cared for by the National Trust. The 18th-century wrought-iron railings at the front of the house are a significant feature of the site as they represent some of the finest work of London smiths of the time.

The hall and stable block are Grade II* listed and well worth a visit, but the garden is a popular attraction. It was laid out as a formal Dutch garden (to complement the house), traces of which can still be seen, including ornamental stone urns and herringbone stone paths partly buried under the grass. A wooded area includes a huge old mulberry tree, and to the rear of the garden is one of London's largest orchards (30 acres/12ha), recently replanted as a community garden.

Look out for the Victorian doghouse which supposedly housed three Dalmatians, used to defend their owner's coaches against highwaymen.

32 ST ANDREWS GARDEN, HOLBORN

Address: 7 Saint Andrew Street, EC4A 3AB (☎ 020-7583 7394, 🖥 standrewholborn.org.uk).
Opening hours: Unrestricted access.
Cost: Free.
Transport: Chancery Lane tube.

Providing a peaceful refuge from the traffic at one of the City's busiest junctions, St Andrew's Garden is the largest public garden in the Holborn area. Screened from the traffic by hedges, trees and artfully planted shrubs, and generously provided with benches, it was developed after the Second World War and was later linked to St Andrew's churchyard. Part of the garden occupies the old burial ground

and some interesting headstones line its walls. A transformation project, to unify the garden spaces and improve disabled access began in 2011.

The church of St Andrew, Holborn can trace its history back to 951. Its medieval incarnation survived the Great Fire of 1666 but was later rebuilt by Sir Christopher Wren, and it was restored to Wren's design following extensive damage during the Blitz. It's the last resting place of Sir Thomas Coram (1668-1751) who established the Foundling Hospital in nearby Bloomsbury.

ST GEORGE'S GARDENS, WC1   33

Address: Access via Handel Street, Sidmouth Street or Heathcote Street, WC1N 2NU (✉ info@friendsofstgeorgesgardens.org.uk, 🖥 friendsofstgeorgesgardens. org.uk).
Opening hours: Daily, 7.30am to dusk.
Cost: Free.
Transport: Russell Square tube.

A wonderful 'secret' garden with a grisly claim to fame, St George's Gardens are hidden between Bloomsbury's Brunswick shopping centre and Gray's Inn Road. The gardens opened in the 1880s atop the 18th-century cemetery which once served St George, Bloomsbury Way and St George the Martyr, Queen Square – they were the first burial grounds to be sited away from their churches and are also where the first recorded case of 'body-snatching' took place in 1777.

Restored in 2001, St George's Garden is now a shady retreat, presided over by plane trees and imposing ivy-clad graves and monuments, including the tomb of Anna Gibson, granddaughter of Oliver Cromwell, and a memorial to Robert Nelson, a leading philanthropist and the first man to be buried here in 1715 (he hoped to encourage others to follow suit!).

Other attractions include a sensory garden, created by the Friends of St George's Gardens, and a splendid collection of ferns, which are among the finest to be found in central London.

34 ST JOHN-AT-HACKNEY CHURCHYARD GARDEN

Address: Lower Clapton Road, E5 0PD (☎ 020-8356 8428/9, 🖥 hackney.gov.uk/st-johns-churchyard.htm).
Opening hours: Unrestricted access. St Augustine's Tower opens on the last Sun of the month, 2-4.30pm.
Cost: Free.
Transport: Hackney Central tube.
Attractions & amenities: Historic church and tower, children's play areas.

The churchyard of St John-at-Hackney is one of the borough's most important heritage sites and the site of Hackney's oldest building. The tower is all that's left of St Augustine's, a medieval church demolished in the 1790s and replaced by the 'new' church of St John. Grade I listed, St Augustine's Tower dates from 1275, and you can climb its staircase for a panoramic view.

 ALLOW...

Allow a few minutes to visit nearby Clapton Square (7.30am to dusk), which is at the centre of an East London conservation area known for its fine Georgian houses.

The area around St John's was a burial ground for over 500 years until closing in 1859. It reopened as a garden in 1894, with its graves grassed over and tombs enclosed in railings – look for the tomb of Sir Francis Beaufort, who developed the Beaufort scale for measuring wind speed. Later additions included a walled 'quiet' garden in 1963. A survey in 1991 identified over 50 species of tree and shrub, including beech, elm and London planes.

An award-winning restoration project in 2006/7, part-funded by the Heritage Lottery Fund, revitalised the churchyard, which is now a vibrant and delightful public space.

35 THAMES BARRIER PARK

Address: North Woolwich Road, Silvertown, London E16 2HP (☎ 020-7476 3741, 🖥 london.gov.uk/priorities/housing/housing-and-land/thames-barrier-park).
Opening hours: From 7am to dusk.
Cost: Free.
Transport: Pontoon Dock DLR.
Attractions & amenities: Café, sports facilities, children's play area.

On the north bank of the Thames, with stunning views of the majestic Thames Barrier, is one of London's best-situated parks. Designed by award-winning French landscape architect Alain Provost and opened in 2000, it was the first riverside park to

be created in over half a century, and is London's first post-modern park.

The park comprises 22 acres (9ha) of lawns, trees, contoured, undulating hedges of yew and maygreen – reflecting the curves of the Barrier – fountains, wildflower meadows, sports and play facilities. A green trench runs through the park, providing a sheltered microclimate for a 'rainbow garden' (strips of coloured plants).

One of its most notable features is the Green Dock: flowers and shrubs chosen to reflect the river's changing range of colours, moods, shades and shapes.

With access to the river, it's a perfect vantage point from which to admire the world's third-largest movable flood barrier (after the Oosterscheldekering and Haringvlietdam in the Netherlands) and the city it protects.

VALENCE PARK   36

Address: Becontree Avenue, Dagenham, RM8 3HT (☎ 020-8227 2332, ▣ lbbd.gov.uk > Parks and countryside).
Opening hours: Daily, 7.15am to dusk. Museum, Mon-Sat, 10am to 4pm (closed on Sun and Public Holidays).
Cost: Free.
Transport: Chadwell Heath rail or Becontree tube and 62 bus.
Attractions & amenities: Manor house, café, shop, fishing lake, sports facilities, children's play area.

Valence House

Valence Park was once the grounds of Valence House, a Grade II* listed manor house that now houses Barking and Dagenham's museum. The park is mentioned as far back as 1290, in connection with Agnes de Valence, a relative of King John, but the house dates from the 15th century. It occupies the north-western corner of the 28.7-acre (11.25ha) park; the remainder is open space for sport and recreation and includes a fishing lake, part of the original moat.

Valence House gardens (around 2.5 acres/1ha) include a herb garden, its central pagoda surrounded by formal beds of roses and herbs, and a Second World War 'Dig for Victory' garden with a replica Anderson shelter. Near the front door of the house are two distinctive trees: a tulip – its yellow flower appears in the Valence House logo – and a ginkgo biloba. Venerable yews and holly hedges screen the gardens from the road, and several oaks thrive in the park, including a spectacular evergreen holm oak.

37   WANSTEAD PARK

> **Address:** Warren Road, Wanstead, E11 2LU (☎ 020-8989 7851 or 020-7332 1911, 🖥 cityoflondon.gov.uk > Green spaces).
> **Opening hours:** Daily, 8am to dusk.
> **Cost:** Free.
> **Transport:** Wanstead tube.
> **Attractions & amenities:** Nature reserve, museum, refreshment kiosk, fishing, golf.

Wanstead Park has a rich history stretching back to Roman times. Its high point was the 18th century when it was home to a grand Palladian mansion, but the estate was sold off and the house demolished in the 1820s to pay the debts of William Wellesley-Pole, the Duke of Wellington's nephew. The park still has traces of its earlier splendour, however, such as its chain of lakes and its glorious follies, including a ruined grotto and a classical temple. The temple is now a museum and opens to the public (☎ 020-7332 1911 for opening times).

Covering around 140 acres (57ha), Wanstead Park has been a public park since 1882 and is Grade II* listed. Its largest lake, the Ornamental Waters, is an important nature reserve, attracting waterfowl such as herons, cormorants and great-crested grebe, while pipistrelle bats skim the water at dusk. Spring brings cascades of bluebells to the woods and wood anemones can also be seen.

38   WEST HAM PARK

> **Address:** Upton Lane, E7 9PU (☎ 020-8472 3584, 🖥 cityoflondon.gov.uk > Green spaces).
> **Opening hours:** Daily, 7.30am to dusk.
> **Cost:** Free.
> **Transport:** Plaistow or Upton Park tube.
> **Attractions & amenities:** Formal gardens, plant nursery, playground, tennis courts, cricket and soccer pitches, other sports facilities.

Winner of multiple awards, including a Green Flag annually since 2000, West Ham Park features ornamental gardens, a plant nursery and a range of sporting facilities, making it one of East London's most popular leisure spots.

It has been run as a public park by the City of London Corporation since 1874, but was originally part of a private estate. Between 1762 and 1780 it was home to physician-philanthropist Dr John Fothergill, who built a botanical garden, often accepting rare plants in lieu of fees. It's appropriate that it now houses an important plant nursery, producing over 200,000 spring and summer bedding plants annually for parks, gardens and churchyards in the City of London.

The ornamental gardens include beds devoted to roses, irises, heathers and rhododendrons, among other plants, and one dedicated to Dr Fothergill. Picnic, wildlife and wildflower areas are dotted around the 77-acre (31ha) park, and there are self-guided walks (which can be downloaded from the website) taking in its historic, floral, arboreal and wild delights.

GARDEN SQUARES   39

From Bloomsbury to Hackney, there are garden squares throughout the City and East End of London, many maintained by local councils and user groups. All provide essential green space for children to play, workers to relax and eat their lunch, and families to picnic. The following squares offer free access to all (see map for locations).

A: Albion Square (E8, dawn to dusk, Haggerston rail) is a delightful Victorian square in a conservation area to the west of Queensbridge Road. The square was built in 1844, while its gardens gained a new lease of life in 1898 when the Metropolitan Public Gardens Association commissioned a new design, consisting of ornamental beds and a fountain, surrounded by four London planes with circular seating around their trunks. A local newspaper claimed it would 'vie in beauty with some of the prettiest gardens in the West End'. Albion Square's gardens have changed little since, and in 1999 won first

prize in the Small Publicly Maintained Garden section of the London Garden Squares Competition.

B: Bloomsbury Square Gardens (WC1, 7.30am to dusk, Holborn tube) occupy one of London's earliest squares, developed by the 4th Earl of Southampton in the 1660s to complement his mansion. The house has long gone, but the gardens still reflect some of Humphry Repton's early 19th-century design of lawns, shrubberies and statuesque trees; while a 2003 refurbishment added new railings and a hornbeam fence, as well as a play area.

At the northern end of Bloomsbury Square Gardens, a bronze statue of Whig politician Charles James Fox (1749-1806), attired as a Roman emperor, gazes towards Russell Square.

C: Brunswick Square (WC1, dawn to dusk, Russell Square tube) was once part of the grounds of the Foundling Hospital, the orphanage founded by Captain Thomas Coram in 1739, and is also where the Knightleys lived in Jane Austen's *Emma*. It became Brunswick Square in the late 18th century, named after Caroline of Brunswick (the Prince Regent's wife), when the gardens were laid out in 1799 with lawns, flowerbeds and trees. Near the centre of the garden is the Brunswick Plane, nominated in 2008 as one of the Great Trees of London by the tree-planting charity Trees for Cities.

D: De Beauvoir Square (N1, unrestricted, Haggerston rail) – actually situated in north London but close to **Albion Square** (see previous page) – is a classically laid out Green Flag garden square with beautiful rose beds and lawn areas, The square offers a range of amenities including a children's play area, seating area, wildlife corner, ranger's hut and bike racks. The square hosts to a number of neighbourhood events – many organised by the De Beauvoir Association (📖 debeauvoir.org. uk) – and there's also a gardening club.

E: Finsbury Circus & Garden (EC2, 8am to dusk, Moorgate tube) is London's oldest public park, dating from the early 1600s when Moor Field was drained and planted with trees, and, at 5.4 acres (2.2ha), the largest within the boundaries of the City. Its name is based on its elliptical shape, which resembles a Roman 'circus'. Grade II listed, it's now noted for its mature London plane trees (some over 200 years old) and a fine Japanese pagoda tree, and for its immaculately maintained bowling green (1925), home to the City of London Bowling Club.

There was uproar when it was revealed that part of Finsbury Circus was earmarked as a worksite for Crossrail, the cross-London railway project, and relief when Crossrail promised to return it to its original condition, following completion of work in 2017.

F: Gordon Square Garden (WC1, 8am to dusk, Euston Square tube) in Bloomsbury was developed in the 1820s by the 6th Duke of Bedford and named after his second wife, Lady Georgina Gordon. Part of the University of London since the 1920s, its a favourite sunbathing spot for students. In the southwest corner there's an area of woodland ground flora, including bluebells, cow parsley and dog violets. Look for the monument to Indian poet-philosopher Rabindranath Tagore (1861-1941) and the old gardener's hut, which now serves as an occasional café.

G: Gray's Inn Gardens (WC1, weekdays noon to 2.30pm, closed Bank Holidays, Chancery Lane tube), also known as The Walks, were laid out by Sir Francis Bacon in 1606 when he was treasurer of the Honourable Society of Gray's Inn, one of the four Inns of Court. In the 17th century the Walks were a fashionable place to see and be seen, and are still open to the public on weekday lunchtimes. The main feature is a broad path between an avenue of red oak trees and mature London planes, and while Bacon's more fanciful designs, such as a

City of London Bowling Club

labyrinth, are long gone, you can still see the Indian bean trees, now bowed with age, grown from slips brought back from Virginia by Sir Walter Raleigh.

H: Lincoln's Inn Fields (WC2, dawn to dusk, Holborn tube) is London's largest garden square with a history dating back to the 12th century. It has been the site of jousting, some notorious duels and the occasional public execution, and became a fashionable garden – said to be planned by Inigo Jones – in the 17th century. A municipal public garden since 1894, it consists of shrubberies, flower beds, tennis courts and an octagonal pavilion/bandstand. Trees include catalpa, ginkgo, holly, mountain ash and laburnum, and there are also some interesting memorials, including a lovely bronze commemorating Margaret MacDonald (1870-1911), social reformer and wife of Ramsey MacDonald.

👁 DON'T MISS!

On the north side of Lincoln's Inn Fields is one of London's most intriguing museums: Sir Joan Soane's Museum (💻 soane.org) showcases the great architect's fascinating collection in his splendid former home.

I: Queen Square (WC1, 7.30am to dusk, Russell Square tube) was once known as Queen Anne Square, although the statue of the regal lady in the north of the garden is now thought to be Queen Charlotte, who nursed her mentally ill husband George III in a house on the square. Dating from 1716, a shady rectangle with a variety of trees, roses and bedding displays, the square has strong medical connections. The National Hospital for Neurology and Neurosurgery and Great Ormond Street children's hospital are both nearby. Look for the sculpture of Sam the cat, perched on a wall – a feline memorial to cat lover and local champion Patricia Penn.

🍴 FOOD & DRINK 🍸

The Queen's Larder: This intimate pub on Queen Square serves typical pub grub, from ploughman's to lamb shank, and has an intriguing claim to fame. Legend has it that Queen Charlotte stored food in its cellar for the King when she was treating his illness in a nearby house.

J: Russell Square (WC1, 7.30am to 10pm, Russell Square tube) is one of London's busiest squares, although its gardens are large enough for you to escape much of the traffic noise. They were laid out in 1800 by Humphry Repton for the 5th Duke of Bedford (the Dukes' surname was Russell), whose Grade II listed statue stands in solitary splendour at the southern end of the square. A re-landscaping in 2000 added a magnificent new fountain with a 30ft (9m) jet, paths and a pergola, plus a new café. Look for the green building at the western corner of the square – it's one of 13 surviving shelters (out of 61) provided throughout London for taxi drivers.

K: Tavistock Square Gardens (WC1, daylight hours, Euston Square tube) in Bloomsbury dates from 1825, when it was developed as part of the Bedford estate. Its layout of London planes and lawns is typical of many City squares; what sets it apart is its large number of memorials which include a bronze of Mahatma Gandhi, busts of writer Virginia Woolf and Dame Louisa Aldrich-Blake, one of the UK's first women surgeons, and a cherry tree in memory of the victims of the Hiroshima nuclear bomb. A refurbishment of the gardens in 2011 included flower beds to reinforce the memorials' themes, including Indian, Japanese and medicinal plants.

40 SMALL CITY GARDENS

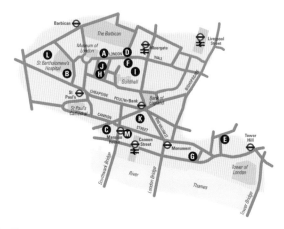

The City of London has some wonderful secret gardens. Some have sprung up in the ruins of old churches and cemeteries, while others have been laid out by members of the guilds who once dominated the City's trades. Often hidden away, they're well worth seeking out, not least for the respite they offer in one of the world's busiest cities. See map for locations.

A: Barber-Surgeons' Hall Garden (EC2, unrestricted access, Barbican or St Pauls tube) is tucked into a defensive bastion of Hadrian's London wall (ca. 300AD), in the shadow of the Museum of London, and harks back to the days when herbs were an essential part of the surgeon's stock-in-trade. There has been a garden here since the 1550s and this one, created in 1987, contains the Worshipful Company of Barbers' physic garden, with 45 different species of plants used to treat wounds, bruises and burns, some of which have an application in modern medicine (the Company's website lists them, 🖥 barberscompany.org). The garden also contains commemorative trees,

including a yellow magnolia planted for the Queen's Golden Jubilee in 2002.

> In medieval times, barber-surgeons were the medics of the battlefield. The link between barbers and surgeons wasn't broken until the 18th century, and the red and white pole outside a barber's shop recalls their gorier glory days – red for blood and white for bandages.

B: Christchurch Greyfriars Rose Garden (EC1, unrestricted access, St Paul's tube) is an enchanting small garden created on the remains of a church on Newgate Street. Several incarnations of Christchurch Greyfriars have stood here since 1306; the last was severely damaged in the Blitz and never rebuilt. The tower still stands, Grade I listed, but its nave is now a rose garden. Redesigned in 2011 in a colour scheme of mainly blue, purple and white, the garden has box-hedged rose beds in place of the original pews, paths where the aisles would have been and tall wooden towers, hung with bird boxes and climbing plants, representing the pillars that once

Salters' Garden

supported the roof. It's a very special place.

C: Cleary Garden (EC4, 8am to dusk, Mansion House tube) is a peaceful garden set back from Queen Victoria Street. Its three tiers reveal an intriguing history, from Blitz bomb damage on the upper section, through medieval London by the stairway, and a section which covers the site of a Roman bathhouse at the lower level. The garden was built in the rubble of a bombed-out house in the '40s, and named after Fred Cleary, who was instrumental in encouraging the creation of new gardens throughout the City. It has shaded wooden arbours, a sunny terrace with a miniature vineyard – a throwback to the Middle Ages when the area was a hub of the wine trade – and provides a variety of wildlife habitats. Sparrows and blue tits nest in the buddleia, and greenfinches, robins, blackbirds and dunnocks are frequent visitors.

D: Salters' Garden (EC2, weekdays 9am to 5pm, Moorgate tube) belongs to one of London's great livery companies, the Worshipful Company of Salters who once traded in… salt! The garden is hidden behind the Salters' Hall in Fore Street, sunk below road level and protected by a stretch of Roman wall. It first opened in 1981, but was redesigned as a knot garden and reopened in 1995 to commemorate the Company's 600th anniversary. It's a formal and classical space, with areas of lawn, hedging, pergolas, fountains and decorative urns; in summer the air is heady with the scent of roses. Note that the garden may be closed in bad weather (☎ 020-7588 5216 to check).

E: Seething Lane Gardens (EC3, weekdays dawn to dusk, Tower Hill tube) are situated near the Tower of London and mark the site of the Navy Office where Samuel Pepys once worked – look for the bronze bust of the great diarist by Karin Jonzen. It's said Pepys buried his wine and Parmesan cheese in the gardens to protect them from the Great Fire in 1666! Seething Lane Gardens were closed for refurbishment in 2012 and were expected to reopen in 2014. Plans focus on attracting wildlife to the area and include a new woodland area, native wildlife planting, a pergola and 'green' walls. To check on progress, contact the City of London Gardens Team (☎ 020-7374 4127).

F: St Alphage Garden (EC2, unrestricted access, Moorgate tube) are typical of the gardens which were resurrected from Blitz bomb damage in the City, which was especially brutal in the area where the Barbican now stands. All that is left of St Alphage's church are the ruins of its 14th-century tower. This has been a public garden since the 1870s and has grassed areas and a magnolia tree, seats and flower beds, all bounded to the north by a high section of the old Roman London Wall – the Salters' Garden (see above) is just on the other side. Part of the garden can only be accessed via a fight of wooden steps.

HIDDEN CORNER

One of the raised walkways which traverse the windy Barbican, **St Alphage's Highwalk** contains an unexpected elevated garden, with contemporary grasses and shrubs, and a bronze sculpture of a Minotaur by Michael Ayrton. It's reached via the Barbican centre and Gilbert Bridge.

G: St Dunstan-in-the-East Garden (EC3, unrestricted access, Monument or Tower Hill tube) is one of the City's most magnificent surprises. Although a church has stood here since at least the 12th century, St Dunstan was all but destroyed in the Blitz. In 1967, the Grade I listed ruins – which include a tower by Wren – and former churchyard were incorporated into a glorious garden. The walls and majestic windows are draped with Virginia creeper and ornamental vine, while exotic plants such as pineapple-scented Moroccan broom and New Zealand flax thrive in the sheltered conditions. In the lower garden is a Japanese snowball that displays breath-taking blossom in late spring. Robins and tits are regular visitors and there's also an 'insect hotel'.

H: St John Zachary Garden (EC2, unrestricted access, St Paul's tube) is on the site of the churchyard and medieval church of St John Zachary, Gresham Street, which was damaged in the Great Fire. It's also called the Goldsmiths' Garden, after the Worshipful Company of Goldsmiths who acquired land here in 1339. It was first laid out as a sunken garden in 1941 and has since been redesigned several times. It contains lawns, trees, a fountain and an unusual sculpture entitled Three Printers (ca. 1957, Wilfred Dudeney), which represents the newspaper process, featuring a newsboy, a printer and an editor.

I: St Mary Aldermanbury (EC2, unrestricted access, Moorgate tube) is a striking garden located next to London's Guildhall. A church has stood here since at least 1181; like many City churches, it was destroyed in the Great Fire of 1666, was rebuilt (by Wren) and finally finished off by the Blitz. Its ruins have made space for a pleasant garden with areas of lawn, flower beds and shrubberies, a variety of trees and an ornamental box-hedged knot garden. There's a bust of Shakespeare, which commemorates not the Bard, but two of his acting troupe – John Heminges and Henry Condell – both buried at St Mary's. After his death in 1616, they collected his works and published them at their own expense; without them we might not know who Shakespeare was!

The remains of Wren's incarnation of St Mary's were taken up in the late '60s and moved to Westminster College in Fulton, Missouri, where they were restored as a memorial to Winston Churchill, who made an important speech at the college in 1946. A plaque was placed in the garden by Westminster College and relates the history of the church.

J: St Mary Staining Churchyard (EC2, unrestricted access, St Paul's tube) in Oat Lane perished in the Great Fire and was never rebuilt. The land lay derelict until 1965 when the City of London Corporation laid out a garden, consisting of a raised area of lawn with a large plane tree, flower beds, shrubs, with tombstones ranged along the back, overlooked by Pewterers' Hall. There's reference to a church standing here as far back as 1189 and to a famous murder which took place in 1278 when Richard de Codeford, accused of robbery, took refuge in the

Walbrook Gardens

were burnt, beheaded or boiled! In 1305, Scottish hero William Wallace was dragged to Smithfield behind a horse, and hung, drawn and quartered, and over 200 Protestants were burnt at the stake here during Queen Mary's (aka Bloody Mary) reign. A public garden since 1872, its centrepiece is a drinking fountain with a bronze figure representing Peace (1873). More recent additions include border planting to provide shrub cover and berries for birds, a 'hotel' for bumblebees and geometric sculptural seating with inscriptions relating to the history of the area.

M: Whittington Garden (EC4, unrestricted opening, Cannon Street rail/tube) on College Street/Upper Thames Street, is named after Richard 'Dick' Whittington, one of the most famous Lord Mayors of London. The garden is alongside the church of St Michael Paternoster Royal, which Whittington had rebuilt at his own expense in 1409 (and was buried there in 1423). The Corporation of London acquired the site in 1955 and the garden was laid out in 1960 with a largely paved area in the west, and grass, flower beds and trees in the east. A small fountain was erected in the west section in the late '60s. The east section is now surrounded by hedge, and remains largely grass, shaded by trees.

church and killed his pursuers with a lance through a hole in the window.

K: Walbrook Gardens (EC4, 8am to dusk, Cannon Street tube/rail) is a recent addition to the City, although they occupy an old site – that of St Swithin, London Stone, established in the 13th century. Norman Foster's Walbrook building was completed in 2010 and towers over this intimate yet formal garden space, which can be challenging to find (the entrance is in Salters' Hall Court, just to the west of St Swithin's Lane). St Swithin was the last resting place of Catrin, daughter of Welsh hero Owain Glyndwr, who was captured in 1409 and taken with her children to the Tower of London during her father's unsuccessful fight for the freedom of Wales. She died in custody in 1413, and a memorial to Catrin and the suffering of all women and children in war stands in the former churchyard.

L: West Smithfield Rotunda Garden (EC1, daylight hours, St Paul's tube) is a pretty and peaceful circular park near Smithfield Market, with a gruesome history. For over 400 years it was a place of public execution, where heretics, rebels and criminals

Guided walks of the City's gardens take place from Apr-Oct from Fri-Sun, led by City of London guides. Fees (2013) are £7 for adults (children free). See the City of London website for more information (🖳 cityoflondon. gov.uk/things-to-do/green-spaces/city-gardens/events-and-activities/pages/guided-walks.aspx).

CHAPTER 3

NORTH LONDON

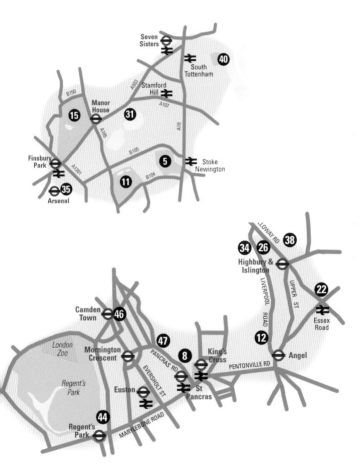

See overleaf for more maps

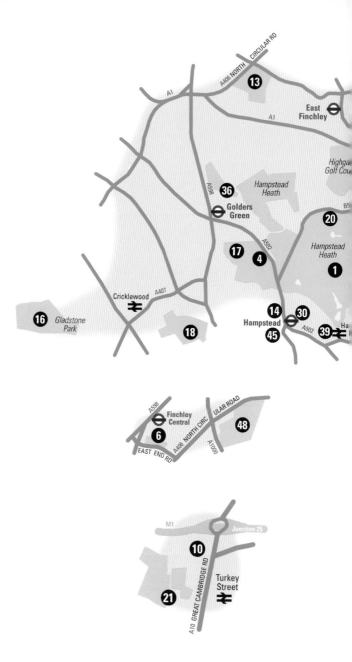

See previous page for key and more maps

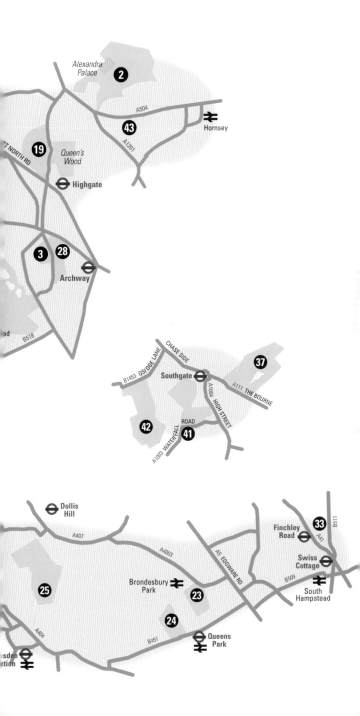

1 HAMPSTEAD HEATH

Address: Spaniards Road, NW3 7JJ (☎ 020-7332 3505, 🖳 cityoflondon.gov.uk > green spaces, hampsteadheath.net and hampsteadheath.org.uk).
Opening hours: Unrestricted access to most areas.
Cost: Free.
Transport: Hampstead & Golders Green tube, and Hampstead Heath & Gospel Oak rail. Buses also serve various parts of the heath.
Attractions & amenities: Three cafés (Golders Hill, Kenwood House and Parliament Hill), playgrounds, swimming ponds, bandstand, wide range of sports facilities.

Hampstead Heath is a large, ancient park between Hampstead and Highgate, covering 790 acres (320ha) and sitting astride one of the city's highest points (440ft/134m). Rambling and hilly, it's one of London's most beloved open spaces, encompassing grassland, woodlands, gardens, ponds, playgrounds and a profusion of sports facilities. It attracts over 7m visitors a year. Along its eastern perimeter are a chain of ponds, including three open-air, public swimming pools, which were originally reservoirs for drinking water from the River Fleet. The Health also encloses the hamlet of Vale of Health (called 'Hatchett's Bottom' until 1801), accessed by a lane from East Heath Road.

The heath was first recorded in 986 when Ethelred the Unready granted one of his servants five hides of land at 'Hemstede'. This same land was recorded in the *Domesday Book* of 1086 as being held by the monastery of St Peter's at Westminster Abbey, then known as the 'Manor of Hampstead'. Westminster held the land until 1133, when control of part of the manor was released to one Richard de Balta; later, during Henry II's reign, the whole of the manor became privately owned by Alexander de Barentyn, the King's butler. Manorial rights to the land remained in private hands until the '40s, when they lapsed under Sir Spencer Pocklington Maryon Wilson, although the estate itself passed to Shane Gough, 5th Viscount Gough.

Over time, plots of land in the manor were sold off for building, particularly in the early 19th century, although much of the heath remained common land. The main part of the

eath – divided into West and East Heaths (separated by Spaniards Road) – was acquired for the people in 1871 by the Metropolitan Board of Works (later the London County Council). Parliament Hill was purchased in 1888 for £300,000 and added to the park; Golders Hill was added in 1898, Kenwood House and grounds (120 acres/48ha) in 1928, and Hill Garden and the Pergola in 1960.

Since 1989, the heath has been managed by the City of London Corporation and lies mostly within the borough of Camden, with the adjoining Hampstead Heath Extension and Golders Hill Park located in the borough of Barnet. The heath is a Local Nature Reserve and a Site of Metropolitan Importance, while part of Kenwood is a Site of Special Scientific Interest. Several parts of the heath – all of which, unlike the rest of the heath, are fenced in and closed at night – are covered separately in this chapter, including **Golders Hill Park** (see page 132), **Hill Garden & Pergola** (page 118) and **Kenwood House** (page 135).

In the southeast corner of the heath, Parliament Hill (322ft/98m) provides a panoramic view over London's skyline that's protected by law. It's considered by some to be the focal point of Hampstead Heath, and the highest part is dubbed 'Kite Hill' due to its popularity with kite flyers. It offers a wide range of sporting facilities including an athletics track, tennis courts and the Parliament Hill Lido. In the northwest corner is the Hampstead Heath Extension, an open space of 125 acres (50ha), which was created from farmland. Its origins can still be seen in the form of old field boundaries, hedgerows and trees. Today it consists mostly of sports pitches – cricket, rugby and soccer – and also includes the Seven Sisters Ponds.

Boudicca's Mound

Near the current men's bathing pond, is a tumulus where, according to local legend, Queen Boudicca (Boadicea) was buried after she and 10,000 Iceni warriors were defeated by the Romans at Battle Bridge in circa 60AD.

Hampstead Heath is an important refuge for wildlife, including Muntjac deer, grass snakes, foxes, rabbits, slow worms, squirrels, terrapins and frogs. It's also home to many bird species (over 180 have been recorded) including common kingfishers, jackdaws, and ring-necked parakeets, while Natterer's, Daubenton's, noctule and pipistrelle bats can be seen over the ponds (the heath is one of London's

Hampstead Heath pond

best places to see bats). It's also home to a quarter of Britain's spider species, some 25 types of butterfly, plus a wide variety of grasshoppers, crickets, dragonflies and damselflies.

🍴 FOOD & DRINK 🍴

The Brewhouse: Situated in Kenwood House, this delightful café serves sandwiches, salads, pastries, soups and stews, plus veggie and children's options, while in summer there's a stand serving ice cream and Pimm's.

   Golder's Hill Café: Another great place for a (homemade) snack or lunch with a good kids' menu.

   Parliament Hill Café: Popular café offering a wide range of food, including jacket potatoes, sandwiches, full English breakfast, fruit, ice cream and cakes.

From the 17th century to the late 19th century there were very few trees on the heath, which supported a mosaic of rich heathland communities, but when it came into public ownership its use as grazing land declined, allowing trees and shrubs to become established. Thus most woodland on the heath is ecologically relatively new and is largely comprised of birch, oak and sycamore, although there are also over 800 identified veteran trees. Today, the heath comprises a mosaic of grassland, woodland, scrub, hedgerows, ponds and wetland habitats, with only remnants of the original heathland habitat; some small areas of acid grassland exist, home to plants such as heath bedstraw, oval sedge and tormentil. The remains of a bog on West Heath contain several species of bog-moss and water horsetail. Over 350 species of fungi have also been recorded, including the rare bracket fungus *Ganoderma lucidum*.

   The hedgerows across the heath are typically dominated by hawthorn, with holly and elder. Some support the high level of diverse species associated with ancient hedgerows, including the rare wild service tree, hornbeam and midland hawthorn, while a good network of hedges remains on the Extension. The heath has been awarded a Green Flag annually since 1998.

   There are more than 25 areas of water on Hampstead Heath. On the east side is a series of eight former reservoirs known as Highgate Ponds, originally dug in the 17th and 18th centuries. They include two single-sex swimming pools, a model boating pond, a wildlife reserve and a fishing 'lake'. In the southwest corner of the heath, towards South End Green, are

Leg of Mutton Pond

Bandstand

three further ponds (called Hampstead Ponds), one of which is a mixed bathing pond. These ponds are the result of the damming of Hampstead Brook (one of the sources of the Fleet River) in 1777 by the Hampstead Water Company, formed in 1692 to meet London's growing water demands.

The heath is home to a range of activities and sports and is extensively used by walkers, runners, swimmers, horse-riders and kite flyers. Facilities include an athletics track, a pétanque pitch, a volleyball court and eight children's play areas, including an adventure playground, plus cricket, rugby and soccer pitches in the Extension. Swimming takes place all year round in two of the three natural swimming ponds: the men's pond which opened in the 1890s and the ladies' pond which opened in 1925. There's even a zoo in Golders Hill Park.

Hampstead Heath has its own 'police' force, consisting of 12 constables, who are responsible for enforcing the heath's bylaws.

2 ALEXANDRA PARK & PALACE

Address: Alexandra Palace Way, N22 7AY (☎ 020-8365 2121,
🖳 alexandrapalace.com and friendsofalexandrapark.org).
Opening hours: Unrestricted access.
Cost: Free.
Transport: Wood Green tube.
Attractions & amenities: Restaurant, cafés, pub, ice rink, boating lake, pitch and
putt golf, children's play area, deer enclosure, conservation area, free parking.

Alexandra Palace

Alexandra Park – named after the Princess of Wales (wife of Edward VII), Alexandra of Denmark – is a beautiful 196-acre (79ha) public park created in 1863 on the former site of Tottenham Wood Farm. The park is best known as the site of Alexandra Palace, but it has much else to offer and is one of London's most beloved green spaces, winning a number of Green Flag awards. Designed by Alexander McKenzie as a park and pleasure ground, it's a delightful mixture of informal woodland, open grassland, formal gardens and attractions. The vast, tree-lined sloping hill has panoramic views over London – on a clear day it's possible to see the Crystal Palace Transmitter on the far southeast side of London.

> The palace – dubbed the 'People's Palace' – was built by the Lucas Brothers, who also built the Royal Albert Hall at around the same time.

Alexandra Palace (Grade II listed) opened in the park in 1873 to provide Victorians with a recreation centre within a green environment, but was destroyed by fire just 16 days later. A new palace opened on 1st May 1875, covering an area of some 7.5 acres (3ha). Centred on the Great Hall – home to the mighty Willis organ driven by two steam engines and

park's nature reserve is a favourite of twitchers and attracts numerous common woodland and parkland birds, both residents and visitors. The park is also home to many ancient trees, particularly oak, and contains a rose garden (constructed by internees during the First World War), a lake and a large enclosure housing a herd of fallow deer.

The park also offers a range of recreation and sports facilities, including an ice-skating rink (open year round), various eateries (see box), a children's play area, skate boarding park, pitch and putt golf course, fishing and boating, and soccer and cricket pitches. It also hosts a farmers' market on Sundays.

vast bellows – it contained a concert hall, art galleries, museum, lecture hall, library, banqueting room and a theatre. There was also an open-air swimming pool (now long closed) and a racecourse (which closed in 1970) with a grandstand, a Japanese village, a switchback ride, a boating lake, and a nine-hole pitch and putt golf course.

In 1935 the east wing of the palace – affectionately nicknamed 'Ally Pally' by Gracie Fields – became the headquarters of the BBC, and it was from here that the world's first public television transmission was made in 1936. It remained the main transmitting centre for the BBC until 1956 and its iconic radio tower is still in use today. The original studios still survive in the southeast wing with their producers' galleries, and the original Victorian theatre is also intact.

In 1980, a fire destroyed the Great Hall and Banqueting Suite, which has since been restored and is now used mostly as an exhibition centre, music venue and conference centre. The

 FOOD & DRINK

Bar & Kitchen: The palace bar offers freshly cooked, traditional menus, with a great indoor area within the Palm Court and some of the best views of London from the garden.

Grove Café: Italian café situated in the picturesque and tranquil Grove, where you can enjoy great coffee, thick Italian hot chocolate, and hot apple juice with cinnamon, plus tasty ciabatta sandwiches.

Lakeside Café: Another café venue serving good coffee and wholesome food, where you can soak up the relaxing atmosphere.

3 HIGHGATE CEMETERY

Address: Swain's Lane, N6 6PJ (☎ 020-8340 1834, 🖥 highgate-cemetery.org).
Opening hours: Mon-Fri, 10am to 4:30pm (3.30pm winter); Sat-Sun, 11am to 4:30pm (3.30pm winter). Tours of the West Cemetery take place on weekdays at 1.45pm (booking required) or at weekends (hourly) from 11am to 3pm (no need to book).
Cost: East Cemetery, £3 adults, £2 students. West Cemetery (accessible only by tour), £7 adults, £5 students; £3 weekend tours, £2 students.
Transport: Highgate or Archway tube.

Highgate Cemetery (Grade I listed) opened in 1839, soon after Queen Victoria's accession to the throne, and was one of London's Magnificent Seven Cemeteries, the others being Abney Park (1840), Brompton (1840), Kensal Green (1833), Nunhead (1840), Tower Hamlets (1841) and West Norwood (1836). Highgate was designed by Stephen Geary (1797-1854) and landscaped by David Ramsey with exotic formal planting. However, it was the stunning architecture that made Highgate the capital's principal and most fashionable cemetery, further enhanced by its unparalleled elevation overlooking London.

In the 19th century, cemeteries were more than simply a place for burials; they were a popular tourist attraction where thousands came to admire the memorials and tombs, and somewhere to be enjoyed for their beauty and tranquillity.

The cemetery covers an area of 37 acres (15ha) and is divided into two parts – the original West Cemetery, and the East Cemetery which opened in 1856 – on either side of Swain's Lane. The former is accessible only by guided tour to protect the monuments and for the public's safety, while the latter can be visited independently and is still open for burials.

In the heart of the West Cemetery is the splendid Egyptian Avenue, which was inspired by the discovery of Egypt's Valley of the Kings in the early 19th century, with vaults on either side of a passageway entered via a great arch. This leads to the eerie Circle of Lebanon (surrounding a huge cedar of Lebanon

Karl Marx tomb

Egyptian Avenue

tree, some 300 years old), a ring of vaults and catacombs, completed in 1842 in the Gothic style. Other highlights include two chapels which were built in the Tudor style – one for Church of England adherents, the other for Dissenters – topped with wooden turrets and a central bell tower.

By the turn of the century the desire for elaborate funerals was waning and by the '30s Highgate was neglected and in decline. It was saved by the Friends of Highgate Cemetery in 1975 and over the last four decades there has been extensive restoration and conservation, including several lavish (listed) monuments. Among the prominent figures buried here are the family of Charles Dickens, Michael Faraday, Christina Rossetti, Sir Sidney Robert Nolan, Douglas Adams, George Eliot, Malcolm McLaren, Sir Ralph Richardson, Max Wall, John Galsworthy and six Lord Mayors of London.

Although the East Cemetery is a pleasant place for a stroll and contains the tombs of many well-known people, including the famous grave of Karl Marx, it's the much murkier and foreboding West Cemetery that's the dark soul of Highgate. It contains a wealth of Gothic monuments overgrown with ivy and moss, in a scene reminiscent of a horror movie. Its jumble of plants, trees and memorials has become a wildlife sanctuary, where foxes, hedgehogs, butterflies, insects and an abundance of bird species thrive in the heart of London.

Apart from being one of London's historical treasures, Highgate Cemetery is a haven of beauty and serenity, a world away from life beyond its walls.

There's only one tour of the West Cemetery a day on weekdays (1.45pm) and it's advisable to book at least a week in advance. Be warned that that the cemetery is on a 1:7 hill and the tour climbs steeply at the start and descends as steeply on the return. The East Cemetery is on a much gentler incline and contains the graves of many of the cemetery's most famous residents. You can obtain a map from the office and discover them for yourself.

4 HILL GARDEN & PERGOLA

Address: Inverforth Close, off North End Way, NW3 7EX (☎ 020-7332 3511, ⬛ cityoflondon.gov.uk > green spaces).
Opening hours: Daily, dawn to dusk.
Cost: Free.
Transport: Golders Green or Hampstead tube.

Pergola

The charming Hill Garden and its beautiful pergola – Grade II listed and 800ft (244m) in length – are among the hidden delights of **Hampstead Heath** (see page 110). The site was formerly part of the gardens of The Hill, a house built in 1807 and owned by the Quaker banking family of Hoare until 1896, when it was sold to George Fisher. Fisher rebuilt the house, set in 5 acres (2ha) of parkland and gardens, and lived here until 1904, when it was sold to William Lever (1851-1925).

It was soap magnate Lever, one of the original Lever Brothers, and a pioneering Liberal MP (later Lord Leverhulme), who commissioned Hill Garden and its extraordinary pergola. The formal Arts and Crafts garden was created between 1906 and 1925 by celebrated landscape architect Thomas Mawson (1861-1933), and is situated at the rear of Inverforth House – as The Hill is now known. Work began on the pergola after Lord Leverhulme acquired land adjoining his property; the first part was finished in 1906 and it was extended in 1911, but it wasn't finally completed until 1925, shortly before his death.

Central to Lord Leverhulme's pergola project was the task of raising the gardens to the required level. As chance would have it, the Hampstead extension to London Underground's Northern Line was being built at the same time, and soon thousands of wagon-loads of soil were making their way to The Hill, with the astute Lord being paid a nominal fee for the material he needed to realise his dream!

Mawson brought architectural treatment and formality to garden design, and Hill Garden and its pergola are the best surviving examples of his work. Once completed, the structure's full length was greater than two soccer pitches and was bisected by a public right of way, over which Mawson built a fine stone bridge. A magnificent Edwardian extravagance, the pergola became the setting for garden parties and summer evening strolls. The pergola walk, which links the formal gardens of the main house and the more gentle lawns of the lower garden, was a master stroke, enhanced by the dramatic contrast between the towering trees of the West Heath and the exotic plants climbing the graceful pergola.

The Second World War and subsequent years weren't kind to the pergola or gardens, and the property was divided in 1960 when London County Council purchased the western part of the garden and the northwest part of the pergola, by which time both were in an appalling state. The area was restored and opened to the public in 1963 as the Hill Garden. In 1991, the part of the pergola owned by the hospital was added to the public gardens (Inverforth House and gardens remain private). Since 1989 the garden has been owned and managed by the City of London Corporation, which restored the pergola in 1995 and laid out further formal gardens to the west.

In 1925, The Hill was purchased by ship-owner Andrew Weir, 1st Baron Inverforth, who lived there until his death in 1955. It was renamed Inverforth House in his honour when he left it to Manor House Hospital.

In late spring and early summer, the raised, covered pergola is festooned with fragrant flowers, including jasmine, buddleia, sage, honeysuckle, vines, clematis, kiwi, potato vine, lavender and wisteria. If you visit during the early evening, you may even see roosting long-eared bats. In contrast to the wild decadence of the pergola, Hill Garden is a beautifully manicured slice of paradise, affording panoramic views of London.

5 ABNEY PARK CEMETERY

Address: Stoke Newington High Street, Stoke Newington, London N16 0LH
(☎ 020-7275 7557, 🖳 abney-park.org.uk).
Opening hours: Daily, 8am to 7pm; closes 4pm in winter. Visitor centre, 9.30am to 5pm weekdays and on some weekends.
Cost: Free.
Transport: Stoke Newington rail.
Attractions & amenities: Arboretum, nature reserve.

Now a memorial park and woodland nature reserve run by the Abney Park Trust, Abney Park was one of London's Magnificent Seven Cemeteries (see **Highgate Cemetery** on page 116), built by the Victorians to cope with London's rapid population increase. It was laid out in the early 18th century on the instructions of Lady Mary Abney and others, becoming a non-denominational garden cemetery in 1840, and also a semi-public arboretum and educational institute.

It was the first wholly non-denominational garden cemetery in Europe and was specifically designed using motifs not associated with contemporary religion. Its impressive entrance reflects the then-popular Egyptian revival style; it's by William Hosking, the first professor of architecture at King's College (London), who also designed Abney Park Chapel (Grade II listed).

The arboretum was intended to be a labelled tree collection for educational walks, and much enhanced the wooded character of the park which already had several exotic trees, some planted in the 1690s. The planting of the original 2,500 arboretum trees and shrubs aimed to be botanical and naturalistic,

rather than purely aesthetic, which led Abney Park to become the most impressively landscaped garden cemetery of its time. Burial rights ceased in 1978 and it's now dedicated to a wide range of projects in the arts, education, conservation and recreation

---

The park's most famous 'resident' is William Booth, founder of the Salvation Army, who lies beneath a huge, striking headstone.

Today, Abney Park is a romantic wilderness in a grittily urban part of London, every bit as atmospheric and interesting as Highgate Cemetery. Its crumbling state adds to its charm, with some magnificent urns, inscriptions, ivy-clad statues and sculptures – leaning, tumbling and falling over, and merging with the planting. The park is full of atmospheric walks and picnic spots, and also rich in wildlife.

AVENUE HOUSE & ARBORETUM   6

Address: 17 East End Road, Finchley, N3 3QE (☎ 020-8346 7812, 🖥 avenuehouse.org.uk and friendsofavenuehouse.org).
Opening hours: Gardens, daily, 7.30am to dusk. House – check public events on the website.
Cost: Free.
Transport: Finchley Central tube.
Attractions & amenities: Arboretum, café, playground, parking.

Avenue House (Grade II listed) is an imposing Victorian (allegedly haunted) mansion in Finchley set in 10 acres (4ha) of grounds. Originally owned by the Bishop of London, the land was subsequently retained by both the Knights Templar and then the Knights Hospitaller, until their estates were seized by Henry VIII in 1540. The first house on the site was built by the Rev Edward Cooper in 1859, and became known as Avenue House.

The estate was purchased in 1874 by Henry Charles (Inky) Stephens, whose father invented the famous blue-black ink. He engaged Robert Marnock (1800-1889), reportedly the best landscape gardener of his time, to design the gardens. Stephens died in 1918, bequeathing Avenue House and its grounds to the people of Finchley. The grounds became a public park in 1928.

The estate contains an arboretum, with rare trees from as far afield as China and California, including a pocket handkerchief tree, redwood, gingko and the memorably-named wing-nut tree. One of the main features of the grounds is The Bothy, built as a large walled garden in the shape of a castle in the late 1870s. It's one of the earliest non-Roman concrete structures in England, though in a state of disrepair. The Bothy Garden, where vegetables were grown for Avenue House, is now a hidden oasis with lawns and a wild garden.

FOOD & DRINK

Al's Cafeteria: This kiosk serves Italian coffee, freshly baked muffins and delicious Mediterranean food, as well as a variety of ice creams and cold drinks. Open year round seven days a week, from 10am to 6pm.

In 1989 the house was ravaged by fire and was refurbished by Barnet Council. It's now run by the Avenue House Estate Trust as a venue for private, community and business functions, meetings and classes.

7 BRUCE CASTLE PARK

Address: Lordship Lane, Tottenham, N17 8NU (☎ 020-8808 8772, ⌨ haringey.gov.uk/brucecastlemuseum).

Opening hours: Gardens, daily, 8am to dusk. House, Wed-Sun, 1-5pm. Closed 25-26th Dec, New Year's Day and Good Friday.

Cost: Free.

Transport: Seven Sisters or Wood Green tube.

Attractions & amenities: Rose garden, museum, playground, sports facilities.

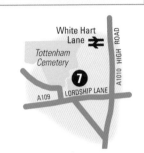

Bruce Castle Park (20 acres/8ha) is home to the only ancient manor house still standing in the Tottenham area. Grade I listed Bruce Castle, which dates back to the 16th century, is constructed of red brick and has a detached tower – both structures are among the earliest examples of brick buildings in England. The house has been substantially remodelled over the years, notably between the 17th and 19th centuries, and is architecturally interesting. Its principal façade has ashiar quoining and tall paned windows, and there are symmetrical matching bays at each end.

The origin of the park's name dates back to the Norman Conquest, when the manor of Tottenham belonged to Waltheof, Earl of Huntingdon, who married the Conqueror's niece. Their daughter, Maud, married David I, King of Scotland, who acquired the Earldom of Huntingdon, and eventually the manor passed to the Bruis (or Bruce) family of Scotland. The family's English lands were seized by Edward I in 1306, after Robert the Bruce became King of Scotland, although the house wasn't renamed Bruce Castle until the 17th century.

Bruce Castle Park became the first public park in Tottenham in 1892, while a famous landmark is a 400-year-old oak tree, a survivor of the ancient forest that once covered the area. A tree trail around the park identifies different species and individual trees thought to be over 200 years old. Awarded a Green Flag annually since 2003, the park contains a formal rose garden and a Holocaust memorial garden, plus a playground, lawn bowls, and tennis and basketball courts. It hosts a variety of events throughout the year, including the Tottenham Community Festival and Carnival in June.

The building and land were purchased in 1891 by Tottenham Urban District Council. Bruce Castle opened as a museum in 1906 housing local history collections, along with an exhibition of postal history.

CAMLEY STREET NATURAL PARK 8

Address: 12 Camley Street, NW1 0PW (☎ 020-7833 2311, 🖥 wildlondon.org.uk).
Opening hours: Apr-Sep, Sun-Fri, 10am to 5.30pm; Oct-Mar, 10am to 4.30pm;
closed Saturdays.
Cost: Free.
Transport: St Pancras tube and rail.
Attractions & amenities: Visitor centre.

Camley Street Natural Park is a stunning, tranquil green haven in the most urban of locations, situated immediately behind St Pancras International Station. The internationally-acclaimed reserve was awarded Green Flag status in 2009 and is a special place for both people and wildlife. Comprising a narrow strip of land (2 acres/0.8ha) bounded by the Regent's Canal (alongside St Pancras Lock), Camley Street is an urban wildlife sanctuary and education centre run by the London Wildlife Trust.

The park opened in 1985 and is an example of the success and importance of urban ecology for environmental and educational purposes in the heart of London. The site was a coal depot from Victorian times until the '60s, when it became derelict, and was acquired in 1981 by the Greater London Council for a lorry/coach park; however, local residents and the London Wildlife Trust

successfully campaigned against this proposal.

A variety of habitats co-exist in the park's relatively small area, including wetlands, marshland, a wildflower meadow, woodland, reed beds around a pond and a garden area, all of which attract a plethora of insects (including many butterflies), amphibians, birds, mammals and a rich variety of plant life.

Some of the reserve's celebrities include the rare earthstar fungi, bats and around 50 bird species, including reed warblers, kingfishers, geese, mallards and reed buntings.

The park is popular with people seeking respite from the noise and bustle of the city, as well as being a hub for London Wildlife Trust volunteers (it has a full-time education programme for Camden schools). There are plans for a pedestrian bridge to span the Regent's Canal from Coal Drops Yard into Camley Street Natural Park. A visitor centre caters for casual visitors and school parties, although tours must be booked.

9 CANONS PARK

Address: Donnefield Avenue, Harrow, HA8 6QT (☎ 020-8424 1754,
🖥 friendsofcanonspark.org.uk and harrow.gov.uk > parks > parks in harrow).
Opening hours: Daily, 8am to dusk.
Cost: Free.
Transport: Canons Park tube.
Attractions & amenities: Gardens, pavilion, café (summer), playground.

Canons Park (Grade II listed and Green Flag endowed) is a delightful segment of 18th-century parkland between Stanmore and Edgware, encompassing 44.5 acres (18ha) and several listed buildings.

The land which became Canons Park belonged, until the Dissolution of the Monasteries, to the Priory of St Bartholomew the Great ('Canons' refers to the canons or monks). In 1709, the estate was acquired through marriage by James Brydges (1673-1744), first Duke of Chandos, who built a palace in 1713-25, designed by James Gibbs. Brydges hired some of the best builders, landscape gardeners and craftsmen of the day to create the splendid grounds, which contained fountains, canals, pools, lakes, avenues, formal gardens and a kitchen garden. Today you can still see the avenue that led from the palace to St Lawrence's Church in the form of a raised causeway along which the duke and his family would proceed to Sunday worship.

Part of the original estate was acquired by Harrow Council in 1936 and became the current Canons Park, combining 18th, 19th and 20th-century landscape designs. The crowning glory is the walled King George V Memorial Garden – part of the duke's original kitchen gardens – which was redesigned in the '30s after the park became public. It reflects the design ideas of that decade with a structure of evergreens highlighted by seasonal displays, featuring a central square pool surrounded by a raised terrace with steps, formal flower beds and a pavilion.

Following a Heritage Lottery Fund grant of almost £1m, the gardens and buildings were comprehensively restored in 2008, including new entrance gates, re-laid paving, replanted flower-beds and stylish topiary.

Today, Canons Park is a lovely haven for both people and wildlife – the Friends of Canons Park organise regular bird-watching walks – with a playground and a café in summer.

CAPEL MANOR GARDENS 10

Address: Bullsmoor Lane, Enfield, EN1 4RQ (☎ 08456-122122,
💻 capelmanorgardens.co.uk).
Opening hours: Nov-Feb, Mon-Fri, 10am to 5pm; Mar-Oct, daily, 10am to 5pm.
Closed 25th Dec to 1st Jan.
Cost: £5.50 adults, £4.50 concessions, £2.50 children (5 and under free), £13.50
families (two adults and up to three children). See website for fees for special
musical and theatrical events.
Transport: Turkey Street rail (then 20 minutes' walk) or by car.
Attractions & amenities: Restaurant, farm, shop.

Capel Manor Gardens is a stunning 30-acre (12.1ha) estate surrounding a Georgian manor house and Victorian stables. It features a variety of richly-planted themed gardens, including historical gardens, an Italianate maze, a Japanese garden, Kim Wilde's Jungle Gym, the front gardens of Sunflower Street and many others.

The history of Capel Manor dates from 1275 when the land was held by Ellis of Honeyland; there's evidence of a manor house at this time, although the one you see today was built in the 1750s. In 1486, Sir William Capel assumed ownership of the estate, which remained in his family (later the Lords of Essex) until the 16th century, when it was surrendered to the crown.

The estate then passed through a succession of owners until, in 1932, Lt Col Sydney Medcalf occupied it until his death in 1958, when he bequeathed the house to the Incorporated Society of Accountants. Colonel Medcalf had a love of horticulture but his great passion was Clydesdale horses; the Manor became a National Centre for Clydesdale breeding and breeders still compete for the Medcalf Cup.

Today, Capel Manor is a college of horticulture and London's only specialist centre for land-based studies. Capel Manor College is a working estate where students gain 'hands-on' experience in all aspects of land-based studies, including horticulture, arboriculture (tree surgery), garden design, floristry, animal care and environmental conservation.

The Animal Corner has Kunekune pigs, poultry, rabbits, pygmy goats and guinea pigs, while Clydesdale horses can be seen working and exercising in the grounds. There's also a varied programme of events throughout the year, while the Hessayon Centre contains a garden gift shop with plant sales in summer.

 FOOD & DRINK

Terrace Restaurant: Serving
everything from breakfast and hot
lunches to ice cream and cakes, with
outdoor seating for sunny days. Or
take a picnic and enjoy it by the lake.

11 CLISSOLD PARK

Address: Greenway Close, N4 2EY (☎ 020-8356 8428, 🖥 hackney.gov.uk/clissold-park.htm and clissoldpark.com).
Opening hours: Daily, 7.30am to 9.30pm (summer), 7.30am to 4.30pm (winter).
Cost: Free.
Transport: Arsenal or Finsbury Park tube.
Attractions & amenities: Gardens, ponds, café, bowling green, bandstand, tennis courts, playground, animal attractions, sports facilities.

Clissold Park is a much-loved public park in Stoke Newington (Hackney), covering 55 acres (22ha), with a rich variety of trees and shrubs, a rose garden and an organic nature garden. The Green Flag park also offers a wide range of facilities, including a playground, paddling pool, sports fields, bowling green, table tennis, basketball and tennis courts, a bandstand, a café and animal attractions (including an aviary, animal enclosures, a butterfly tunnel and terrapins in the lakes).

Clissold House (Grade II* listed) was reputedly designed by Joseph Woods (1776-1864) for his uncle, the Quaker banker Jonathan Hoare (1752-1819). In 1811 the house was sold to the Crawshay family of iron makers; Eliza Crawshay inherited the property on her father's death in 1835, when she married the Reverend Augustus Clissold (1797-1882), from whom the house and park take their name. On Clissold's death, the estate was purchased by developers, but activists John Runtz and Joseph Beck persuaded the authorities to buy it and create a public park, which opened in 1889. The two ponds in the park are named Beckmere and Runtzmere in honour of the two principal founders.

Hackney Council (the current owner) and the Heritage Lottery Fund have invested some £9m in restoring the house and park to their former glory, which was completed in 2011.

The project reinstated original design features to the house and included a new café with improved access for disabled users, restored function rooms, and smaller rooms for private hire and community use. The park has been landscaped, ponds and part of the New River restored, and the facilities improved, including a landscaped play area, a wheels park, and a games area for five-a-side football and basketball.

Clissold is one of London's most beautiful and well-equipped parks, where even the delightful benches are special.

CULPEPER COMMUNITY GARDEN 12

Address: 1 Cloudesley Road, N1 0EG (☎ 020-7833 3951, 🖵 culpeper.org.uk).
Opening hours: Mon-Fri, 10am to 5pm; weekend times vary.
Cost: Free.
Transport: Angel tube.
Attractions & amenities: Plant sales, events, 'open' days.

Culpeper Community Garden is a green retreat in the midst of Islington's inner city bustle; a beautiful public space serving both as a city park and an environmental community project. Named after the famous 17th-century herbalist Nicholas Culpeper (1616-1654), who published his works in Islington, the garden began as a joint project between the Free School on White Lion Street, a local alternative school for excluded children, and Penton Primary School (now closed), in order to provide somewhere children could learn to grow and care for plants and vegetables. Work began in 1982 to transform a derelict, rubbish-filled site into the lovely public space you see today.

Managed by and for local people, Culpeper – a registered charity – is a unique project where people from all walks of life come together to enhance their environment. It employs part-time workers who develop projects with community groups and support volunteers, working with local children and schools; it also coordinates communal fundraising and social and gardening activities.

Culpeper is an organic garden comprising a lawn, ponds, rose pergolas, ornamental beds, vegetable plots, seating and a wildlife area. It contains a rich and varied array of plants: shrubs, trees, a wealth of herbaceous perennials, and a wide variety of herbs (appropriately) and seasonal vegetables. There are some 50 plots for community groups, children and local people without gardens, plus raised beds for disabled gardeners. Different habitats have been created, including a wildlife area with native species, which is home to a large frog population, insects, butterflies and birds. There's also a drought-resistant garden – a new garden for the changing climate!

Culpeper has won many awards over the years, including 'best display in a public space in London' three times, awarded by the London Gardens Society, and 'best communal garden in London', bestowed by London in Bloom.

13 EAST FINCHLEY CEMETERY

Address: East End Road, N2 0RZ (☎ 020-8567 0913, 🖳 westminster.gov.uk > communityandliving > burials).
Opening hours: Nov-Feb, Mon-Fri, 8.30am to 4.30pm; weekends and Public Holidays 11am to 4pm. Mar-Oct, Mon-Fri, 8.30am to 6pm; weekends and Public Holidays 11am to 6pm.
Cost: Free.
Transport: East Finchley tube.

East Finchley Cemetery is a relatively unknown Victorian cemetery, and one of London's most beautiful. It dates from 1855 (the crematorium opened in 1937) and ought to be on the list of London's 'must-visit cemeteries' but is often over-looked in favour of the Magnificent Seven (see **Highgate Cemetery** on page 116). Originally called St Marylebone Cemetery, its name was changed to East Finchley when Westminster City Council re-acquired it in the early '90s. The cemetery contains over 22,000 private graves and is still used for burials today.

There are a number of splendid bronzes, including the tomb of Australian engineer Sir Peter Nicol Russell (1816-1905) near the entrance, which depicts a young engineer being lifted to heaven by an angel, with a bust of Sir Peter on a pillar above them. It's by Sir Edgar MacKennal, who also designed the effigies of Edward VII and Queen Alexandra in St George's Chapel at Windsor Castle. Two more notable bronzes – facing each other to the northwest of the main chapel – adorn the graves of Thomas Tate (a reclining youth pointing to heaven) and Harry Ripley (a mourning woman). The 'chapel' (Grade II listed) at the centre of the cemetery is, in fact, a mausoleum for Lord Borthwick, owner of *The Morning Post*.

Although a number of grave markers and monuments are broken and decayed, East Finchley Cemetery has generally been superbly maintained, attested to by the award of a Green Flag annually since 2007. It's also a local nature reserve and contains a number of specimen trees, including two splendid Cedars of Lebanon planted on the front lawn in 1856.

Notable burials include conductor Leopold Stokowski, Sir Robert Harmsworth (newspaper publisher, with a memorial by Edwin Lutyens), Lord Northcliffe (founder of the *Daily Mail*), Melanie Appleby (of pop duo Mel and Kim), scientist Thomas Henry Huxley, and artist and cartoonist Heath Robinson. There are also many war graves from both world wars.

FENTON HOUSE GARDEN 14

Address: Hampstead Grove, Hampstead, NW3 6SP (☎ 020-7435 3471,
🖥 nationaltrust.org.uk/fenton-house).
Opening hours: 5th Mar to 30th Oct, Wed-Sun, 11am to 5pm.
Cost: Garden £2. House, £6.50 adults, £3 children, £16 families. Free to National
Trust members.
Transport: Hampstead tube.
Attractions: House, museum.

Affluent, leafy Hampstead is full of substantial, attractive properties, of which Fenton House is one of the earliest, largest and most architecturally important; a charming 17th-century merchant's house built in idealised Queen Anne style. The house – now owned by the National Trust – was built around 1686 and has been virtually unaltered over 300 years of continuous occupation. It's named after the Fenton family, who bought it in 1793 and made some Regency alterations that give the house its current appearance. Fenton House is home to a superb collection of early keyboard instruments, fine paintings, porcelain, 17th-century needlework pictures and Georgian furniture.

Country Life magazine described Fenton House as 'London's most enchanting country house'.

The house is set in beautiful walled and terraced gardens – virtually unchanged since the 18th century – which combine formal borders and a sunken rose garden with a working kitchen garden and a 300-year-old apple orchard. The garden is laid out on the side of a hill and divided into upper and lower levels. It's an almost rural haven in a heavily populated part of London, and is noted for its sunken walled section with a glasshouse, vegetable beds, culinary herb border, lawns and flower beds. The various flowering shrubs and hardy perennials are at their best in late summer and autumn.

The herb border was created in late 1999 and includes myrtle, hyssop, chives, rosemary, thyme and lavender, to name just a few, plus various annual herbs that change from year to year. The orchard – sewn with spring bulbs, including bluebells – of agreeably gnarled apple trees produces over 30 different varieties. Apple Day, held in late September, gives the public the opportunity to savour some of its rare and delicious apples, along with goodies such as apple-blossom honey.

The grounds also have splendid wrought-iron gates, a lead cistern dating from 1723 and a number of fine garden statues.

15 FINSBURY PARK

Address: Endymion Road, Seven Sisters Road and Green Lanes, N4 (☎ 020-8489 0000, 🖥 haringey.gov.uk > parks and open spaces).
Opening hours: Daily, dawn to dusk.
Cost: Free.
Transport: Manor House tube.
Attractions & amenities: Arboretum, gardens, lake, café, concerts, art exhibitions, sports facilities.

Finsbury Park (Grade II listed) is a beautiful 115-acre (46ha) public park in the borough of Haringey – one of London's first great Victorian parks. Officially opened in 1869, Finsbury Park was one of many 'people's parks' created to provide Londoners with open spaces as an antidote to the city's ever-increasing urbanisation. Today it's one of London's most diverse parks with a rich tapestry of landscapes, serving a wide range of communities.

The Parkland Walk (🖥 parkland-walk. org.uk) starts in Finsbury Park – a lovely 4.5mi (7.2km) linear green pathway following the route of the old railway line from Finsbury Park to Alexandra Palace.

Throughout the late 19th and early 20th centuries, the park was a respectable and beautifully manicured space in which people would relax and exercise; in the early 20th century it also became a venue for political meetings, including pacifists' rallies during the First World War. The park deteriorated after the Second World War, although still much loved and used by the local community; it was belatedly restored to its former glory after a £5m Heritage Lottery Fund award in 2003. Finsbury Park now has a mixture of open ground, formal gardens, avenues of mature trees and an arboretum containing rare trees. It was awarded the prestigious Green Flag in 2007 and has retained it ever since.

Finsbury Park has long been an established music venue, attracting many famous artists and bands, including Jimi Hendrix (1967), Ian Dury and The Blockheads and Morrissey and Madness (1992), Oasis (2002) and Bob Dylan (1993 and 2011).

The park offers a wide range of sports facilities including soccer pitches, a bowling green, an athletics track, an outdoor gym, and tennis and basketball courts. Unusually for London, the park also provides pitches for American football, softball and baseball.

GLADSTONE PARK

Address: Dollis Hill Lane, NW2 (☎ 020-8937 5619, 🖥 brent.gov.uk > sport, leisure and parks > park finder and gladstonepark.org.uk).
Opening hours: Unrestricted access, except walled garden (dawn to dusk).
Cost: Free.
Transport: Dollis Hill tube.
Attractions & amenities: Walled garden, arboretum, gallery, café, bowling green, playgrounds, sports facilities.

Gladstone Park is a beautiful 97-acre (39ha) refuge in Dollis Hill, administered by the borough of Brent. It has a diverse environment, including a formal garden, duck pond and arboretum, with varied terrain comprising woodland, hedgerows and open ground that constantly changes with the seasons. The hill rises to 213ft/65m and on clear days offers a panoramic vista, including fine views of Wembley Stadium.

The core of Gladstone Park was formed from the parkland which surrounded Dollis Hill House; this was once an extensive estate, although the derelict house was sadly demolished in 2012. In 1898, the house and land south of Dollis Hill Lane were acquired by Willesden Rural District Council for £50,000 and opened as a public park by the Earl of Aberdeen in 1901. It was named after the Liberal leader and Prime Minister William Gladstone, who was often a guest at Dollis Hill, as was the great American writer Mark Twain.

Many of the park's features date from the turn of the 20th century, such as the fine tree-lined avenues, lake and walled garden. Additional features included a swimming pool, opened in 1903 (now a bowling green), flower beds and a formal terraced garden. There's a Holocaust Memorial (Paula Kotis, 1968) in the northwest of the park.

The tranquil walled garden – a former winner of the London in Bloom competition and recipient of many Green Flag awards – is a lovely spot to relax and enjoy the fine lawns, flowerbeds, shrubs and trees that give it such a unique atmosphere.

Gladstone Park offers a range of sports facilities, including tennis courts, soccer pitches, a rugby pitch, a cricket pitch, netball courts and a bowling green. Other facilities and attractions within the park include two playgrounds, obstacle course, zip slide, tree carvings, duck pond, terraced garden, wildlife area and allotments.

17 GOLDERS HILL PARK

Address: West Heath Avenue, Golders Green, NW11 7QP (☎ 020-7332 3511, 🖥 cityoflondon.gov.uk > green spaces > Hampstead Heath).
Opening hours: Daily, 7.30am to dusk (ranges from 4.30pm in mid-winter to 10pm in mid-summer). Butterfly House, Apr-Aug, daily, 2-4pm; Sep-Oct, weekends only, 2-4pm; closed Nov-Mar (see website for exact dates).
Cost: Free.
Transport: Golders Green tube.
Attractions & amenities: Gardens, zoo, butterfly house, café, bandstand, children's play area, sports facilities.

Golders Hill Park is a formal park opened in 1898, which adjoins the western part of **Hampstead Heath** (see page 110), and has been managed as a separate part of the heath by the City of London since 1989 (unlike the rest of the heath, Golders Hill Park is closed at night). It's on a site formerly occupied by Golders Hill House, a large 18th-century house (built in the 1760s by Charles Dingley) that was destroyed during the Second World War.

The main characteristic of the park is a large expanse of grass (great for games), dotted with specimen trees, a beautiful formal English flower garden, a Mediterranean garden, a walled garden, and a water garden with a number of ponds. The ponds are stocked with marsh and water plants, and are home to a large number of water birds, including black and white swans. Formal paths wind their way around the park, criss-crossing and meandering beneath beautiful trees, past water features and through secret vales.

A major attraction is the children's zoo. Free to enter, it plays an important role in educating visitors about the habitats and wildlife of Hampstead Heath, and also has a growing collection of rare and exotic birds and mammals, including laughing kookaburras and ring-tailed lemurs.

There's also a butterfly house, which offers a close-up of many British and tropical species.

The park has an excellent café (try the delicious home-made ice-cream), a bandstand and children's play area, and offers a variety of sports and leisure facilities, including tennis courts, a croquet lawn, golf practice nets and a putting green.

During the summer, children's activities are organised and throughout June and July there's live music on the bandstand (brass bands, jazz, etc.) on Sunday afternoons.

Golders Hill Park is everything an urban park should be. Note, however, that unlike most of Hampstead Heath, you must keep your dog on a lead due to the animals.

HAMPSTEAD CEMETERY 18

Address: Fortune Green Road, West Hampstead, NW6 1DR (☎ 020-7527 8300, 🖥 camden.gov.uk > cemeteries and thefriendsofhampsteadcemetery.com).
Opening hours: Weekdays from 7.30am, Sat from 9am, and Sun and Public Holidays from 10am. Closing time is around dusk, i.e. 4pm from Nov-Jan and 8.30pm from May-Jul (see website for exact times).
Cost: Free.
Transport: West Hampstead tube or rail.
Attractions & amenities: Specimen trees, wildlife area, parking.

Hampstead Cemetery is a beautiful historic cemetery, situated in Finchley, and jointly managed by Islington and Camden Cemetery Services. Opened in 1876 on a 20-acre/8ha site (extended to 26 acres/10.5ha in 1901) and divided into eastern and western sections, it contains some 60,000 graves but is now closed for burials.

The cemetery has an entry lodge and a pair of Gothic-style mortuary chapels (Grade II listed), made of Kentish ragstone and Bath stone. The southern chapel was used for burials in consecrated ground south of the main avenue, while the other was for burials in unconsecrated ground to the north.

A large number of Celtic crosses are found in the area to the southwest of the chapel, marking the presence of several Scottish families. The north-eastern corner contains some notable examples of modern and Art Deco stonemasonry – including 18 listed by English Heritage – and several graves noted for their humorous or bizarre inscriptions.

The eastern part of the cemetery is home to the so-called Bianchi Monument, a large triangular grave for the Gall family, executed in the finest Art Deco style. The most prominent feature of the grave – a stylised sculpture of an angel raising her hands to heaven – has become famous in its own right, and often adorns the covers of local guidebooks. The nearby tomb of James

Wilson ('Wilson Pasha'), Chief Engineer to the Egyptian Government (1875-1901), is executed in red marble and has a striking Egyptian appearance.

The cemetery has a large number of trees, including ash, cedar, yew, oak, Scots pine, lime, sycamore, Norwegian maple, silver birch, Lombardy poplar, purple cherry-plum, weeping willow and Swedish whitebeam.

A wildlife area in the north-eastern section of the cemetery has been planted with shrubs and wildflowers that are particularly attractive to wildlife, and attracts a wide variety of birds (both residents and visitors).

19 HIGHGATE & QUEENS WOODS

Address: Muswell Hill Road, N10 3JN (☎ 020-8444 6129 for Highgate Wood, 020-8489 1000 for Queen's Wood, 🖥 cityoflondon.gov.uk > green spaces, haringey.gov.uk > parks and open spaces and fqw.org.uk).
Opening hours: Highgate Wood, daily, 7.30am to sunset; this can be as early as 4.30pm in winter and as late as 9.45pm in summer. Queen's Wood, unrestricted access.
Cost: Free.
Transport: Highgate tube.
Attractions & amenities: Organic garden, rare trees, two cafés, playground, information centre, sports facilities.

Highgate Wood and Queen's Wood (separated by Muswell Hill Road) are two imposing preserved segments of the ancient Forest of Middlesex, which once covered much of London and is mentioned in the *Domesday Book*.

In 1886, the City of London Corporation acquired Highgate Wood, then known as Gravelpit Wood, for public use. The wood covers 70 acres (28ha) and is rich in oak, holly and hornbeam, plus the rare wild service tree – an indicator of ancient woodland. The wood is home to over 50 other tree and shrub species and is rich in wildlife, including five species of bat, over 70 bird species and over 250 types of moth.

Queen's Wood is owned and managed by the borough of Haringey. It covers an area of 51 acres (21ha) and was known as Churchyard Bottom Wood until being purchased by Hornsey Council in 1898, when it was renamed Queen's Wood in honour of Queen Victoria. Like Highgate Wood, it's a rich stretch of ancient woodland, featuring English oak and the occasional beech, which provide a canopy above cherry, field maple, hazel, holly, hornbeam, midland hawthorn, mountain ash, lowland birch and the rare wild service tree. Queen's Wood has a greater diversity of flora and fauna than Highgate Wood; it's

wilder, with greater structural diversity and a denser shrub layer.

In addition to soccer and cricket pitches, Highgate Wood also has a playground, a café and an information centre, while Queen's Wood has a café and organic community garden.

 FOOD & DRINK

Queen's Wood Café: An excellent community café, child- and dog-friendly, serving home-cooked food with a good range of veggie options, and highly-rated by both locals and visitors (🖥 queenswoodcafe.co.uk). A bonus is that it's licensed! Opens 10am to 5pm weekdays, 9am to 6pm weekends (closes an hour earlier in winter).

KENWOOD HOUSE 20

Address: Hampstead Lane, Hampstead, NW3 7JR (☎ 020-8348 1286 or 0870-333 1181, 🖳 english-heritage.org.uk > properties).

Opening hours: Estate, 7am to dusk. House closed until autumn 2013 for major renovations, although the gardens, gift shop and Brewhouse café remain open (9am to 5pm). See website for more information.

Cost: Entry to the grounds is free. Check website for fees to see the house.

Transport: Archway or Golders Green tube, then 210 bus.

Attractions & amenities: Gardens, lakes, sculptures, house, gallery/museum, restaurant, shop, concerts.

The 112 acres (45ha) of landscaped parkland enclosing Kenwood House (managed by English Heritage) lies to the north of **Hampstead Heath** (see page 110). In contrast to the natural heath, the park around Kenwood House was created by the great English landscape gardener Humphry Repton (1752-1818) and was designed to be seen from a planned circuit walk that provides a series of evocative views, contrasts and 'surprises'. Although bordered on three sides by Hampstead Heath, the estate was maintained as a designed landscape until the '50s with a different character from the heath. One third of the estate (Ken Wood and North Wood) is semi-natural ancient woodland and a Site of Special Scientific Interest, home to many birds and insects and the largest pipistrelle bat roost in London.

Highlights include the walled garden with its kidney-shaped butterfly bed and ivy arch, leading to a raised terrace with stunning views over the lakes. The inner and outer circuit routes take you around lawns, over bridges and through woods, following the original walks laid out by Repton. The gardens near the house contain sculptures by Reg Butler, Barbara Hepworth and Henry Moore, among others.

The park is famous as the site of Kenwood House (Grade II* listed), an elegant villa built in the 17th century and owned for over 200 years by the family of William Murray, the 1st Earl of Mansfield (1705-1793). It was remodelled between 1764 and 1773 by Robert Adam, who transformed the original brick house into a majestic neoclassical villa. Brewing magnate Edward Cecil Guinness, first Earl of Iveagh (1847-1927), purchased Kenwood House and the estate in 1925, and bequeathed the house, land and part of his stunning collection of old masters to the nation (on display in the house).

The park is noted for its annual picnic concerts in June and July (see 🖳 picnicconcerts.com).

21 MYDDLETON HOUSE GARDENS

Address: Bulls Cross, Enfield, EN2 9HG (☎ 01992-702230, ⌨ leevalleypark.org.uk > gardens).
Opening hours: Mon-Fri, 10am to 4.30pm (3pm Oct-Mar). Also noon to 4pm on Sun and Bank Holiday Mon from Easter to Oct. See website for exact dates and times.
Cost: Free. Guided walks from £3 to £4.50 (see website).
Transport: Best reached by car from the M25, junction 25.
Attractions & amenities: Conservatory, tea room, visitor centre.

Myddelton House was built around 1818 by Henry Carrington Bowles (1763-1830) in the then fashionable Suffolk white brick. It was named Myddelton House in honour of Sir Hugh Myddelton (1560-1631), an engineering genius who created the New River to supply London with fresh water; a section of the river bisected the garden from 1613 until 1968.

When Bowles died in 1830 the house passed to his son, who bequeathed it in 1852 to his nephew Henry Carrington Bowles Treacher. The garden was created by Henry's youngest son, E A (Edward Augustus or 'Gussie') Bowles (1865-1954), a renowned botanist, author, artist and Fellow of the Royal Horticultural Society – and one of the great gardeners of the 20th century. He developed the remarkable garden as a self-taught horticulturist and became an expert on many plants, particularly snowdrops and crocuses, which earned him the soubriquet The Crocus King.

Secreted away near Enfield, this wonderful garden was neglected for 30 years, hidden under layers of ivy and bramble. It was restored to its former glory, with Heritage Lottery funding, in 2011.

On his death, the house and gardens passed to the Royal Free Hospital School of Medicine and the London School of Pharmacy, which grew a range of medicinal plants there. In 1967 it was purchased by the Lee Valley Regional Park Authority as its headquarters.

Myddelton House Gardens cover an area of 6 acres (2.4ha) and contain an impressive range of flora and fauna. Within the gardens are the national collection of award-winning bearded irises and 'special' areas which include the Lunatic Asylum (home to unusual plants), Tom Tiddler's Ground (for variegated specimens), Tulip Terrace and the Kitchen Garden. They also contain a beautiful carp pond, a Victorian conservatory, a rock garden, plus a number of historical artefacts collected by Bowles, including pieces from the original St Paul's Cathedral and the Enfield Market Cross.

NEW RIVER WALK 22

Address: Canonbury Grove, N1 (☎ 020-7527 2000, 🖳 islington.gov.uk > parks and green spaces).
Opening hours: Daily, 8am to dusk.
Cost: Free.
Transport: Highbury & Islington tube or Essex Road rail.

New River Walk is a delightful linear public park of 3.48 acres (1.4ha) – running from Islington to Canonbury – that's part of the New River Path and a tranquil oasis for wildlife. The New River was an aqueduct commissioned in 1613 by Sir Hugh Myddleton (1560-1631) – his statue stands at the southern tip of Islington Green – to bring water from the River Lee in Hertfordshire to central London.

The New River Path – developed between 1991 and 2003 at a cost of over £2m – is 28mi (45km) long, following the course of the New River from Hertford to Islington, linking the inner city to the open countryside. It's waymarked throughout its length by signs displaying the NR Path logo.

The Walk follows the New River as it runs above ground between St Pauls Road and Canonbury Road in Islington. This charming park is around 4mi (7km) in length, exploring some of Islington's many and varied squares and garden spaces. Much of the route is along service paths on private land running beside the watercourse, while other sections follow public rights of way; the 'heritage' section south of Stoke Newington runs through parks and along streets.

The park is a haven for wildlife and is landscaped with native English plants and specimen trees, including swamp cypress, dawn redwood and weeping willows; signboards provide information about the local flora and fauna. The river teems with life and you're likely to encounter ducks, coots and moorhens, plus – if you're lucky – rarer species such as sparrowhawks, grey wagtails, firecrests and grey herons.

> The narrow pathway winds intriguingly over pretty bridges, while benches are strategically placed for rest stops and to enjoy the views.

A popular stroll along the New River Walk is from Canonbury Square to Newington Green, where you can enjoy lunch in one of the area's many excellent eateries.

23 PADDINGTON OLD CEMETERY

Address: Willesden Lane, Kilburn, NW6 7SD (☎ 020-8902 2385, 🖥 brent.gov.uk
> births, marriages and deaths > deaths > list of Brent cemeteries).
Opening hours: Daily, 9am to between 4 and 8pm (see website for seasonal
closing times).
Cost: Free.
Transport: Kilburn or Brondesbury Park tube.

Paddington Old Cemetery is a lovely small Victorian cemetery – covering an area of 25 acres (10ha) – with a pair of stunning chapels. Opened in 1855, primarily to bury the dead of Paddington (despite being situated in Kilburn), it was named for the Paddington Burial Board who opened it.

The Old Cemetery was one of the first to be opened by the Burial Board, established following the 1852 Metropolitan Interment Act to address the acute problem of over-flowing urban churchyards. Designed by Thomas Little (1802-1859) – who was also responsible for **Nunhead Cemetery** (see page 262) – the original layout of pathways in the shape of a horseshoe still remains. Specimen trees were planted along the paths, many of which still exist, including oak, lime, horse chestnut, yew, field maple, London plane and Scots pine. Today there are over 500 mature trees, which provide a sanctuary for wildlife in this heavily built-up area.

An apiary is situated within the cemetery – the bees are essential for the cross-pollination of the abundant wildflowers – and 'tombstone honey' is a favourite with locals.

Little also designed two lodges, now in private use, and a fine pair of chapels (Grade II listed) with a *porte-cochère* (coach gate) and central belfry in 13th-century Gothic style, constructed from Kentish ragstone and

linked by arches. The original cemetery is almost full but a new section has been opened in the north which allows its continued use. In the eastern corner is an overgrown area known as 'God's Acre' (marked by a stone cross), which is now given over to nature.

A war memorial lies close to the western entrance, next to formal rose beds, and there are also rose gardens near the eastern lodge. The cemetery is enclosed within brick perimeter walls and has imposing iron gates with piers topped by draped urns.

QUEEN'S PARK 24

Address: Kingswood Avenue, Kilburn, NW6 6SG (☎ 020-8969 5661, 🖥 cityoflondon.gov.uk > green spaces).
Opening hours: Daily, 7am to dusk. Pets corner: weekdays 11am to 5pm, weekends and Bank Holidays, 1 to 5.30pm.
Cost: Free.
Transport: Queen's Park tube.
Attractions & amenities: Café, pets corner, playground, bandstand, various sports facilities.

The park was the original home of Queen Park Rangers FC, although the football club later moved to Shepherds Bush in west London.

Bandstand

Queen's Park (30 acres/12ha) was created in 1887 in celebration of Queen Victoria's Golden Jubilee on land that was chosen as the site of the annual Royal Agricultural Show in 1879. Managed by the City of London Corporation, it's a fine example of a well-loved city park, retaining much of its original structure and early features, including the bandstand. It provides a welcome green space in Brent, one of London's most densely populated boroughs. The park offers a wide range of facilities, including six all-weather tennis courts, a pétanque pitch, an ornamental garden and a café.

The original layout of the park, with elliptical paths in the form of a figure of eight, was reinstated in 1999, meeting in the centre where the '60s café now stands (it replaced an earlier refreshment pavilion built

in 1890). Around the paths are mown grass with clumps of trees and shrubs, areas with formal bedding displays and a children's gymnasium. The fine 19th-century wrought-iron bandstand, restored in 1994, was erected in 1891; tennis courts were added in 1937, while to the north is a pitch and putt course dating from 1966. The park contains many fine trees, including willow, horse chestnut and lime – a Woodland Walk was created in 1999 – while London plane trees line the boundary with Harvist Road. East of the café is an ancient oak that pre-dates the park.

The Green Flag park contains excellent children's play facilities, including a pets corner (added in 1990), paddling pool and sandpit. The park has also done much to encourage wildlife in recent years, with wild grass and wildflower areas (and bat boxes), which have led to an explosion in the bird population.

25 ROUNDWOOD PARK

Address: Harlesden Road, NW10 3SH (🖥 roundwoodpark.org).
Opening hours: Daily, 8am to dusk.
Cost: Free.
Transport: Dollis Hill or Willesden Junction tube.
Attractions & amenities: Gardens, café, wildlife area, aviary, playground, bowling green, basketball court.

Roundwood Park (Grade II listed) is a beautiful, tranquil green space in the London borough of Brent, covering an area of over 26 acres (10ha). Now Brent's flagship Green Flag park, it was originally known as Hunger Hill Common Field and was part of the Roundwood House Estate (the house was built around 1836 to the south of the current park). In 1892, a section of the estate was sold to Willesden Local Board to create a public park, which opened in 1895.

It was designed by local council surveyor Oliver Claude Robson (who also designed nearby **Gladstone Park** – see page 131). Robson installed five miles of drainage under the park and planted some 15,000 trees and shrubs. His design also included numerous paths, a mock-Tudor gardener's lodge, a children's gymnasium, greenhouses, a bandstand, and fine wrought-iron gates and railings.

Today, Roundwood Park has many imposing specimen trees, including a tulip tree, while London planes and hybrid poplars define its structure, standing in groups as well along the paths. There are also scattered poplar, oak and hawthorn, plus some lovely original flower beds and floral displays. A wrought iron cupola from the Olympia Garden Show was erected for the park's centenary in 1995. In addition, there's an aviary, fish pond and wildlife area, which attracts many bird species.

Roundwood Park has been the setting for many public events and activities since it opened, including numerous religious and political open-air meetings, circuses and concerts. It once even hosted a model steam railway.

Roundwood Park was planned as a peaceful environment, therefore sports activities are limited, although there's a bowling green which dates back to 1924 and a rather more modern basketball court. There's also an excellent café, Roundwood Lodge, which is open all year round.

ST MARY MAGDALENE GARDENS 26

Address: Holloway Road, Islington, N7 8LT (⊟ stmarymagdalenegardens.org.uk).
Opening hours: Daily, 8am to dusk.
Cost: Free.
Transport: Highbury & Islington tube.

St Mary Magdalene Gardens were originally burial grounds laid out two centuries ago around a handsome early Victorian neo-classical chapel of ease. At the close of the 19th century, the grounds were transformed into a public park. Many tombs and headstones were removed, the area enlarged and formal rose gardens added, while the chapel of rest became St Mary Magdalene's Church (also worth a visit), as it remains today.

The 20th century saw many changes and over time the park has evolved and its usage altered. Burial rituals have given way to informal leisure activities, promenading to jogging and dog-walking, and relaxed family picnics to hasty packed lunches. But the park is still a quiet place to sit and relax or read, a safe place for children to play, a place of peace and sanctuary, somewhere to stroll beneath the trees or smell the roses – and even a venue for occasional drunkenness (as it was in the 1850s when inquests were held in the local pub)!

The gardens are home to a number of majestic London plane trees (some are over 250 years old), mature lime and ash trees, and native shrubs that have risen up around the church, creating a huge green canopy across the park. These oldest-living residents have become the mainstay of a rich city ecology, giving this walled public space a sense of protection and seclusion unrivalled in Islington, all the more remarkable for being in such a densely populated borough.

Around the park, the environment has also changed, and the gardens are now bordered by Holloway Road/the A1, one of London's busiest thoroughfares, and surrounded by local households and estates with no green space of their own. As such, it's an important and irreplaceable community resource.

27 TRENT COUNTRY PARK

Address: Cockfosters Road, Enfield, EN4 0PS (☎ 020-8379 1000, 🖥 trentcountrypark.com).
Opening hours: Daily, 8 or 8.30am (Sun) to dusk.
Cost: Free.
Transport: Cockfosters or Oakwood tube.
Attractions & amenities: Adventure park, café, golf, fishing lakes, horse-riding circuit, cycling trail, plus other sports facilities.

Trent Park Mansion

Trent Country Park covers an area of 413 acres (167ha), comprising undulating meadows, babbling brooks, tranquil lakes, ancient woodland and imposing historical sites. It forms part of London's green belt and provides a peaceful retreat on the outskirts of the city.

The park is a relic of the Royal Hunting Forest of Enfield Chase, mentioned in the *Domesday Book*. In the 14th century it was one of Henry IV's royal hunting grounds, and has survived almost unchanged over subsequent centuries. In 1777, George III gave the site to his favourite doctor Richard Jebb for saving the life of his younger brother, the then Duke of Gloucester. It isn't clear what his ailment was but it occurred at Trento in the Italian Alps, hence the name of the park. A deer park and lake were laid out, and an old lodge converted into Trent Place, which was enlarged over the years and later rebuilt.

In 1951 the entire estate was purchased by Middlesex County Council and in 1973, much of it was opened to the public as a country park. It was also home to one of Middlesex University's campuses between 1992 and 2012.

Remaining features of the original landscaping include an impressive avenue of lime trees, an obelisk, ornamental lakes and a water garden (renovated in the '90s). Some of the woodland is pre-17th century and includes fine oak and hornbeam specimens, with some birch, hazel, beech, holly, sweet chestnut, and plantations of Scots and Corsican pine, western hemlock and larch. The wealth of birdlife includes three species of woodpecker, plus nuthatch, treecreeper and hobby, while two large lakes and many small ponds are home to a variety of water birds. The park also has Muntjac deer.

Today, visitors can enjoy Trent Country Park's large open spaces for walking, jogging, cycling, horse-riding, golfing, or just relaxing in the tranquil, picturesque surroundings.

WATERLOW PARK · 28

Address: Lauderdale House, Highgate Hill, N6 5HG (☎ 020-7974 8810, 💻 waterlowpark.org.uk and lauderdalehouse.co.uk).

Opening hours: Park, daily, dawn to dusk. Lauderdale House, Tue-Fri, 11am to 4pm, Sat 1.30-5pm, Sun, midday to 5pm. Café, Tue-Sun, 10am to dusk.

Cost: Free.

Transport: Archway or Highgate tube.

Attractions & amenities: Gardens, house, arts & education centre, café, children's play area, sports facilities.

Waterlow Park is situated in Highgate and bordered on two sides by **Highgate Cemetery** (see page 116). Within the park is Lauderdale House, built in 1582 for Sir Richard Martin (d. 1617), Master of the Mint and three-times Lord Mayor of London. It was inherited in 1645 by the Earl of Lauderdale and has been associated with Samuel Pepys and Nell Gwyn, among others.

> Nestled on a hillside to the south of Highgate Village, Waterlow Park has some of the best cityscape views in London, but retains a sense of peace and serenity.

Lauderdale's last private owner was Sir Sidney Waterlow (1822-1906), after whom the park is named; he gave the house and grounds to the London County Council in 1889 'for the enjoyment of Londoners' and as 'a garden for the gardenless'. The 29 acres (11.7ha) of grounds became a public park and the house was restored in 1893 and served for 70 years as a tearoom and park-keepers' flats, but was almost totally destroyed by fire in 1963. It lay derelict for 15 years, until the local community established the Lauderdale House Society and restored the house. It's now an arts and education centre (see website), with an excellent café.

Within the park you'll find a potpourri of formal terraced gardens (one of Britain's earliest examples); three ponds fed by natural springs; tree-lined walkways and mature shrub beds; herbaceous borders and ornamental bedding; and verdant expanses of lawn. The park supports a number of important ecological habitats and a rich variety of wildlife, and also boasts tennis courts, a natural children's play area and an ever-changing events programme. In the summer it hosts outdoor theatre and music performances.

Managed by Camden Council, Waterlow Park – returned to its former glory after extensive restoration in 2005 – belongs to a select group of parks awarded Green Flag status and is one of London's best-kept secrets.

Lauderdale House

29 BENTLEY PRIORY NATURE RESERVE

Address: Stanmore, HA7 3LX (☎ 020-8954 2918 for nature reserve,
💻 bentleypriory.org and harrowncf.org/bp_home.html).
Opening hours: Unrestricted access.
Cost: Free.
Transport: Stanmore tube, but best reached by car.

Bentley Priory Nature Reserve lies to the south of the 18th-century Bentley Priory, named after an Augustinian priory that stood here in the Middle Ages. Bentley Priory is famous for being the headquarters of Royal Air Force Fighter Command during the Second World War, and a Battle of Britain museum was due to open here in 2013.

The 163-acre (66ha) reserve is a Site of Special Scientific Interest, consisting of a mosaic of ancient woodland, unimproved natural grassland, scrub, wetland, streams and an artificial lake – an unusual combination of habitats in Greater London. The reserve contains a number of woods, including Heriot Wood, where the dominant tree is

hornbeam, a species characteristic of ancient woodlands, while to the west of Summerhouse Lake stands the 'Master', a mighty oak that's at least 500 years old.

The reserve is noted for its abundance of coarse grasses, which includes traditional grassland that has never been treated with fertilisers, and therefore is rich in wildflowers. There's also a host of birdlife, including buzzards, spotted flycatcher, bullfinch, whitethroat, garden warblers, blackcaps, chiffchaffs and willow warblers.

30 BURGH HOUSE & GARDEN

Address: New End Square, NW3 1LT (☎ 020-7431 0144, 💻 burghhouse.org.uk).
Opening hours: Buttery café & garden, Wed-Sun 11am to 5.30pm, Sat-Sun from 9.30am. House & museum, Wed-Fri and Sun, noon to 5pm. Museum closed Saturdays.
Cost: Free.
Transport: Hampstead tube.
Attractions & amenities: House, museum, gallery, café.

Burgh House (Grade I listed) – built in 1704 in the time of Queen Anne – is a handsome building and one of the oldest houses in Hampstead. Named after the Reverend Allatson Burgh who purchased it in 1822, nowadays it houses Hampstead

Museum and a particularly fine art collection.

From 1906 to 1924, Burgh House was the home of art specialist and author Dr George Williamson, who in 1908 commissioned Gertrude Jekyll to design the garden behind the house. The house was purchased by Hampstead Borough Council in 1947 and the sloping terraced garden was allowed to become derelict. However, it was restored in 1979 and re-stocked with over 100 varieties of plants.

Improvements to the garden continued in the '80s and in later phases plants favoured by Jekyll were added, such as old varieties of rose. Full of delightful nooks and crannies, today the lovely garden is home to the licensed Buttery café (☎ 020-7794 2905) – an enchanting place to enjoy a coffee or lunch and justifiably popular with Hampstead locals.

EAST RESERVOIR COMMUNITY GARDEN 31

Address: 1 Newnton Close, N4 2RH (☎ 020-8802 4573, 💻 wildlondon.org.uk/page/reserves).
Opening hours: Mon-Fri 10am to 5.30pm; closed weekends.
Cost: Free.
Transport: Stamford Hill rail or Manor House tube.

Stoke Newington East and West Reservoirs were constructed in 1833 to purify water from the New River and to act as a water reserve. While the West Reservoir is now a leisure facility, the London Wildlife Trust has created a community garden between the New River and the East Reservoir. Complete with a fully-equipped eco-classroom with a living roof, it provides a base for school visits and a range of community projects. Visitors can take part in a number of activities, including bird watching, guided bat and bird walks, arts and craft workshops, landscape design and construction, wild walks, pond and river dipping, and mini-beast hunts along the nature trail.

The diverse habitats include a canalised river (New River), summer meadow, woodland copse, stag beetle

sanctuary, grassland, scrub, open water (reservoir), reed beds, wildlife pond and a community garden. The reservoir is home to a profusion of wildlife and is particularly rich in birdlife, including great crested grebe, common tern and reed bunting (see 💻 snrbirds.org.uk).

32   FORTY HALL & ESTATE

Address: Forty Hill, Enfield, EN2 9HA (☎ 020-8363 8196, 🖥 fortyhallestate. co.uk).

Opening hours: Daily except Mondays (see website for times).

Cost: Free (charges apply for tours and special events).

Transport: Turkey Street rail or catch the 191 bus from Enfield Town, Enfield Chase or Southbury rail.

Attractions & amenities: Gardens, museum, gallery, lakes, café, shop, farm, free parking.

Forty Hall (Grade I listed) is Enfield's 'Jewel in the Crown' and one of England's finest historic houses. It was built by Sir Nicholas Rainton (1569-1646) in 1632 and is set in its own estate. In 1894, the estate was purchased by Henry Carrington Bowles, whose descendants sold it to the borough of Enfield in 1951. It opened to the public in 1955 and today the hall is home to Enfield's local history museum.

The estate extends to 260 acres (107ha), containing a walled garden, formal and informal gardens, a lime walk, lakes, lawns, woodland, meadows and a farm. The parkland also contains the rare archaeological remains of Elsyng Palace, a 14th-

century Tudor hunting lodge used by Henry VIII and Elizabeth I. Both hall and estate underwent a major restoration in 2011-2012 and, together with the surrounding area of Forty Hill, they comprise a conservation area with many superb buildings and a distinct historic village style, much loved and used by the local community.

33   FREUD MUSEUM & GARDEN

Address: 20 Maresfield Gardens, NW3 5SX (☎ 020-7435 2002, 🖥 freud.org.uk).

Opening hours: Wed-Sun, noon to 5pm.

Cost: £6 adults, £4.50 senior citizens, £3 concessions (students, children 12-16, unemployed and disabled), under-12s free.

Transport: Finchley Road tube.

Attractions & amenities: House, museum, tea/coffee, shop.

The Freud Museum is an interesting, atmospheric museum, housed in the former home of Sigmund Freud and his family after they fled the Nazi annexation of Austria in 1938. Built in 1920 in Queen Anne style, it's a

striking, handsome red-brick house, which remained the Freud family home until 1982, when Anna Freud, Sigmund's youngest daughter (he had six children), died and left the house and its contents as a museum.

Both Sigmund and Anna loved the garden, which is largely as they would have known it, from the terracotta flower pot, containing a red geranium (with Anna Freud's trowel still beside it), to the circular flower bed to the right of the garden, and the curved bench and tables on the shaded left-hand side of the garden. The large pine tree at the rear of the garden was knee-high to Anna Freud when planted, while the roses, clematis, plum and almond trees are all original plants from the time when the Freuds came to live at Maresfield Gardens.

FREIGHTLINERS FARM & GARDEN 34

Address: Sheringham Road, N7 8PF (☎ 020-7609 0467, ⌨ freightlinersfarm.org.uk).
Opening hours: Tue-Sun, 10am to 4.45pm (closes at 4pm in autumn/winter months); closed Mondays, except on Bank Holidays, and during the Christmas/New Year period.
Cost: Free (but donations are encouraged).
Transport: Holloway Road tube or Highbury & Islington rail.
Attractions & amenities: Garden, café, shop.

Freightliners Farm is an outstanding urban farm in the heart of Islington, one of only half a dozen in inner London, which allows individuals and groups to learn from and interact with their environment and each other through animal care, horticulture and sustainable living practices. The farm was founded on 1.2 acres (0.5ha) of former wasteland behind King's Cross Station in 1973 – its name came from the railway goods vans that originally housed the animals.

Freightliners has a wide variety of animals, ranging from cows and sheep to rare breed pigs and goats, plus chickens, ducks, geese, turkeys, guinea fowl, quail, pigeons, doves, rabbits and guinea pigs, while in the animal village there's a children's petting area. The farm also has five beehives, and visitors can buy delicious honey and products made from beeswax, such as candles.

There's an ornamental garden and a kitchen garden, where visitors can relax and obtain gardening tips and ideas. The Strawbale café (Thu-Sun 10am to 3.45pm) sells local produce at sensible prices.

35 GILLESPIE PARK & ECOLOGY CENTRE

Address: 191 Drayton Park, N5 1PH (☎ 020-7527 4374, 🖥 islington.gov.uk > parks and green spaces > Islington Nature Reserves).
Opening hours: Mon-Fri, 8am to dusk; closed on Arsenal stadium event days.
Cost: Free.
Transport: Arsenal or Finsbury Park tube.
Attractions & amenities: Organic gardening, courses, events, disabled access.

Gillespie Park is a beautiful 7-acre (2.8ha) Local Nature Reserve created in 1983 on the site of the Great Northern Railway sidings, which fell out of use around 1960. The Ecology Centre is a visitor and education centre where you can discover more about wildlife gardening and green living, and obtain advice on sustainable living. The centre's green features include a wind turbine, green roof, sun pipes and wind catchers, waste water treatment, eco kitchen, biomass boiler and much more. It also runs events and festivals and takes school bookings.

The park has a remarkable diversity of habitats, including woodland, meadow and ponds, and is home to a plethora of wildlife, including many rare species; a total of some 250 plants, almost 100 bird species and some 25 varieties of butterflies have been recorded. Visit in the spring or summer when the ponds are thronged with frogs, newts and dragonflies, and the meadows are alive with wildflowers and insects.

36 GOLDERS GREEN CREMATORIUM GARDENS

Address: Hoop Lane, Barnet, NW11 7NL (☎ 020-8455 2374, 🖥 crematorium.eu/golders_green_crematorium.html).
Opening hours: Daily 9am-6pm (summer), 9am-4pm (winter).
Cost: Free.
Transport: Golders Green tube.

Far from being morbid, Golders Green Crematorium is an inspiring and fascinating place. It was London's first crematorium (dating from 1902) and is one of the oldest in Britain, designed by Sir Ernest George (1839-1922). The cremations of many of the great names of British history have taken place at Golders Green over the last century, including people from the worlds of politics, film, theatre, music and the arts. A map of the Gardens of Remembrance and information about some of the people who were cremated here is available from the office.

The 12 acres (4.9ha) of gardens were designed by William Robinson (1838-1935) and provide a beautiful and tranquil environment. There are several large tombs, two ponds and other water features, a bridge, a large crocus lawn and a special children's section, which includes a swinging bench. There are also two cremation chapels and a chapel of remembrance. The gardens contain many beautiful statues and mausoleums, including the Lutyens-designed Philipson family mausoleum and the Martin Smith mausoleum (Paul Phipps), which are among several Grade II listed monuments.

GROVELANDS PARK 37

Address: Bourne Hill, Southgate, N14 6RA (🖳 enfield.gov.uk > parks, trees, allotments and nature > parks and n21.net/friends-of-grovelands-park-winchmore-hill-n21-london.html).
Opening hours: Daily, 8am to dusk (8.30am Sun). See website for seasonal closing times.
Cost: Free.
Transport: Southgate tube or Winchmore Hill rail.
Attractions & amenities: Café, playground, fishing lake, pitch and putt, bowling green and various other sports facilities.

Grovelands Park was originally a heavily wooded area close to the southern border of Enfield Chase, a hunting forest formed in the 14th century. In the late 1700s, Southgate became a fashionable place for wealthy London merchants to build their mansions. The earliest known owner of the Grovelands Estate was Mr Walker Gray, who purchased 230 acres (93ha) of land in 1796 and engaged John Nash to build a fine neo-classical villa (now a hospital) and Humphry Repton to landscape the estate.

In 1911, Southgate Urban District Council purchased 64 acres (26ha) of land from the Grovelands Estate for a public park, which opened in 1913. Today, the Green Flag park comprises an original wooded area with oak, beech, birch and hornbeam (among other species), a large lake, grassland and formal gardens. The lake and woodlands attract an abundance of birds and other wildlife, while the park's facilities include several soccer pitches, a playground, basketball court, bowling green, nine-hole golf course and a pavilion.

38 HIGHBURY FIELDS

Address: Highbury Crescent, N5 1RR (☎ 020-7527 2000, 🖥 islington.gov.uk > parks and green spaces).
Opening hours: Unrestricted except for playground, 8am to dusk.
Cost: Free.
Transport: Highbury & Islington tube/rail.
Attractions & amenities: Wildlife area, café (summer), playground, toilets, pool/fitness area, tennis and netball courts, floodlit soccer pitch.

Highbury Fields is the largest open space (29 acres/11.75ha) in the borough of Islington, extending north from Highbury Corner almost as far as Highbury Barn and divided in half by the northernmost curve of Highbury Crescent. The park was created from farmland in 1885 when Islington Vestry and the Metropolitan Board of Works jointly acquired around 25 acres (ca. 10ha) for a public park, which was enlarged in 1891. The park is surrounded by elegant – and highly desirable – Georgian and Victorian townhouses, home to many famous residents over the years, including painter Walter Sickert and statesman Joseph Chamberlain.

Highbury Fields is scattered with fine oak, horse chestnut and lime trees, while London planes line the perimeter of the park and its principal walks. The park contains a range of recreational facilities, including 11 tennis courts (seven floodlit) and the Highbury Pool and Fitness Centre. There's also a fine Art Nouveau Boer War memorial (1905) by Bertram McKennal, featuring a wreath, cannons and the captured standards of defeated enemies.

39 KEATS HOUSE & GARDEN

Address: Keats Grove, Hampstead, NW3 2RR (☎ 020-7332 3868, 🖥 cityoflondon.gov.uk > attractions around London).
Opening hours: Mar-Oct, Tue-Sun, 1-5pm; Nov-Feb, Fri-Sun, 1-5pm, Tue-Thu, pre-booked groups only. Closed Mondays and Good Friday. See website for exact dates.
Cost: Access to the garden is free. See website for museum costs.
Transport: Hampstead Heath rail or Hampstead tube.
Attractions & amenities: House, museum.

Keats House (Grade I listed) is a shrine to one of the leading poets of the English Romantic movement, John Keats (1795-1821), who lived here for just 17 months from 1818, before travelling to Italy where he died of tuberculosis aged just 25. The house was built between 1814 and 1816 and was originally two separate properties, combined in 1838 by the actress and one-time favourite of King George IV, Eliza Jane Chester. The house is now a museum devoted to Keats.

The garden is one of the most romantic in London and is planted to reflect its Regency heritage. It's here that Keats is said to have written *Ode to a Nightingale* while sitting under a plum tree (a plaque records the spot where the tree once stood). The garden was re-designed in 2009 with new fruit trees, plants and shrubs in keeping with the Regency period, with borders reflecting aspects of Keats's poetry: melancholy, autumn and nightingale. The garden also contains a mulberry tree thought to date from the 17th century.

MARKFIELD PARK & BEAM ENGINE MUSEUM 40

> **Address:** Markfield Road, Tottenham, N15 4RB (☎ 01707-873628, ⌨ haringey.gov.uk > parks and open spaces and markfieldpark.org.uk).
> **Opening hours:** Park, unrestricted access. Beam Engine Museum, Oct-Mar, second Sun of the month, 11am to 4pm; Apr-Sep, second and fourth Sun of the month, 11am to 5pm.
> **Cost:** Free.
> **Transport:** Tottenham Hale tube and rail, and South Tottenham rail.
> **Attractions & amenities:** Gardens, museum, café, playground, sports facilities.

Markfield Park is a lovely 18.8-acre (7.6ha) Green Flag park located within the Lee Valley Regional Park in the borough of Haringey, which was officially opened as Markfield Recreation Ground King George's Field in 1938. It's situated on a flood plain with two major watercourses flowing through it; the culverted Stonebridge Brook and the

open channel of the Old Moselle Brook, which discharge into the River Lee.

The park is famous for the Markfield Beam Engine and Museum (⌨ mbeam.org), a Site of Industrial Heritage Interest. The Tottenham and Wood Green sewage treatment works and pumping station was opened here in 1864, while the 100hp Markfield Beam Engine was built between 1886 and 1888.

The park – which was restored and upgraded along with the museum in recent years – contains various different areas and facilities, including soccer pitches, open grass and picnic areas, a playground, rose and community gardens, a lawn bowls club, BMX area and even graffiti walls. There's also a café with free wi-fi in the museum.

41 MINCHENDEN OAK GARDEN

Address: Waterfall Road, Southgate, N14 7JN (⌨ enfield.gov.uk/directory_record/5732/minchenden_oak_gardens).
Opening hours: 8am to dusk (8.30am Sun). See website for seasonal closing times.
Cost: Free.
Transport: Southgate tube.

Minchenden Oak Garden was created in 1934 as an evergreen Garden of Remembrance, on land adjacent to the old graveyard of Christchurch. It lies on the former site of the Minchenden Estate, one of the great estates in the area owned by the Duke of Chandos. Minchenden House was built around 1747 by John Nicholl, from whom Chandos purchased it as his country house.

A relic of the grounds of Minchenden House remains today in the form of the Minchenden or Chandos Oak, an ancient pollarded oak tree, said in the 19th century to be the largest in England with a girth of over 27 feet (8.2m). Edward Walford reported that in 1873 its spread was 'no less than 126 feet, and it's still growing'. This mighty tree is thought to be a survivor of the ancient Forest of Middlesex and could be up to 800 years old.

The beautiful walled garden is laid out with lawns, hedges and a variety of evergreen shrubs and trees, including magnolia, and is a peaceful haven with seating around the oak tree.

42 NEW SOUTHGATE CEMETERY

Address: Brunswick Park Road, New Southgate, N11 1JJ (☎ 020-8361 1713, ⌨ newsouthgatecemetery.co.uk).
Opening hours: Daily, 7am to 5.15pm (gates), but 24-hour access via adjacent pedestrian gate.
Cost: Free.
Transport: Arnos Grove tube or New Southgate rail.

New Southgate Cemetery and Crematorium (formerly the Great Northern London Cemetery) is regarded as one of the most beautiful and well maintained in England. Established in 1856, many of its 60 acres (24ha) resemble a country park, with tree-lined drives and gardens. The cemetery was laid out on a concentric plan with a Gothic chapel in the centre, and contains many mature trees, particularly in the southern, older section, while oak, horse chestnut, sycamore and yew are found in the newer area, which is more open. The cemetery is classified as a Local Nature Reserve.

The various burial sections reflect the diversity of the local community, with separate areas for Greek Orthodox, Roman Catholic and Caribbean communities. Monuments include a late 19th-century obelisk erected by the Society of Friends and a walled garden with a large marble column surmounted by a golden eagle, which is dedicated to Shoghi Effendi, the Baha'i leader who died in 1957 on a visit to London.

PRIORY PARK 43

Address: Middle Lane, N8 8LN (☎ 020-8489 0000, 🖳 haringey.gov.uk > Parks and Open Spaces or fopp-n8.org.uk).
Opening hours: 7.30am to dusk. FunYums café, 9.30am to dusk.
Cost: Free.
Transport: Hornsey rail then bus.
Attractions & amenities: Café, pavilion, paddling pool, tennis and basketball courts, bowling green, playground, tennis courts.

Priory Park (16 acres/6.5ha) in Hornsey is named after The Priory, a house built in the 1820s for the Warner family. Land was purchased from the estate in 1891 by Hornsey Local Board for a public park, which opened in 1899 – when it was named Middle Lane Pleasure Grounds – and was enlarged in 1926 when the western section (9 acres) was added and the park was renamed Priory Park.

The large granite fountain at the north end was installed in 1909, a gift from the Dean and Chapter of St Paul's Cathedral; made from 50 tons of Lamorna granite, it's now used as a planter. The original eastern section of the park preserves much of its early landscaping, with lovely bedding displays, serpentine walks, perimeter shrub beds, and mature silver birches and plane trees. The Philosophers Garden, named after a debating society that used to meet here, is a tranquil area with sculptures, a sundial, water feature and a tree seat.

A Green Flag park since 2003, it has a café, playgrounds, paddling pool, bowling green, and tennis and basketball courts.

44 ROYAL COLLEGE OF PHYSICIANS GARDEN

Address: 11 St Andrews Place, NW1 4LE (museum ☏ 020-3075 1543, garden tours ☏ 020-7935 1174, 🖥 www.rcplondon.ac.uk/museum-and-garden).
Opening hours: Mon-Fri, 9am to 5pm, excluding Public Holidays and event days (see website). Tours of the garden take place from Mar-Nov, first Wed of the month at 2pm.
Cost: Free. Guided tours £5 per person.
Transport: Great Portland Street, Regent's Park or Warren Street tube.
Attractions & amenities: Museum

The Royal College of Physicians (RCP) of London was founded in 1518 as the College of Physicians by charter of Henry VIII, acquiring its 'Royal' prefix in 1674. The College moved to its current RIBA prize-winning home in Regent's Park in 1964, which was designed by Sir Denys Lasdun (1914-2001) and is Grade I listed. The museum's extensive collections cover both the history of the college and that of the profession.

The RCP has had a medicinal garden since 1965, which can be visited when the museum is open. It was extensively replanted by Mark Griffiths in 2005-6 with sponsorship from the Wolfson Foundation, and now contains over 1,300 therapeutic plants. Eight gardens were planted along St Andrews Place in 2006-7 with box parterres containing plants from the *Pharmacopeia Londinensis* published by the RCP in 1618. The RCP conducts tours of the medicinal garden from March to November (see box) – bookable on the day at reception – and group tours by appointment.

45 ST JOHN AT HAMPSTEAD GRAVEYARD

Address: Church Row, NW3 6UU (☏ 020-7794 5808, 🖥 hampsteadparishchurch.org.uk).
Opening hours: Daily, 9am to 5pm.
Cost: Free (but donations are welcome).
Transport: Hampstead tube.

St John-at-Hampstead (dedicated to St John the Evangelist) is a sumptuous Georgian Church of England church with a stunning interior. There's likely to have been a church on this site for over 1,000 years, when a charter was granted to the Benedictine Monks of Westminster in 986, although the current building dates from 1747.

Perhaps more famous today than the church is its tranquil, magnificent graveyard, whose monuments and gravestones include many of great historic significance, particularly that of romantic painter John Constable. Other notables buried here include novelist and historian Walter Besant, writer and comedian Peter Cook, actress Kay Kendall, Labour Party leader Hugh Gaitskell, John Harrison, inventor of the marine chronometer (and discoverer of longitude), and various members of the distinguished du Maurier family.

The churchyard is designated a Site of Nature Conservation Importance and noted for its wildlife, providing a refuge for many rare and protected plants and animals.

ST MARTIN'S GARDENS   46

> **Address:** Camden Street and Pratt Street, NW1 0HR (☎ 020-7974 1693,
> ⌨ camden.gov.uk > parks and gardens > great parks in Camden and
> stmartinsfriends.blogspot.co.uk).
> **Opening hours:** Daily, dawn to dusk.
> **Cost:** Free.
> **Transport:** Camden Town tube.
> **Attractions & amenities:** Children's play area, wildlife area.

St Martin's Gardens were created in 1889 to provide a green haven and recreational space in the midst of the busy urban environment of Camden Town. The site was previously Camden Town Cemetery, which closed in 1856, before becoming public gardens in

1889. The many gravestones were cleared and removed to the perimeter, although a few remain in situ. The garden layout had a central mound and large plane trees on the boundaries, all of which may date from the 1889 layout, including the boundary to the Almshouses (1818), where there was also a clipped privet hedge. A small area with graves is fenced off with railings.

Following the formation of The Friends of St Martin's Gardens in 2005, the park underwent a major restoration and was re-dedicated as a public garden on 10th June 2006 by The Countess of Rosebery. The Green Flag gardens are now a well-balanced mixture of trees, grassland, shrub beds and wildflower borders, with a children's play area surrounded by a wildflower meadow.

47 ST PANCRAS GARDENS

> **Address:** 191 Pancras Way, NW1 1UL (☎ 020-7424 0724, ⌨ posp.co.uk/old-st-pancras and camden.gov.uk > parks and gardens > parks and open spaces).
> **Opening hours:** Open daily from around 9am to dusk.
> **Cost:** Free.
> **Transport:** St Pancras tube.
> **Attractions & amenities:** Historic church and churchyard.

Hardy's Tre

S t Pancras Gardens were once part of the burial ground of St Pancras Old Church, which remains adjacent to the public garden. The beautiful and historic (Grade II* listed) C of E church is dedicated to the Roman martyr St Pancras, after which the surrounding area is named. It's thought to be one of the oldest sites of Christian worship in England; remnants of medieval features and references in the *Domesday Book* (1086) suggest it pre-dates the Norman Conquest of 1066.

The recently restored gardens are the largest green space in the locality, with some fine mature trees. They were laid out in their current form in 1890-91 and have a geometric layout with paths, mature trees, grass and a rose garden, with a number of monuments remaining. Many important people were buried here, including Sir John Soane and his family and the composer Johann Christian Bach (buried in a pauper's grave in 1782). An ash tree in the gardens – known as 'Hardy's Tree', after the poet Thomas Hardy – has grown among the gravestones in such a way that the stone and wood have fused.

ST PANCRAS & ISLINGTON CEMETERY

48

Address: 278 High Road, East Finchley, N2 9AG (☏ 020-7527 8300,
🖥 islington.gov.uk > Cemeteries).
Opening hours: Daily, Feb-Nov, 9am to 5pm; Dec-Jan, 9am to 4pm.
Cost: Free.
Transport: East Finchley tube.

This was the first publicly-owned cemetery in London, established in 1854 when St Pancras Burial Board purchased over 88 acres (35ha) of Horse Shoe Farm on Finchley Common. It was extended to over 182 acres when a further 94 acres (38ha) were added in 1877 – the whole being divided between Islington and Camden (formerly St Pancras) – making it the largest cemetery in London; it also had the largest number of interments at around one million!

St Pancras & Islington is a lovely traditional Victorian cemetery (still active) – with two chapels, one of which has a magnificent spire (1853) – surrounded by lawns, flower beds and

mature specimen trees, including lime, cedar, monkey puzzle and cypress. It represents a cross section of London from the 1850s, with a host of styles of monuments and mausoleums, among which is the Mond mausoleum – one of the most magnificent in any public cemetery in the city. Parts of the cemetery, designated a local nature reserve, are completely overgrown, creating a diverse habitat for flora and fauna.

CHAPTER 4

WEST LONDON

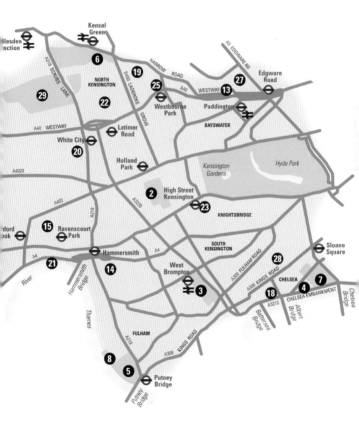

1 CHISWICK HOUSE & GARDENS

Address: Burlington Lane, Chiswick, W4 2RP (☎ 020-8742 3905, ☐ chgt.org.uk and chfriends.org.uk).

Opening hours: Gardens, daily, 7am to dusk. Conservatory, mid-Mar to mid-Oct, daily, 10am to 4pm. House, 1st Apr to 31st Oct, Sun-Wed and Bank Holidays 10am to 5pm; closed 2nd Nov to 21st Dec, except for pre-booked tours; closed 22nd Dec to 31st Mar.

Cost: Gardens and conservatory, free. House, £5.70 adults, £5.10 concessions, £3.40 children (5-15), £14.80 families, free for under-5s.

Transport: Turnham Green tube or Chiswick rail.

Attractions & amenities: Museum, conservatory, sculptures, café, shop, sports facilities.

Nestled unexpectedly in affluent Chiswick suburbia is a glorious piece of Palladian Italy, with expansive, enchanting gardens in which to wander, wonder and become happily lost. Chiswick House was completed in 1729, the vision of the 3rd Earl of Burlington (1694-1753), who'd been inspired by the architecture he saw during his 'grand tours' of Italy. One of England's finest examples of neo-Palladian design, i.e. modelled on the architecture of ancient Rome and 16th-century Italy, it was intended as a showcase for art and a venue for entertaining. Its design echoes that of classical temples – the result of a collaboration between the Earl and architect William Kent (1685-1748) – and is where the Earl played host to such 18th-century luminaries as Alexander Pope and Handel.

There's much to see in the house, highlights of which include eight beautiful landscape views of Chiswick by the Dutch artist Pieter Andreas Rysbrack; the Chiswick Tables, which are some of the best examples of English neo-Palladian furniture; the Blue Velvet Room Ceiling, an ornate blue and gold representation of the goddess of architecture; the Coffered Dome in the Upper Tribunal; carvings of the pagan Green Man in the fireplaces of the Green Velvet Room; and a splendid lead sphinx, to name only a few.

The 65 acres (26ha) of gardens (Grade I listed) are of huge historical significance as the birthplace of the

freer, more luscious design: straight lines were out and curves and clusters in. 'Natural' spaces were created, their informality highlighted by the careful addition of sculpture and other architectural details, including an Ionic temple and Doric column.

English Landscape Movement, i.e. the style of sweeping elegance which replaced the earlier formality, and was the inspiration for great gardens from Blenheim Palace to New York's Central Park. They offer grand vistas and hidden pathways, dazzling flower displays and a wealth of architectural delights.

The Western Lawn, which slopes gently down from Chiswick House to the artificial river, was a revolutionary feature in its day, and one of the defining features of the English Landscape Movement, opening up the bordering parkland and making it part of the garden. A lacework of meandering paths was introduced, which meant visitors could wander the grounds for an hour or more without retracing their steps.

In recent decades the gardens fell into decline, not helped by the footfall of over one million visitors a year, until an ambitious £12m refurbishment project, completed in mid-2010,

🍴 FOOD & DRINK 🍷

Chiswick House Café: The café (which won the RIBA London Building of the Year Award in 2011) serves delicious sandwiches, soups and the best of modern British cooking, which can be taken indoors or outdoors. It opens daily, from 9am to between 4 and 6pm, depending on the season.

Picnics: Specific areas have been set aside for picnics, including the Western Walled Garden and the fenced lawn in between the Classic Bridge and the Ionic Temple.

Created in 1729 by Lord Burlington and William Kent, assisted by Charles Bridgeman (1690-1738), the gardens were inspired by the romance of classical Italian landscape painting and conceived as a single, living artwork. They replaced the formality of the existing Renaissance garden with a

'Term' statues

The Conservatory

restored them to their 18th-century glory. The restoration recovered the original vistas and design from decades of disrepair, and repaired and restored the statuary and buildings. The result is an inspiring balance between a historic landscape and a public park. A new café and play area were also created, miles of paths renewed and over 1,600 trees planted.

Highlights of the gardens include:

The Conservatory: Designed by Samuel Ware (1781-1860) and completed in 1813, it was the longest ever built at 302ft (96m) and was the forerunner of several large glasshouses, culminating in the magnificent Crystal Palace (see **Crystal Palace Park** on page 258). The Conservatory is famous for its large collection of camellias, some of which survive from those originally planted in 1828, thought to be the oldest in the Western world. They are celebrated with a Camellia Festival in March.

The Exedra: A lawn lined by alternating cypresses and stone urns, closed by a semicircular dark yew hedge – known as the Exedra – formed a backdrop to Burlington's collection of ancient Roman and 18th-century sculpture. The statues of three figures are copies of antique statues said to

represent Caesar, Pompey and Cicero (the originals are in Chiswick House). The statues of the lion and lioness, completed around 1733, were probably sculpted by Pieter Scheemakers.

The Lake: This was originally a stream called the Bollo Brook, which formed the boundary of Lord Burlington's estate. After the estate was extended in 1726-27, the Brook was widened and canalised and, in 1737, 'naturalised' by landscaping its edges to give the illusion of a river. It's crossed by an elegant stone bridge, built for the 5th Duke in 1774 to a design attributed to James Wyatt.

The Italian Garden

This semi-circular garden was designed by Lewis Kennedy in 1812 for the 6th Duke. Bordered by evergreens, with geometric flower beds cut in grass, it became an example of the massed bedding system and 19th-century experiments in colour theory.

The Orange Tree Garden: This garden, in the shape of an amphitheatre, surrounds a circular pool with an obelisk in the centre, and an Ionic Temple behind. It was created in

Sphinx by John Cheere

around 1726 when orange trees were planted in tubs on the garden terraces. To the right of the garden is a tomb with a Latin inscription, the translation of which begins: 'Under this stone lies Lilly, my dear hound…' It's thought that the dog may have belonged to Georgiana, Duchess of Devonshire (wife of the 5th Duke).

Various: Among the many other famous features of the gardens are:

◆ **The Cascade:** An Italian Renaissance-style waterfall descending a series of rock steps through three archways, dating from around 1738.

◆ **The Doric Column:** Thought to have been designed by Lord Burlington in about 1720, the Doric Column was once surmounted with a copy of the famous statue of Venus de Medici from the Uffizi Gallery in Florence. The rose garden has been replanted and a new carved statue of the Venus now graces the column.

◆ **Inigo Jones Gateway:** Designed by Jones for Beaufort House in Chelsea in 1621 and acquired by Lord Burlington in 1738, when his friend Hans Sloane was demolishing the house.

◆ **The Obelisk:** Erected in 1732, the Obelisk has an ancient Hellenistic sculpture of a man and a woman built into its base, which was given to the young Burlington in 1712.

◆ **The Raised Terrace:** Constructed from the soil excavated from work on the lake, the terrace was planted with all manner of sweet shrubs, including roses and honeysuckle, and afforded visitors spectacular views across the Thames to the pagoda in Kew Gardens.

There are a number of sports facilities in the gardens that are open to the public,

including a cricket pitch and pavilion (home to Chiswick & Latymer Cricket Club), a sports field and tennis courts.

 DON'T MISS!

Patte d'oie

Patte d'oie, French for 'goose-foot', denotes three radiating avenues, like the webbed foot of a goose, each terminating in a small building. It was one of the earliest designs of the landscaped garden in around 1716, and was thought to reproduce the layout of an ancient Roman garden. Today, the right-hand avenue is the only one to survive and leads to the Rustic House.

2 HOLLAND PARK

Address: Ilchester Place, Kensington, W8 7QU (☎ 020-7361 3003, 🖳 rbkc.gov. uk > leisure and libraries > parks and gardens).
Opening hours: Daily, 7.30am until half an hour before dusk.
Cost: Free.
Transport: Kensington High Street or Notting Hill tube.
Attractions & amenities: Gardens, ecology centre, statuary, restaurant, café, playground, sports facilities.

Kyoto Garden

Holland Park (the area) is an affluent, fashionable part of west London, dotted with large Victorian townhouses and upmarket restaurants and shops. It's one of the capital's most expensive residential districts and therefore an appropriate location for arguably London's most peaceful and romantic park. Yet it's a park that's either unknown or ignored by most (other than local residents).

At 54 acres (22ha), Holland Park – managed by the Royal Borough of Kensington and Chelsea since 1986 – is one of the capital's smallest public parks, but also one of the most interesting, with plenty to offer. A Green Flag winner since 2001, its treasures include beautiful views, glorious gardens, galleries, sports facilities, an

ecology centre, some of London's best children's play facilities, a restaurant and café, large areas of woodland, a pride of peacocks and a stunning Japanese garden. The park is also a favourite picnic spot, with plenty of secluded hideaways in a variety of environments.

 DON'T MISS!

Statues

The park contains a number of striking sculptures, including Tortoises with Triangle and Time by Wendy Taylor (in the Dutch Garden), Boy with two Bear Cubs by John Macallan Swan (adjacent to the remains of Holland House) and a statue of the 3rd Lord Holland by George Frederic Watts, which stands in a pond in the woodland. There's also an elegant bronze fountain, Sibirica by William Pye, in the Iris Garden.

Holland Park used to be the grounds of Cope Castle, one of the area's first great houses with an estate extending to some 500 acres (200ha) – from Holland Park Avenue as far as the

Holland House

site of today's Earl's Court tube station. A large Jacobean mansion dating from the early 17th century, it was built for Sir Walter Cope (1553-1614), James I's Chancellor. Sir Walter's daughter Isabel inherited the property, which was renamed Holland House after she married Henry Rich, 1st Earl of Holland in 1616. (He was executed for his Royalist activities by Cromwell's Puritans in 1649.)

The area remained a rural backwater until the 19th century, when it mostly consisted of the grounds of Holland House, although in the later decades of the century the owners sold off the outlying grounds for residential development, and the district which evolved took its name from the house.

Holland House was almost totally destroyed during a German bombing raid in 1940 and the ruins and grounds were purchased by London County Council in 1952 from the last owner, the 6th Earl of Ilchester, in order to create a public park. Some remnants of the former estate's structures remain in the park, including the 19th-century stable, lodge, orangery and ice house, while elements of the landscaping and formal gardens are still visible, such as the Dutch Garden, Iris Garden, Lime Walk and a woodland area. The Orangery, an elegant building in the heart of the park, is now a gallery (and can be hired for private functions), while the former ice house has been transformed into a contemporary exhibition space for small-scale works, with an annual programme of exhibitions.

Ecology Centre

The Ecology Centre at Holland Park promotes awareness and understanding of biodiversity and the local environment through formal and informal education. It hosts a series of events; activities, educational visits and workshops for schools; plus a wildlife club for children. The centre has an on-going programme of informative talks and walks on environment and wildlife topics, 'open' days in the wildlife area, training events and workshops.

Today, the remaining single-storey south front and the east wing of Holland House comprise the London Holland Park youth hostel, possibly the capital's most attractive. In the summer, open-air opera and theatre performances

are staged by Opera Holland Park (operahollandpark.com) under a temporary canopy, with the remains of Holland House as a backdrop.

The park can roughly be divided into three areas: the northern half is semi-wild woodland (including a wildlife or 'nature' reserve to which the public has only limited access) where the sounds of the city all but disappear; the central part – around the remains of Holland House – is more formal, with a number of garden areas; while the southern

part is used mainly for sport. There's woodland with paths and open glades north of Holland House, an arboretum to the northwest of the house, and formal gardens to the southwest.

FOOD & DRINK

Belvedere Restaurant (☎ 020-3641 8320): Occupying what was once the Summer Ballroom of Holland House, the Belvedere is an elegant, romantic restaurant in a glorious location in the centre of the park, surrounded by flower gardens and lawns. The menu is classic French with a few British dishes thrown in, such as fish and chips and a Sunday roast.

Holland Park Café (daily, 9.30am to 5.30pm): A calm and tranquil oasis, the self-service café serves fresh, home-made seasonal food, including take-away snacks and lunch boxes for kids.

One of the highlights of Holland Park is the beautiful Kyoto Garden, a Japanese garden donated by the Chamber of Commerce in Kyoto in 1991 to celebrate the Japan Festival, held in London in 1992. Refurbished in 2001, the garden is immaculately

Belvedere Restaurant

Walking Man, Sean Henry

including magnificent maples – is at its best in spring and autumn, offering an ever-changing variety of vivid colours.

The park has a good range of sports and recreational facilities, including a giant chess set, one of London's best-equipped playgrounds, parading peacocks (unusual for a London public park) and an excellent restaurant and café (see box). There's also a variety of sports facilities, including tennis courts, soccer pitches, golf and cricket practice nets, and a netball court. The park is also an arts venue with two gallery spaces (the Orangery and Ice House), an open-air theatre and sculpture exhibitions (the Napoleon Garden provides a space for contemporary sculpture – see **Statues** box).

maintained and is regarded as one of London's most tranquil places. It has a lovely pond, with stepping stones, and a 15ft (4.5m) waterfall which feeds a pond stocked with colourful koi carp. A beautiful stone path outlines the pond with a little bridge and viewing platform, which crosses the pond at the base of the falls. The garden's elegant plantings of Japanese shrubs and trees –

3 BROMPTON CEMETERY

Address: Fulham Road, SW10 9UG (☎ 020-7352 1201, 🖳 royalparks.org.uk/parks/brompton_cemetery and brompton-cemetery.org).
Opening hours: Daily, 8am to 8pm (summer) and 8am to 4pm (winter). Guided tours (two hours) are held on certain days (see website), for which there's a 'donation' of £5 per person.
Cost: Free.
Transport: West Brompton tube.

In the mid-19th century, London's existing burial grounds, mostly churchyards, had long been unable to cope with the number of burials, and were a health hazard and an undignified way to treat the dead. Parliament established the creation of seven large, private cemeteries around London, which came to be known as the 'Magnificent Seven' (see **Highgate Cemetery** on page 116), one of which was Brompton.

Brompton Cemetery (39 acres/15.8ha) is one of Britain's oldest and most distinguished garden cemeteries (Grade I listed), containing some 35,000 monuments (including 27 that are Grade II listed and one that's Grade II* listed), which adorn over 200,000 burial sites. Brompton was closed to burials between 1952 and 1996, but is once again a working cemetery, with plots for interments and a Garden of Remembrance for cremated remains.

The West London and Westminster Cemetery, as it was then known, was established in 1836 and opened in 1840. Designed by Benjamin Baud (1807-1875), the grounds were laid out by landscape gardener Isaac Finnemore. Time, money and strong opinions conspired against the completion of Baud's grand design, but the site embodied his vision of the cemetery as an open-air cathedral, with a tree-lined Central Avenue as its nave; the domed Chapel, in honey-coloured Bath stone, as its high altar; and two long colonnades embracing the Great Circle (reputedly inspired by the piazza of St Peter's in Rome). Below the colonnades are catacombs, conceived as a cheaper alternative to a burial plot, entered via a pair of ornate 'snake doors', decorated with symbols

 DON'T MISS!

The tomb of Frederick Richards Leyland (1831-1892), ship-owner and patron of the Pre-Raphaelites, by Edward Burne-Jones, is a unique example of Arts and Crafts funerary design and a fine example of Pre-Raphaelite sculpture.

of death; the catacombs weren't a success and fewer than 500 were sold. The Chapel, colonnades and Brompton Road gate are all now Grade II* Listed.

People from all walks of life are buried here, including no fewer than 13 Victoria Cross holders (the Royal Hospital Chelsea acquired a plot when the Old Burial Ground at the hospital closed to burials in 1855). Among its famous 'residents' are author Beatrix Potter – she lived in The Boltons nearby – who took the names of many of her animal characters from tombstones in the cemetery. It's also the last resting place of civil servant and inventor Henry Cole, ship-owner Samuel Cunard, actor Brian Glover, author and broadcaster Bernard Levin, suffragette Emmeline Pankhurst, auctioneer Samuel Leigh Sotheby, and cricketer and publisher John Wisden.

Today, the cemetery is managed by the Royal Parks and is the only Crown Cemetery still used for burials, although it's more popular as a public park than a place to mourn the dead. There's notable and dominant planting of lime trees along the northwest and southeast avenues, with scattered mature weeping silver lime, holly, holm oak, cedar of Lebanon and yew. As well as its many attractions, the cemetery provides an oasis in all seasons and is a rare haven of peace, beauty and tranquillity in a part of London with few other green spaces.

The Gothic splendour of Brompton Cemetery has proved irresistible to film-makers and has been the backdrop for many period dramas, romantic comedies and thrillers, including the 1997 version of Henry James' *The Wings of the Dove*, *Finding Neverland* and Guy Ritchie's 2009 re-telling of *Sherlock Holmes*. The chapel on the Fulham Road side of the cemetery appears as a Russian church in *GoldenEye*, Pierce Brosnan's first Bond movie.

4 CHELSEA PHYSIC GARDEN

Address: 66 Royal Hospital Road, Chelsea, SW3 4HS (☎ 020-7352 5646,
🖳 www.chelseaphysicgarden.co.uk).
Opening hours: Mar-Apr to 31st Oct, Tue-Fri, Sun and Bank Holiday Mon, noon
to 6pm; 3rd Jul to 4th Sep until 10pm; closed Mon and Sat.
Cost: £9 adults; £6 students, unemployed and children aged 5-15 (a maximum of
two children are permitted per adult).
Transport: Sloane Square tube.
Attractions & amenities: Café (no free public access), shop.

This gem of a 'secret' garden in the heart of London is a historic, living museum as well as a haven of beauty and relaxation. It was founded in 1673 – when a 3.5-acre (1.4ha) plot of land with a 100m (328ft) river frontage on the Thames was leased by the splendidly-named Worshipful Society of Apothecaries of London, so that its apprentices could study the medicinal properties of plants. It's London's oldest botanical garden and Britain's second-oldest, after the one at the University of Oxford which was founded in 1621.

 FOOD & DRINK

Tangerine Dream Café: The garden's acclaimed, licensed café – where you can dine al fresco in the beautiful garden – serves a range of fresh homemade food, including light lunches and afternoon teas.

The location of the Chelsea Physic Garden – Physic refers to the science of healing – was carefully chosen; its proximity to the river tempers the weather and gives it a relatively warm microclimate, which helps the survival of non-native plants. These include Britain's largest outdoor fruiting olive tree (30ft/9m high) and the world's northernmost outdoor grapefruit. The river also served as a transport link, for the movement of botanists and plants. The garden had steps down to the water at its southern gate and a boathouse was built in the southeast corner, which once housed the Apothecaries' livery barge.

In decline by the early 18th century, the Physic Garden was essentially re-founded after the Apothecaries were granted a lease for £5 per year in perpetuity by Sir Hans Sloane (his statue is at the centre of the garden), who purchased the Chelsea Manor in 1712. Sloane appointed botanist Philip Miller as gardener in 1722, who made the garden world-famous during his almost 50 years in charge. He was particularly influential through his correspondence with leading botanists

of his day – who brought many plants to the country for cultivation at Chelsea – and his writings such as his *Gardener's Dictionary*.

The garden has had an important educational role since its inception and in the 18th century became one of the world's leading centres of botany and plant exchange, a role which has expanded in modern times with the renewed interest in natural medicine. Its Garden of World Medicine is Britain's first garden of ethnobotany (the study of the botany and plant use of different ethnic and indigenous groups), and incorporates a new Pharmaceutical Garden which displays plants of proven medicinal use. There's also a Historical Walk of plants introduced by past curators, a Victorian fernhouse and glasshouses with Mediterranean plant collections.

The Chelsea Physic Garden contains some 5,000 types of plant, concentrating on medicinal plants and rare and endangered species. There are different environments suitable to different types of plant, most notably the pond rock garden built from old building stones from the Tower of London, and Icelandic lava (collected by Sir Joseph Banks, who also contributed many seeds to the garden, gathered on his travels) mixed with bricks and flint. This odd construction is Grade II listed and dates from 1773, making it the oldest rock garden in England open to the public (and probably the oldest man-made rock garden in Europe).

The Chelsea Physic Garden has beautifully-scented aromatherapy and perfumery borders, and a vegetable plot that concentrates on rare and unusual vegetables. It also boasts England's first greenhouse and stove, built in 1681.

5 FULHAM PALACE & GARDENS

Address: Bishop's Avenue, Fulham, SW6 6EA (☎ 020-7736 3233,
🖥 fulhampalace.org).
Opening hours: Gardens, daily, dawn to dusk, including Christmas Day. Walled
garden, Mon-Fri, 10.15am to 4.15pm; Sat, 10.15am to 3.45pm; Sun and Bank
Holidays, guided tours only. Museum, Sat-Wed, 1-4pm. Guided tours (2pm) of the
palace and gardens on the second and fourth Suns and third Tue of each month
(see website for additional dates).
Cost: Palace and grounds free. Guided tours £5.
Transport: Putney Bridge tube or Putney rail.
Attractions & amenities: Walled garden, café, museum, gallery, various
entertainments.

Fulham Palace (Grade I listed) is a well-kept local secret; an unexpected, tree-surrounded haven in west London, with lovely gardens in a tranquil riverside setting. It's one of London's oldest and most historically significant buildings, yet strangely little known outside the local area. The palace was the country home of the Bishops of London for many centuries and excavations of the grounds have revealed several former buildings, including evidence of settlement dating back to Roman and Neolithic times.

The site – 13 acres (5.3ha) of the original 36 remain – was once enclosed by the longest moat (drained in 1921-4) in England, reputedly the largest in Europe, providing direct access to the Thames. The surviving layout is mainly 19th century, with an earlier walled garden and some 18th-century landscaping. It includes many rare trees, such as an ancient evergreen oak (*Quercus ilex*), estimated to be at least 450 years old and designated one of the 'Great Trees of London'. It may have been planted by Bishop Grindal (1559-1570), who sent grapes grown at the palace to Elizabeth I each year. The most celebrated gardening Bishop was Henry Compton (1632-1713), who developed a famous collection of plants, both hardy and exotic, and gave the palace gardens world significance. The grounds were landscaped for Bishop Terrick in the 1760s during the rebuilding of the house, when the formal enclosed gardens were replaced with open lawns providing views to the river.

The land is recorded as belonging to the Bishop of London in 700AD and the palace was the bishop's country house from at least the 11th century (possibly earlier) and their main residence from the 18th century until 1975. Much of the surviving palace dates from 1495 and encompasses a variety of different building styles and periods on one site.

FOOD & DRINK

Drawing Room Café: Licensed café open for breakfast, lunch and afternoon tea, serving home-made food, including soups, sandwiches, bangers and mash, cakes and cream teas.

picnic spot, with lawns, unusual tree species (including black American walnut, cork and Virginian oak), and an 18th-century walled herb garden with an orchard and a wisteria-draped pergola. There are regular displays of sculpture and other art works in the gardens, while in summer there are special events such as 'movies on the lawn'.

Fulham Palace also has a shop, a museum that traces the site's long history with displays of archaeological finds, models and paintings, a contemporary art gallery and a café (see box) overlooking the grounds. Today, the palace – which is said to be haunted by the ghosts of Protestant heretics who were persecuted in the Great Hall – is owned by the Church Commissioners and leased to Hammersmith & Fulham Council and the Fulham Palace Trust.

The grounds of Fulham Palace have served a variety of purposes, notably providing food for the household and a beautiful garden for relaxation, recreation and hospitality. Bishop Creighton (1843-1901) exhausted his guests by taking them for fast walks around the garden, while Bishop Winnington-Ingram (retired 1939) had a grass tennis court on the southwest area of the lawn. A bachelor, he opened up his house to convalescent children from the East End slums and allowed fetes in the grounds. After the Second World War, the estate had to be run on more cost-effective lines and the gardens went into a gradual decline until being taken over by Hammersmith & Fulham Council and opened to the public in 1976.

Today, the award-winning (and recently restored) gardens are an ideal

Tudor Walled Garden

6　KENSAL GREEN CEMETERY

Address: Harrow Road, Kensal Green, W10 4RA (☎ 020-8969 0152,
🖥 kensalgreencemetery.com and kensalgreen.co.uk).
Opening hours: Apr-Sep, Mon-Sat 9am to 6pm; Sun 10am to 6pm. Oct-Mar,
Mon-Sat 9am to 5pm; Sun 10am to 5pm. Bank Holidays, including Christmas Day,
10am to 1pm. Guided tours most Suns at 2pm; those on the first and third Sun of
the month (the only days available from Nov to Feb) also take in the vaults.
Cost: Free. Guided tours (two hours), £7 'donation', £5 concessions.
Transport: Kensal Green tube or rail.

A nondescript, slightly shabby part of northwest London, Kensal Green is home to one of the capital's most beautiful (if ramshackle) and distinguished cemeteries with a lovely rose garden. The access point to the cemetery is unpromising, from traffic-choked Harrow Road, with its fast-food outlets and secondhand shops – but enter the gates and you're transported to the countryside. This is a place where it pays just to wander, getting slightly lost and stumbling across a wealth of visual and architectural treats.

The cemetery is crammed with mature shrubs and trees, with two conservation areas and an adjoining canal, which help make it one of inner London's richest and most important wildlife habitats, home to many bird species and other wildlife.

Kensal Green opened in 1833, making it London's oldest public burial ground. It's one of London's 'Magnificent Seven' Victorian cemeteries – see **Highgate Cemetery** on page 116 for a full list – all of which are covered in this book. At 77 acres (31ha), it's also the largest and the most opulent, containing around 250,000 graves. It's also home to the West London Crematorium and its extensive gardens.

The cemetery was designed by John Griffith and the grounds by Richard Forrest, head gardener at **Syon Park** (see page 229), and was laid out as an informal landscape park with a number of formal features. It had well-kept lawns and a large number of specimen trees, including plane, cedar, chestnut, beech, lime, holm oak, poplar and yew.

Today, vast tracts of the grounds have been set aside as nature and wildlife reserves, hence their sometimes overgrown and unkempt appearance. The eastern end has a butterfly and bee garden and plants to attract insects, such as bergamot, hyssop, rosemary and sage.

Kensal Green contains a heady mix of architectural styles, with

Kensal Green has three atmospheric catacombs: the Colonnaded Catacomb on the north wall and others beneath the Dissenters and Anglican Chapels, the latter of which is the largest working catacomb in the country with a capacity of 4,000 coffins. After the funeral service a hydraulic mechanism, restored to full working order in 1997, would dramatically lower coffins from the chapel to the catacombs below. You can visit the vaults as part of a guided tour conducted by the Friends of Kensal Green (⌨ kensalgreen.co.uk), which start from the Anglican Chapel at 2pm on Sundays – it's advisable to bring a torch!

an interesting blend of Georgian splendour, Victorian decadence, 19th-century Gothic and modern styles; there seems little order or pattern to its layout, and its graves, which date from the 1700s to the 1990s, are often sited close together. There are a great number of buildings, tombs, memorials and mausoleums – many of them Grade II or II* listed. From the outset, prominent members of 19th-century society sought burial plots here, erecting fine monuments, many of which were created by well-known sculptors, including Basevi, Burges, Cockerell, Gibson, J B Papworth, Owen Jones and Eric Gill. Thus the cemetery has more free-standing mausolea than any other in England, the majority of which were constructed while their 'subjects' were still alive.

👁 DON'T MISS!

Kensal Green has a number of famous 'residents' you might wish to seek out, including the Brunel family of engineers who have a surprisingly understated tomb in a quiet corner of the cemetery. It's also the last resting place of authors Wilkie Collins, William Makepeace Thackeray and Anthony Trollope, playwright Terence Rattigan and three descendants of George III.

7 ROYAL HOSPITAL CHELSEA & RANELAGH GARDENS

Address: Royal Hospital Road, Chelsea, SW3 4SR (☎ 020-7881 5324, 🖳 chelsea-pensioners.co.uk).

Opening hours: Grounds, Mon-Sat from 10am (Sun 2pm) until between 4.30pm (winter) and 8.30pm (summer). Ranelagh Gardens close daily from 12.45-2pm. Hospital (courtyards, chapel, museum and Great Hall), Mon-Sat, 10am to noon and 2 to 4pm. The gardens are closed in May for the Chelsea Flower Show (for dates, see 🖳 rhs.org.uk/shows-events).

Cost: Free. Tours (for groups of up to 40) Mon-Fri, 10am and 1.30pm, £70.

Transport: Sloane Square tube.

Attractions & amenities: Royal Hospital, shop, museum, plus sports facilities (soccer, netball, sports pavilion) and toilets in the South Grounds.

Ranelagh Gardens (and South Grounds) make up the grounds of the Royal Hospital Chelsea, a secluded and picturesque retreat with shady walks, home to the famous Chelsea Flower Show (see below).

The Royal Hospital was founded by Charles II for veteran soldiers and designed by Sir Christopher Wren – it's been suggested that Charles was persuaded to build a hospital for veterans by his mistress, Nell Gwyn, whose father had been made destitute by the Civil War. The hospital was founded in 1682, but delays and mismanagement during the build meant it wasn't completed until 1692, by which time William III was on the throne. The first 476 'in-pensioners', as they became known, were admitted soon after.

Chelsea Pensioners

Today, the hospital is home to around 400 pensioners, who receive board, lodging, nursing care and a distinctive red uniform. However, much of the site is open to visitors, including the Great Hall, Octagon, chapel, courtyards and grounds. There's also a small museum dedicated to the hospital's history.

The Royal Hospital is built around three courtyards, the central one opening to the south, the side courtyards to the east and west. The building remains almost unchanged from Wren's original, except for minor alterations by Robert Adam between 1765 and 1782, and the stables, which were added by Sir John Soane in 1814.

The Earl of Ranelagh, appointed hospital treasurer by James II, had managed to lease almost a third of the grounds – the area now known as Ranelagh Gardens – and had a house built there in 1688. Both house and gardens were purchased by a syndicate in 1741, and opened to the public. To recoup the extravagant construction costs of £16,000 (£2.5m in today's money!), the owners charged a substantial entry fee and so the gardens attracted a wealthy crowd, with balls, concerts and dinners staged almost daily. For a while, Ranelagh overtook Vauxhall Pleasure Gardens in popularity, until the fashionable set abandoned it entirely in the early 1800s.

Wren's magnificent formal gardens were swept away from 1850 to 1868 when the Chelsea Embankment was constructed, and the current Ranelagh Gardens date from 1860, when they were laid out as a public park by John Gibson.

Today, the South Grounds consist of sports facilities, while the Royal Hospital grounds are home to the Chelsea Playground (operated by Kidsactive), which provides a safe and secure playground for children with disabilities and special needs.

Ranelagh Gardens and the South Grounds are also the venue for the celebrated RHS (Royal Horticultural Society) Chelsea Flower Show which takes place in May. Highlights include avant-garde show gardens designed by leading names, with a Floral Marquee as the centrepiece. It's the world's leading flower show, founded in 1913 and attended by some 160,000 visitors annually (numbers are limited by the capacity of the 11-acre/4.5ha site). It's also one of London's premier social events and very much somewhere to see and be seen (book well in advance) – the horticultural world's equivalent of Paris Fashion Week!

 FOOD & DRINK

Nearby Restaurants

The Orange (37-39 Pimlico Road, ☎ 020-7881 9844): Welcoming gastropub with great ales, food and service. Delicious pizzas.

The **Surprise** (6 Christchurch Terrace, ☎ 020-7351 6954): Comfortable (sofas, fireplaces, etc.) 'gastro' pub specialising in fresh modern British cuisine.

Tinello (87 Pimlico Road, ☎ 020-7730 3663): Tasty, reasonably-priced, contemporary Italian food. Rave reviews.

Royal Hospital Chapel

8 BISHOP'S PARK

Address: Bishop's Avenue, Fulham, SW6 3LA (☎ 020-8748 3020, 🖥 lbhf.gov.uk > parks and friendsofbishopspark.com).
Opening hours: Daily, 7.30am to dusk.
Cost: Free.
Transport: Putney Bridge tube.
Attractions & amenities: Café, children's play areas, beach, bowling green, sports facilities.

Bishop's Park (Grade II listed) was opened by the London County Council in 1893, on land previously known as Bishop's Walk, Bishop's Meadow and West Meadow, which was formerly part of the lands of the adjacent moated **Fulham Palace** (see page 172). The land was given to Fulham District Board of Works by the Ecclesiastical Commissioners, as Lords of the Manor of Fulham, on condition it be used and maintained for public recreation.

The park was extended in 1894 with the inclusion of Pryors Bank gardens, which contains stone figures depicting Adoration, Protection, Grief and Leda, presented by the sculptor James Wedgwood. The river wall was extended to Putney Bridge and a refreshment pavilion built on the site of the house, and the garden opened in 1900. Today, the east garden contains a fountain and modern statuary, while to the west are formal terraces with rose gardens. Pryors Bank – which remains a distinct garden within Bishop's Park – contains a memorial to local volunteers in the International Brigade who lost their lives in the Spanish Civil War.

There were further additions to the park in 1903, and today it extends to 22 acres (9ha). However, it retains much of its original design and the main entrance in the northeast on Bishop's Avenue still has its early 20th-century iron gates and railings. This green thoroughfare, which also leads to Fulham Palace, has mature plane trees along its length, while to the northwest are two bowling greens (1908). The park also has two splendid lodges.

The park's facilities include tennis courts; a bowling green and clubhouse (sports pavilion); playgrounds; a beach, waterplay and ornamental lake; and a café and public toilets. The park underwent major renovation in 2011, when the lake was restored to its original design.

 FOOD & DRINK

Bishops Garden Café: Housed in an Edwardian Pavilion (Grade II listed) and open seven days a week (8am to 9pm in summer – 6pm in winter), the café offers healthy, locally-sourced produce and homemade dishes.

BOSTON MANOR HOUSE & PARK　9

Address: Boston Manor Road, Brentford, TW8 9JX (☎ 0845-456 2796/456 2800.
🖥 hounslow.info > parks and open spaces and fobm.org.uk).
Opening hours: Park, 8am to dusk. House, staterooms and dining room 'open'
weekends and Bank Holidays from Apr to Oct, 2.30 to 5pm.
Cost: Free.
Transport: Boston Manor tube.
Attractions & amenities: Walled garden, lake, café (weekends), children's play
area, bowling green, sports facilities.

Boston Manor House (Grade I listed) **is** one of west London's lesser-known gems, a splendid Jacobean manor house built in 1623 occupying 20 acres (8ha) of beautiful parkland, now Boston Manor Park. Situated on ground that slopes gently down to the River Brent (from which Brentford gets its name), the house was built for Lady Mary Reade, a young widow who remarried not long after its completion. Her second husband was Sir Edward Spencer of Althorp, Northamptonshire, an ancestor of the late Diana, Princess of Wales. The house and estate was sold to Brentford Urban District Council in 1924, when the land became a public park. Boston Manor House has undergone restoration and a number of rooms are open to the public.

Due to its unique architecture and decoration, the house is often used as a setting for period films.

The estate had fine gardens, which in 1918 included a walled garden, glasshouses, a temperate house and vinery, and a 650ft (200m) herbaceous border. The original grounds extended from the Thames in the south to the railway line in the north, with the lake appearing on maps at the end of the 18th century.

The park – now bisected by the M4 motorway – is a regular Green Flag winner, and contains mature cedars (including a magnificent cedar of Lebanon, thought to date back to the 1700s) and other trees planted by the Clitherows, the family who owned Boston Manor from the 1670s to 1923. In addition to the lake, with its wild fowl and island, there are ornamental lawns, herbaceous borders, a nature trail with a wildflower meadow, and a 'secret garden'. In recent years the park has been refurbished, including paths, replanting and tree works.

Sports facilities include three tennis courts, a basketball court, soccer pitches and a bowling green, plus a large children's play area. The Pavilion Café, run by volunteers, opens from 9am to 4pm at weekends.

10 EASTCOTE HOUSE GARDENS

Address: Eastcote High Road, Eastcote Village, HA5 2EQ (☎ 01895-556000, ⌨ hillingdon.gov.uk > parks and open spaces and eastcoteparkestate.org.uk/gardens.htm).
Opening hours: Unrestricted.
Cost: Free.
Transport: Eastcote or Pinner tube, then bus.
Attractions & amenities: Walled garden, dovecote, stables, organised walks, car park.

Eastcote House Gardens is a tranquil Green Flag public park of 9 acres (3.6ha), located east of historic Eastcote Village and included within the village's conservation area. The gardens incorporate the 17th-century walled garden, dovecote and coach house (all Grade II listed) of Eastcote House, which was demolished in 1962. Today, the gardens and outbuildings are maintained by a group of volunteers, the Friends of Eastcote House Gardens (formed in 2008), in partnership with the local authority.

Eastcote House was first recorded in 1507 and was the principal residence of the Hawtrey-Deane family from 1527 until 1930. Parts of the estate were sold for housing developments in the late 19th century, and Ruislip-Northwood Urban District Council purchased the house and remaining grounds in 1931 for use as a public open space.

Planting includes notable Scots pine, oak, and Wellingtonia on the rising lawn, while in the old orchard there are yew, laurel and holly shrubberies, as well as traditional mulberry, fig, apple, walnut and medlar trees.

The gardens are much loved and used by the local community and have been painstakingly preserved and improved in the last few decades. The herb garden was planted with Artemisia, catmint, santolina and curry plants in 1977 to celebrate the Silver Jubilee of Queen Elizabeth II; a small topiary garden of box and yew was planted in 1983, while lilacs, weeping cherries and hibiscus were added the following year along the garden wall near the coach house. A pergola covered with laburnum and wisteria was introduced in 1986 and two iron gates and a sundial were added soon after. In the '90s, the orchard was supplemented by black mulberry, walnut and quince trees.

Ecological surveys have found 50 types of tree in the gardens, plus numerous species of birds, many mammals and a host of insects. Bats have been found in the coach house, but aren't believed to be nesting there long-term.

GUNNERSBURY PARK 11

Address: Popes Lane, Brentford, W3 8LQ (☎ 020-8992 1612, ⌨ hounslow.info/arts-culture/historic-houses-museums and hounslow.gov.uk > leisure and culture > local history and heritage).

Opening hours: Daily, 11am to 5pm (Nov-Mar, 11am to 4pm); closed 25-26th Dec and 1st Jan.

Cost: Free.

Transport: Acton Town tube.

Attractions & amenities: Gardens, two mansions, museum, arts centre, café, bowling green, various sports facilities.

Gunnersbury Park – the name derives from Gunylda, the niece of King Canute who lived here until she was banished from England in 1044 – contains two early 19th-century mansions, one of which (the Large Mansion) is Grade II* listed. The park is a former 18th-century estate with formal gardens developed by Princess Amelia (favourite daughter of George II) in the late 18th century, and extended by Baron Lionel de Rothschild and his family in the 19th and early 20th centuries, when it was famous for its gardens.

In 1925, 186 acres (75ha) of the estate, including two mansions (designated 'large' and 'small') and some outbuildings, were purchased by the boroughs of Acton and Ealing and opened to the public in May 1926. Although its horticultural features were maintained, there was increasing emphasis on sports and recreation, with facilities including a bowling green, golf course and a playground. A number of earlier landscape features and historic buildings remain, including the Potomac (round) pond with Pulhamite rock work, Princess Amelia's 18th-century bath house, a 19th-century orangery, and Gothic ruins and stables. The park also contains many exceptional mature trees, open grassland, and formal Japanese and Italian gardens.

> The museum occupies a suite of grand reception rooms designed by Sydney Smirke (1798-1877) in 1835-6, and has a servants' wing with magnificent original Victorian kitchens (open to the public weekends, April to October).

Since 1929, the large mansion has been the home of Gunnersbury Park Museum, the local history museum for the boroughs of Ealing and Hounslow, while the small mansion is an arts centre. The park's facilities include a café, bowling green, 18-hole pitch and putt golf course, two large play areas (with soccer, rugby and cricket pitches) and 15 tennis courts.

12 GUNNERSBURY TRIANGLE NATURE RESERVE

Address: Bollo Lane (opposite Chiswick Park tube), Chiswick, W4 5LW (☏ 020-7261 0447, ⌨ wildlondon.org.uk).
Opening hours: Unrestricted access. The visitor centre opens most days in summer (except Mondays) and two days a week in winter.
Cost: Free.
Transport: Chiswick Park tube.
Attractions & amenities: Visitor centre.

Gunnersbury Triangle is a 6.2-acre (2.5ha) local nature reserve consisting of woodland, meadow, marsh and pond. It became one of the London Wildlife Trust's first reserves when it was saved from development by a vigorous local campaign in the '80s. Cut off from the surrounding area by railway tracks in the late 19th century, the area had developed into a lively ecological community, and was the only genuinely wild place for miles around and greatly cherished by the local populace.

The triangular area now occupied by the reserve was delineated by three railway lines, two belonging to the District Line and one to the now defunct London and South Western Railway (LSWR). In the '40s the area was used as railway allotments, but they were later abandoned and the disused land was colonised naturally by grasses and trees. Over subsequent decades, it has become a sheltered birch and willow woodland with attractive pond, marsh and meadow.

> The London Wildlife Trust runs guided visits such as 'fungus forays', and on 'open' days staff and volunteers organise activities to allow visitors to learn more about nature conservation in a relaxed environment.

Secreted away behind a five-bar gate on Bollo Lane, the reserve opens up before you as if by magic as you wind among wild cherry and rowan, under archways of hazel branches, to a pond where damselflies and dragonflies flit in early summer. Gunnersbury supports a wealth of plants, birds and other wildlife, including hedgehogs, pipistrelle and noctule bats, ramshorn snails and brown-banded carder bees. You can follow the marked nature trail, listening for birds or the rustle of a hedgehog, seeking out the tunnels of field voles, and spotting interesting spiders, ladybirds and butterflies (from April onwards, holly blue, peacock and brimstone butterflies abound). In this triangle of tranquillity, busy west London feels a million miles away.

LITTLE VENICE 13

Address: Warwick Crescent, Maida Vale, W2 6NE.
Opening hours: Unrestricted access.
Cost: Free.
Transport: Warwick Avenue tube.
Attractions & amenities: Restaurants, cafés, pubs, canal-side walks, boat trips.

Little Venice is a beautiful, tranquil survivor from a time when London was a collection of villages and suburbs. The term 'Little Venice' was allegedly coined by the poet Robert Browning (1812-1889) who lived nearby and compared the area with Venice, Italy (others claim it was used ironically by Lord Byron). It's used rather loosely, but technically speaking it's the area at the point where the Paddington arm of the Grand Union Canal meets the Regents Canal (termed Browning's Pool with Browning's Island at its centre). Nowadays it's generally used in a wider context to describe an area of around a square mile in London's Maida Vale district, although the name didn't come into general use until after the Second World War.

When visiting Little Venice you may wish to drop into nearby Clifton Nurseries (5A Clifton Villas, W9 2PH, ⌨ clifton.co.uk) garden centre, a much loved London institution established in 1851.

Apart from being one of London's most exclusive residential areas, Little Venice is an unexpected haven of calm and beauty. The canal is lined with weeping willows and flanked by graceful stucco Regency mansions, many designed by noted architect John Nash. Houseboats in bright red, dark green and navy blue dot the canal (Richard Branson used to live here); some have window boxes bursting with flowers, while others are adorned with elaborate nameplates. Ducks, geese and herons drift languidly by.

This tranquil waterside area feels a long way from the surrounding hub of central London and brings to mind the words of the Water Rat in Kenneth Grahame's book *The Wind in the Willows*: 'There is nothing – absolutely nothing – half so much worth doing as simply messing about in boats.' You can take a cruise to Camden Lock or alternatively enjoy a delightful walk there along the towpath (around 2 miles/3km).

Little Venice boasts the Puppet Theatre Barge, the Cascade Floating Art Gallery and many attractive cafés, pubs and restaurants.

14 MARGRAVINE CEMETERY

Address: Margravine Gardens, W6 8RL (☎ 020-7385 3650, 🖳 lbhf.gov.uk > parks and open spaces and margravinecemetery.org.uk).
Opening hours: Daily, 9am (10am on Sun) to 4-8pm (see website for seasonal closing times).
Cost: Free.
Transport: Barons Court tube.

Margravine Cemetery, opened in 1868, takes its unusual name from the title of Elizabeth Craven (1750-1828), writer and socialite, who lived in Hammersmith in the late 18th century. She was wife of the Margrave of Brandenburg-Ansbach and Bayreuth (a margrave was a military commander in medieval times) and known as the Margravine.

The burial ground – labelled Hammersmith Cemetery on most maps – covers 16.5 acres (6.7ha), and was designed by local architect George Saunders, who also contributed a modest Gothic style lodge and two chapels (one of which survives). It was declared a Garden of Rest in 1951 when Hammersmith Council, concerned at its dilapidated state, decided to remove as many memorials and tombstones as possible and lay the cleared land to grass. By 1965 the 'clear-up' operation was completed, leaving behind the fascinating mix of grave stones and grass, tombstones, turf and trees that you see today. The cemetery also forms part of the Barons Court Conservation area, designated in 1989.

Although not bursting with spectacular memorials, Margravine has a number of distinctive monuments, three of which are listed. Most striking is the impressive Young family mausoleum, a single story building in Gothic style, the spectacular Fletcher family's throne, and bandmaster Tom Brown's (damaged) cello. Remarkable in both name and monument is the splendid 'pillow' gracing the grave of Sextus Gisbert van Os. There's also a screen wall commemorating almost 200 service personnel buried in registered war graves.

Today, Margravine is one of Hammersmith's most important public open spaces and well used by local residents – particularly as a short cut between Baron's Court tube station and Charing Cross Hospital!

Margravine is a lovely, well-maintained Green Flag cemetery, with over 300 beautiful trees and a plethora of wildflowers, benches and grassy areas for a relaxing picnic. It's also home to a profusion of wildlife, including two species of bat.

RAVENSCOURT PARK · 15

Address: Ravenscourt Park, W6 (☎ 020-8748 3020, 🖥 lbhf.gov.uk > parks and open spaces and s295963082.websitehome.co.uk/forp).
Opening hours: Daily, 7.30am to sunset, e.g. 10pm (summer) and 4.30pm (winter).
Cost: Free.
Transport: Ravenscourt Park tube.
Attractions & amenities: Gardens, tea house, play areas, bowling and putting greens, sports facilities.

Ravenscourt Park is a beautiful 32-acre (13ha) public park and garden established in 1888, designed by JJ Sexby on land surrounding Ravenscourt House. The origins of the park lie in the medieval manor and estate of Palingswick (or Paddenswick), first recorded in the 12th century. A manor house was rebuilt in 1650 and in 1747 was sold to Thomas Corbett, who named it Ravenscourt, probably derived from the raven in his coat of arms, which was itself a pun on his name – *corbeau* is French for raven.

The park offers a wide range of leisure facilities, including tennis and basketball courts, bowling and putting greens, multiple play areas and a tea house. Annual events include a spectacular bonfire night, Carter's Steam Fair and an alfresco opera season.

In 1812, the house and estate were purchased by George Scott, who employed leading landscape architect Humphry Repton to design the gardens, and encouraged the building of houses along their edges. In 1887, the estate was purchased by the Metropolitan Board of Works (later the London County Council), which established a public park in 1888. Ravenscourt House was demolished after being severely damaged during the Second World War; only the stable block remains and is now the park's café.

A Green Flag park, Ravenscourt combines attractive landscaping with a range of wildlife habitats. Its crowning glory is the magical, scented walled garden, secreted in the northeast corner of the park. Originally the kitchen garden of the house, it's laid out in a traditional Victorian symmetrical design with rose beds and arches, and exotic herbaceous beds featuring yuccas, giant poppies, irises and gunnera. It's bordered below the wall with shrubs, while scented plants such as lavender and honeysuckle make it a real treat for the nose as well as the eyes. The garden is a wonderful, Zen-like retreat, with benches and bowers.

16 RUISLIP WOODS

Address: Ruislip, Hillingdon, HA4 7XR (☎ 01895-250635, 🖳 hillingdon.gov.uk > parks and open spaces and ruislipwoodstrust.org.uk).
Opening hours: Unrestricted access.
Cost: Free.
Transport: Ruislip tube, M13 or 331 bus or by car.
Attractions & amenities: Lido, walks.

Ruislip Woods is an area of rare, ancient woodland in Hillingdon surrounding the lake known as Ruislip Lido. Extending to 726 acres (294ha), the woods were designated a National Nature Reserve in 1997, the first of its kind in Greater London. The reserve comprises four woods – Park Wood, Mad Bess Wood and Copse Wood in Ruislip, and Bayhurst Wood in Harefield – as well as Poor's Field and Tartleton's Lake in Ruislip.

Ruislip Lido

> The woods offer a quiet haven for recreation, including walking, running, cycling and horse riding, while Ruislip Lido – a 60-acre (24ha) lake with sandy beaches and a narrow gauge railway – lies on the woods' edge.

Following the Norman Conquest of England in 1066, Ernulf de Hesdin was given the manor of Ruislip, which he passed to Bec Abbey in 1087. King's College, Cambridge, became lords of the manor in 1451 and owned the woods until 1931, when Park Wood was sold to the local authority. Adjoining woodlands were added later, creating Ruislip Woods.

The woods are rich in rare flora and flora including many ancient forest trees such as English oak, sessile oak, hornbeam, beech, silver birch, the wild service tree, aspen, rowan, field maple, crack willow, wild cherry, hazel and holly. Wild flowers are also found in abundance and include common knapweed, harebell, rosebay willowherb, heather, bluebells, wood anemone, yellow archangel, snowdrops and honeysuckle. Among the many species of birds that inhabit or visit the woods are mute swan, Canada goose, magpie, robin, green woodpecker, jay, nuthatch, lesser spotted woodpecker, greater spotted woodpecker, cuckoo, sparrow hawk, tree creeper, tawny owl, willow tit and woodcock. Resident mammals include badger, fox, hedgehog, stoat, weasel and mink, plus several species of bat.

The Ruislip Woods Trust organises a number of walks throughout the year, and self-guided walks can be downloaded from Hillingdon Council's website.

WALPOLE PARK 17

Address: Mattock Lane, W5 5EQ (☎ 020-8567 1227, 🖥 ealing.gov.uk > parks and open spaces and walpolefriends.org).
Opening hours: Park, 7.30am to evening (5.30 to 10pm, depending on the time of year). House, Tue-Fri 1-5pm, Sat 11am to 5pm, closed Sun, Mon and Bank Holidays.
Cost: Free.
Transport: Ealing Broadway tube.
Attractions & amenities: Gardens, pond, manor house, museum, café, playgrounds, sports facilities.

Walpole Park (30 acres/12ha) was once part of the estate of a house now known as Pitzhanger Manor, which stands on the northeast side of the park. It's Ealing's flagship cultural venue, comprising the Grade I listed manor house and the PM Gallery, west London's premier contemporary arts venue.

In 1800, the architect Sir John Soane (1753-1837) – designer of the Bank of England and the Dulwich Picture Gallery – purchased the house and estate and built a country residence which he used as a showcase for his idiosyncratic architectural style. He sold the house in 1810, after which it had a succession of owners including the daughters of Spencer Perceval (1762-1812), the only British prime minister to have been assassinated. In 1899, Perceval's grandson Sir Spencer Walpole sold it to Ealing District Council.

The grounds were opened to the public as Walpole Park in 1901, while the house became Ealing's public library. Over time, the building was restored and extended, and it's been home to the Pitzhanger Manor (PM) Gallery since 1996.

Walpole Park (Grade II listed) contains an ornamental bridge remodelled by Soane, a pond (on whose banks he allegedly fished with his friend, JMW Turner), a rose garden and a community kitchen garden. The borough surveyor, Charles Jones, designed the tree-lined avenues, paths and flower beds in the wider park, and planted the area around the pond with plants and shrubs. As Walpole is a formal park, it isn't a major attraction for wildlife, although it's edged with diverse plants and trees that provide a habitat for a variety of birds and mammals. The magnificent cedars on the west lawn date from the 18th century.

In 2011, the park received a grant from the Heritage Lottery Fund to recreate its Regency planting and kitchen garden, protect its heritage trees and restore its listed architecture, including Soane's bridge.

18 CARLYLE'S HOUSE & GARDEN

Address: 24 Cheyne Row, SW3 5HL (☎ 020-7352 7087, 🖥 nationaltrust.org.uk/carlyles-house).
Opening hours: Mar-Oct, Wed-Sun 11am to 5pm. See website for exact dates.
Cost: £5.10 adults, £2.60 children, £12.80 families. Free to National Trust members.
Transport: Sloane Square tube.

Thomas Carlyle (1795-1881) was one of the Victorian era's greatest writers – he's even said to have inspired Dickens. Carlyle moved to London from Scotland in the 1830s and to Cheyne Row in 1834, where he lived until his death in 1881 (his wife Jane died in 1866). In May 1895, the house was purchased by public subscription and was transferred to the National Trust in 1936.

Inside this beautiful, atmospheric house you gain a vivid picture of life in a middle-class Victorian home, although the building itself is older – built in 1708 – and a typical Georgian terraced house. It has a small, tranquil walled garden, where Carlyle would sit and write.

Both Thomas and Jane tended the garden, which was planted with flowers and vegetables, a cherry tree, grape vine and walnut tree, lilac bushes, hawthorn, ash, jessamine, wallflowers and mint, as well as plants that reminded Jane of their native Scotland. It has been replanted with species mentioned in the Carlyles' writings, including walnut, figs, grape vine, nettles, ivy and box hedging.

19 EMSLIE HORNIMAN PLEASANCE

Address: Bosworth Road, W10 5EH (☎ 020-7361 3003, 🖥 rbkc.gov.uk > parks and gardens and www.londongardenstrust.org/features/voysey2006.htm).
Opening hours: Daily, 7.30am to dusk. When closed, Voysey Garden can be visited on request to the council.
Cost: Free.
Transport: Westbourne Park tube.
Attractions & amenities: Gardens, playground, sports facilities.

The Emslie Horniman Pleasance – the word derives from French and means 'a secluded garden' or 'enclosed plantation' – is a lovely small park measuring just 1 acre (0.4ha) and containing a delightful walled Arts and Crafts garden.

The pleasance is named after Emslie John Horniman (1863-1932), politician, philanthropist and heir to the Horniman's Tea dynasty, who donated the land in 1911. The park opened in 1914 and was designed by architect

Charles Voysey (1857-1941) and Madeline Agar (1874-1967) to include an area of grass, trees and shrubs, plus a formal Spanish-style walled garden, now Grade II listed and named the Voysey Garden. It's Voysey's only design of a park, and he intended it to be part garden, part playground, appealing to adults and children alike.

After decades of neglect, the park was restored to its former glory in the '90s. It also contains tennis courts, five-a-side football pitches, an all-weather sports area, plus a kiosk during summer months.

Nowadays the park is famous as the starting point for the Notting Hill Carnival in August.

HAMMERSMITH PARK 20

Address: South Africa Road, White City, W12 7PA (☎ 020-8753 4103,
🖳 lbhf.gov.uk > parks and open spaces).
Opening hours: Daily, 7.30am to dusk.
Cost: Free.
Transport: White City or Wood Lane tube.
Attractions & amenities: Japanese gardens, playground, sports facilities.

Tucked behind the BBC's former flagship Television Centre building, Hammersmith Park was built on land reserved as open space when the former White City Exhibition Grounds, built to house the 1908 Olympics, were redeveloped in the '40s and '50s.

The park was laid out over 6 acres (2.4ha), with tennis courts and a playground, and opened in November 1954. In the south is a garden with a water feature that was once part of a much larger lagoon. A key feature is the Garden of Peace, created in 1910 as part of the Japan-British Exhibition, and restored in 2008. Set among bamboo and pagoda trees, it consists of two large ponds connected by a stone bridge with rocks forming a small waterfall; some of the original plants and trees imported from Japan can still be seen.

The park also boasts a paddling pool, children's play area, boating lake, soccer pitch, playground, tennis courts, basketball courts and an all-weather sports area.

21 KELMSCOTT HOUSE GARDEN

> **Address:** 26 Upper Mall, Hammersmith, W6 9TA (☎ 020-8741 3735,
> 🖥 williammorrissociety.org).
> **Opening hours:** Thu-Sat, 2-5pm.
> **Cost:** Free.
> **Transport:** Ravenscourt Park tube.

Kelmscott House, an attractive Georgian building, was the home of William Morris from 1879 until his death in 1896. Built in around 1780, it was originally called The Retreat, but Morris renamed it after Kelmscott Manor, his home in Oxfordshire, and sometimes travelled between the two by boat (those were the days!). He founded the Kelmscott Press in a nearby property in 1890.

Morris was a keen gardener, and part of his former garden remains to the rear of the house. A small lower garden has a variety of ferns that thrive well in its shady micro-climate, while the upper walled garden has lawns, shrubs, flower beds and trees, many of which are mentioned in Morris's writing in the 1880s and '90s. The house is now a private residence but the areas which house the William Morris Society – the coach house and basement – can be visited, as can the garden.

The garden of 26 Upper Mall is also where the inventor Sir Francis Ronalds (1788-1873) constructed the world's first electric telegraph in 1816.

22 KENSINGTON MEMORIAL PARK

> **Address:** St Marks Road, W10 6DG (☎ 020-7361 3003, 🖥 rbkc.gov.uk > parks
> and gardens).
> **Opening hours:** Daily, 7.30am to dusk.
> **Cost:** Free.
> **Transport:** Ladbroke Grove tube.
> **Attractions & amenities:** Gardens, café, pagoda, adventure playground, toilets,
> various sports facilities.

Kensington Memorial Park – originally called St Mark's Park – opened in 1923 on land acquired by the Kensington War Memorial Committee to create a tribute to those who fell in the First World War. London County Council designed the park mainly as a playground, although other recreational and sports facilities have been added over the years. Recreational facilities range from playgrounds – including an excellent adventure playground and a water play facility – to tennis courts, soccer and cricket pitches, and a large open area of grass.

The park covers over 6.5 acres (2.63ha) and still has its original railings and perimeter tress. There are some beautiful cherry trees, and a line of elegant Lombardy poplars and various avenues. There are also formal areas of planting, including a pergola railed off from the main sports area, and a garden with shrub beds either side

with two areas of circular rose beds, a central palm tree set into the lawn and a central circular stone feature, possibly once a fountain.

KENSINGTON ROOF GARDENS 23

Address: 99 Kensington High Street, Kensington, W8 5SA (☎ 020-7937 7994, 🖥 roofgardens.virgin.com).
Opening hours: Open to the public on selected dates unless booked for a private function; check on the website or telephone. Babylon restaurant, daily, noon to 2.30pm (lunch); Mon-Sat, 7-10.30pm (dinner).
Cost: Free.
Transport: High Street Kensington tube.
Attractions & amenities: Restaurant, club, lift, need to negotiate some steps.

Utterly unexpected, these exotic gardens perched on the roof of a former department store are one of London's hidden secrets. They include a stream stocked with fish, 70 fully grown trees and even four flamingos – all just 100ft (30m) above a busy shopping street.

Covering 1.5 acres (0.6ha), Kensington Roof Gardens are the largest of their kind in Europe. They were laid out between 1936 and 1938 by Ralph Hancock, and are divided into three distinct areas: a Spanish garden, modelled on the medieval gardens of the Alhambra; a Tudor garden with archways, wisteria, roses and lavender; and an English walled garden, which includes around 100 species of tree (some are from the original planting and, incredibly,

grow in just 5ft/1.5m of soil). There's even a pond with the aforementioned flamingos and some ducks. Panoramic views of south and west London can be seen through windows in the surrounding wall and from the 7th floor restaurant.

Grade II listed, Kensington Roof Gardens have been owned by Sir Richard Branson since 1981 – note the Virgin flags flying from the roof – and were re-opened in 2009 after extensive refurbishment.

Spanish Garden

24 MANOR HOUSE GROUNDS

Address: The Green, Southall, UB2 4BH (☎ 020-8825 6999, 🖥 ealing.gov.uk > parks and open spaces).
Opening hours: Daily, 7.30am to dusk.
Cost: Free.
Transport: Southall rail.

An unexpected find in the centre of multicultural Southall, with its Asian restaurants and sari shops, is this stunning 16th-century, timber-framed, Elizabethan manor house. Originally called The Wrenns, it was located in the hamlet of Southall – a far cry from today's busy suburb – and was purchased in 1572 by Francis Awsiter who rebuilt it as an Elizabethan mansion. It remained in his family until 1821.

The house, now Grade II* listed, was purchased by Norwood council in 1913 and its magnificent grounds opened as public gardens. They provide a peaceful retreat, with some lovely yew trees and an old mulberry, said to have been planted by Henry VIII.

Various amenities were laid out in the '20s and '30s, including new gardens, a bowling green and a cottage for the park superintendent, and the overall layout has changed little since. It comprises a series of yew-hedged areas including an Arts and Crafts sunken garden with pool, a circular pond and circular stone-built flower garden, rockery, shrubberies (yew, laurel and rhododendron) and yew topiary, and seasonal floral displays.

25 MEANWHILE GARDENS

Address: Elkstone Road, W10 5NT (☎ 020-8960 7894, 🖥 meanwhile-gardens.org.uk).
Opening hours: Unrestricted access.
Cost: Free.
Transport: Westbourne Park tube.
Attractions & amenities: Playhut, skate park.

Meanwhile Gardens (4 acres/1.6ha) was established as a community garden in 1976 on former derelict land along the Grand Union Canal, after sculptor Jamie McCullough asked Westminster City Council for permission to turn it into a park. Permission, albeit temporary, was granted – hence the garden's name – but the unique gardens have continued to thrive and are now an oasis in this densely populated part of North Kensington, and a tribute to the many volunteers who made the project possible.

Delightful Meanwhile Gardens feature various landscapes, including a wooded area and wildlife garden with a bridge, path, pond and seating, and a scented courtyard for quiet contemplation. In contrast, there's a popular skate park (the first of its kind in London) and a playhut, built to provide a safe, stimulating play and learning environment for children.

The gardens are also a venue for the Wildlife Garden Project run by Kensington and Chelsea MIND, which uses horticultural training to help the recovery and social integration of people with mental health problems.

PITSHANGER PARK 26

Address: Meadvale Road, Ealing, W5 (☎ 020-8825 6999, 🖳 ealing.gov.uk > parks and open spaces).
Opening hours: Unrestricted access.
Cost: Free.
Transport: Perivale tube.
Attractions & amenities: Allotments, playground and play centre, golf course, lawn bowls, sports facilities, car park.

Pitshanger Park – the name comes from an Anglo-Saxon word meaning 'wooded slope frequented by kites' – is a large (52 acres/21ha) formal park in Ealing, bordered to the north by the River Brent and Ealing Golf Course. The river acts as a sanctuary for local flora and fauna, and key species include water vole, kingfisher, native black poplar, orchids and adder's tongue fern.

The park was once part of the estate of Pitshanger Manor Farm, from which Ealing Town Council acquired land for a public park in 1905 (further land was added in 1913). By 1914 the park was laid out with a bowling green, tennis courts, cricket pitches and a perimeter path planted with horse chestnuts. In 1976 Pitshanger became part of the Brent River Park – a curving linear park along 4 miles (7km) of the Brent Valley – following proposals by the Brent River and Canal Society to improve the Brent Valley river corridor.

The area's main summer event, Party in the Park, is held in the park in June.

27 REMBRANDT GARDENS

> **Address:** Warwick Avenue, W2 1XB (☎ 020-7641 5271, 🖥 westminster.gov.uk > parks and open spaces).
> **Opening hours:** Daily, 8am to dusk.
> **Cost:** Free.
> **Transport:** Warwick Avenue tube.
> **Amenities:** Deckchairs, disabled WC.

A peaceful spot with splendid views over **Little Venice** (see page 183), Browning's Pool and the Paddington Arm of the Grand Union Canal, Rembrandt Gardens is at the junction of Warwick Avenue and Harrow Road. A Green Flag winner since 2007, the gardens are quite formal, consisting of lawns, shrubs and bedding displays, with beech, rowan and silver birch trees, plus a raised terrace and pathways leading down to the towpath. There are also areas set aside to attract wildlife, and on summer evenings you may see bats flitting about.

In the '50s, local residents, including the artist Feliks Topolski, led a campaign to prevent a row of artists' studios being demolished, and its success paved the way for Warwick Avenue Gardens. The name was changed in 1975 when a collaboration between Westminster and Amsterdam resulted in 5,000 tulips being donated to Westminster; the council responded by re-naming the canal-side garden after the great Dutch master.

28 ST LUKE'S GARDEN

> **Address:** Sydney Street, SW3 6NH (☎ 020-7351 3003, 🖥 rbkc.gov.uk > parks and gardens and chelseaparish.org).
> **Opening hours:** Daily, 7.30am to dusk.
> **Cost:** Free.
> **Transport:** South Kensington or Sloane Square tube.
> **Attractions & amenities:** Beautiful church, playground, games area.

St Luke's (Grade I listed) was built in 1824 to cater to an increasing congregation, which had out-grown its parish church (now Chelsea Old Church). Designed by John Savage (1799-1852), it's built of Bath stone with flying buttresses and Gothic perpendicular towers along the nave and to the east end.

The large burial ground which surrounded the church was converted into a public garden (Grade II listed) in 1881, with the gravestones forming a

boundary wall. The garden has paths, lawns, island beds and many fine mature trees, including plane, acacia, hawthorn, tree of heaven, lime, sorbus, catalpa, chestnut, holm oak, sycamore and weeping ash. Today, the delightful gardens are famous for their beautiful flower beds and magnificent trees (visit in spring when they're in blossom), and its many seats offer a welcome respite from the bustling streets. There's also a nearby playground and games area.

> The church has associations with many famous people, not least Charles Dickens, who married Catherine Hogarth here in 1836.

WORMWOOD SCRUBS 29

Address: Scrubs Lane, W12 (☎ 020-7983 4000, 🖥 lbhf.gov.uk, scrubs-online. org.uk and friendsofwormwoodscrubs.org.uk).
Opening hours: Unrestricted access.
Cost: Free.
Transport: White City tube.
Attractions & amenities: Nature reserve, pony centre, stadium, various sports facilities.

Wormwood Scrubs (also the name of a notorious nearby prison) – the name derives from the 15th-century word Wormholtwode, meaning 'a snake-infested wood' – is the largest open space (ca. 200 acres/80ha) in the borough of Hammersmith and Fulham and one of the largest areas of common land in London. Known locally as the Scrubs, it's been a public open space since 1879.

Little Wormwood Scrubs

Originally part of Wormwood Scrubs, LWS (21 acres/8.8ha) was cut off when the West London Railway was constructed in 1844. Open daily (7.30am to dusk) and managed separately by the Royal Borough of Kensington and Chelsea, it consists mostly of grassland with a number of children's playgrounds.

In 2002 the Scrubs was designated a Local Nature Reserve and is home to an important population of common lizards and some 20 varieties of butterfly; it also attracts over 100 bird species. Although still predominantly grassland, in recent years thousands of trees have been planted to benefit diversity and encourage wildlife.

The common boasts a wide range of sporting facilities – soccer, cricket and rugby pitches, a pony centre catering for disabled riders and the Linford Christie Stadium athletics centre. There's also an area set aside for model aircraft flying.

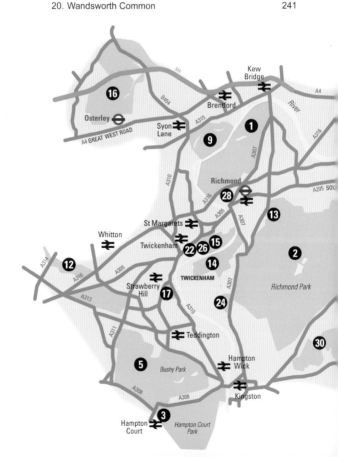

CHAPTER 5

SOUTHWEST LONDON

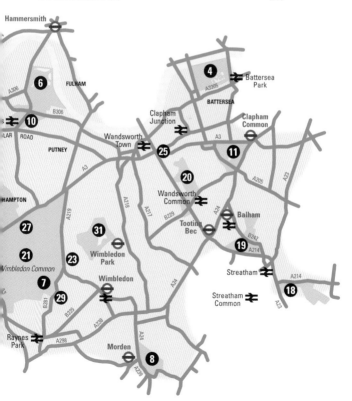

1 ROYAL BOTANIC GARDENS, KEW

Address: Royal Botanic Gardens, Kew, TW9 3AB (☎ 020-8332 5655, ⌨ kew.org).

Opening hours: Daily, 9.30am to 3.45pm (winter) and 7.30pm (summer weekends); see website for exact dates and times. Closed 24-25th Dec.

Cost: £14.50 adults, £12.50 concessions, children (16 and under) free when accompanied by an adult. Fee includes admission to most attractions. Free guided walking tours leave from Victoria Gate at 11am and 1.30pm daily.

Transport: Kew Gardens tube.

Attractions & amenities: Greenhouses, historic buildings, galleries, museum, lake, guided walks, two restaurants, two cafés, shops.

Palm House

The Royal Botanic Gardens, Kew – better known simply as Kew Gardens – comprise around 300 acres (121ha) of gardens and botanical greenhouses. Created in 1759, the gardens welcome some 2m visitors annually, and have been a UNESCO World Heritage Site since 2003.

Kew's rich horticultural and scientific history is interwoven with its royal heritage and historical importance. It houses the world's largest and most diverse botanical collections, including reference collections. The gardens contain some 50,000 plants from throughout the world, including over 14,000 trees, while the Herbarium has over 7 million specimens. The gardens also contain six magnificent glasshouses, where tropical and sub-tropical plants are kept in climatic conditions. Kew doesn't just conserve plants, but also coordinates the Millennium Seed Bank Project in Wakehurst Place (West Sussex), where seed samples from over 30,000 species – some 1.8 billion seeds – are stored.

Kew Gardens cannot be appreciated in just one visit and reveals something new every time you explore. As well as must-see attractions such as the Palm House and Pagoda, it has areas devoted to all types of flora, from azaleas and bluebells to roses and rhododendrons. The 'show' is

Frederick, Prince of Wales), founded the botanic gardens at Kew in 1759, although they had their roots in the exotic garden at Kew Park, which was the home of the Capel family in the latter half of the 17th century. The botanic gardens originally covered just 10 acres (4ha) south of the Orangery. Adjacent to them were two 18th-century gardens, while to the south were royal pleasure gardens and kitchen gardens dating from 1729, designed by Charles Bridgeman for Queen Caroline (later redesigned by Capability Brown). At the northern end, the grounds were landscaped by Sir William Chambers, who also built several garden structures, including the famous Chinese pagoda in 1762.

ever-changing at Kew and each season brings new surprises, from the massed ranks of spring bulbs to the spectacular display of autumn leaves.

Lancelot 'Capability' Brown (1716-1783) – who became England's most renowned landscape architect – applied for the position of master gardener at Kew in 1758 and was rejected. In 1764 he was appointed Master Gardener at Hampton Court.

History: Princess Augusta, Dowager Princess of Wales (widow of

After Princess Augusta died in 1772, her son George III inherited Kew and the botanic gardens were enlarged. Sir Joseph Banks, president of the Royal Society and botanical adviser to George III and Queen Charlotte, introduced many new and exotic plants. However, the collections grew somewhat haphazardly until the appointment in 1771 of the first collector, Francis Masson, who travelled as far afield as Africa and the Americas, gathering specimens.

In February 1913, the Tea House pavilion at Kew was burnt down by suffragettes Olive Wharry and Lillian Lenton, one of a series of arson attacks in London as young women fought for the right to vote.

In 1841, Kew Gardens were acquired for the nation and, under the first director, botanist William Hooker, the site was extended to 270 acres (109ha) and later enlarged to its current

size. The gardens were re-landscaped by William Nesfield, a watercolour painter turned landscape gardener, who overlaid much of the work of Bridgeman, Brown and Chambers, and created many of the avenues and vistas we see today. At the same time, Decimus Burton designed the main entrance gates and two glasshouses: the Palm House (1844-48) and the Temperate House (1859-62, extended in 1898/99). Iron-maker Richard Turner worked with Burton on the Palm House and also designed the Water Lily House in 1852. The Marianne North Gallery was built in the late 1880s to house the artist's botanical collection of paintings (see page 203).

> Plant material can sometimes provide important clues or evidence in criminal cases, and Kew provides advice to police forces around the world. In one famous case, Kew's forensic science department was able to ascertain that the contents of the stomach of a headless corpse found in the Thames contained a highly toxic African bean.

To mark Queen Victoria's Diamond Jubilee, the Queen's Cottage grounds were added to the Royal Botanic Garden in 1898, an area of around 37 acres (15ha) that had rarely been visited by the royal family and had become a wilderness and a haven for birds. The gift was made on the condition that it would be kept in its natural state and it remains a conservation area only open to the public on special occasions.

Historic Buildings: The grounds of Kew Gardens contain many historic buildings, including four Grade I and 36 Grade II-listed structures. These include **Kew Palace**, built by Dutch merchant Samuel Fortrey in around 1631. The recently restored palace (aka 'The Dutch House') was leased by George III in the 18th century and was a place of sanctuary for him and his family during his 'madness'. The nearby royal kitchens remain intact almost 200 years after they were last used by George's wife, Queen Charlotte, who died at the palace in 1818. Behind the palace is the **Queen's Garden**, a formal 17th-century garden conceived in 1959. **Queen Charlotte's Cottage**, built in the southwest corner in around

1722, was a wedding present from her husband.

Kew's wealth of attractions also includes the **Chokushi-Mon** or 'Imperial Envoy's Gateway', a scale replica of the gateway of the Nishi Hongan-ji temple in Kyoto, made for the 1910 Japan-British Exhibition at White City in London; **Minka House**, a traditional Japanese wooden townhouse originally erected in around 1900 in a suburb of Okazaki; the ten-storey octagonal **Pagoda** which stands 163ft (50m), or 253 steps, high; and the **Orangery**, designed by Sir William Chambers in 1761 and the largest 'classical' building in Kew (now a restaurant).

> During the construction of the Princess of Wales Conservatory, a time capsule was buried, containing the seeds of basic crops and endangered plant species, plus key publications on conservation.

Davies Alpine House: Opened in March 2006, this is the third version of an alpine house at Kew since 1887. Although it's a small building, just 52ft (16m) in length, the arching roof reaches 33ft (10m) high to allow the natural airflow necessary for plant ventilation. It features special glass to maximise light, automatic blinds that activate when the sun's too hot, plus a system that blows a continuous stream of cool air over the plants. Only some 200 of Kew's 7,000-plus alpines are on show at any time.

Herbarium: The Kew herbarium is one of the largest in the world containing some 7 million specimens from all regions, especially the tropics. It was begun in the mid-19th century and is located in Hunter House, just outside the main gate. Researchers can visit by appointment.

The Lake & Sackler Crossing: Conceived by director Sir William Hooker as an 'open flow of water through a portion of the Pleasure Grounds', the lake was created in 1856 in the centre of the gardens. The minimalist bridge – the Sackler Crossing – which crosses the lake was added in 2006 and is named in honour of philanthropists Dr Mortimer and Theresa Sackler, whose donation made it possible, Designed by John Pawson, it comprises a sweeping double curve of black granite, with sides formed of bronze posts. The crossing forms part of a path designed to encourage visitors to see more of the gardens.

Palm House: This iconic building was designed by Decimus Burton and built by Richard Turner between 1844 and 1848, and was the world's first large-scale structure made of wrought iron, containing 16,000 hand-blown panes of glass. The 62ft (19m) high central nave is surrounded by a walkway halfway up, which allows visitors to view the palm tree crowns.

Princess of Wales Conservatory: Kew's third major conservatory – extending to 48,500ft² (4,500m²) – was

Alpine House

designed by Gordon Wilson and opened in 1987 by the late Diana, Princess of Wales to commemorate her predecessor Augusta's associations with Kew. It houses ten computer-controlled micro-climatic zones containing mostly dry and wet tropical plants, including a wide variety of orchids, water lilies, cacti, lithops, carnivorous plants and bromeliads, among other species.

Rhizotron: This below-ground attraction (its name derives from the Greek *rhiza*, which means 'root') opened at the same time as the Treetop Walkway (see below) and illustrates the relationships that exist between tree roots, the soil and organisms such as nematodes, beetles, woodlice and bacteria.

Temperate House: Commissioned in 1859 and designed by Decimus Burton and Richard Turner, the Temperate House is the world's largest surviving Victorian glass structure. It's twice the size of the Palm House – covering an area of 52,500ft² (4,880m²) and rising to 632ft (19m) – with a central viewing gallery allowing visitors to gaze down on the collection. There are plants and trees from all the world's temperate regions, including citrus, tea plants and the famous Chilean wine palm, raised from a seed in 1846 and now over 58ft (17.6m) tall.

Water Lily House: The hottest and most humid of the houses at Kew, it was originally built in 1852 to showcase a giant Amazon water lily (the *Victoria amazonica*), which was transported from South America to Kew in phials of clean water. It now houses many different heat-loving plants and closes during the winter months.

The Kew Explorer is a free 72-seater road-train service that takes a circular route around the gardens. A commentary is provided by the driver and there are several stops.

Xstrata Treetop Walkway: One of Kew's most popular attractions, the Walkway (2008) takes visitors on a 200m (660ft) journey through the treetops, 18m (59ft) above the ground – you ascend and descend via stairs, although there's also a lift. The floor of the walkway is made from perforated metal and flexes as it's walked upon, so don't be surprised if you sway in the breeze.

Among Kew's many other attractions are a library, a number of galleries and a museum, all described below:

Water Lily House

Cambridge Cottage: Also known as Kew Gardens Gallery, the cottage displays exhibitions of botanical art by past and contemporary artists and other subjects, including iconic London Transport posters which since 1908 regularly featured trips to Kew.

Oculus Block

Sculptor David Nash sourced the wood for this imposing sculpture – four eucalyptus trunks naturally fused together – from northern California.

Kew Palace

Library & Archives: The library and archives at Kew comprise one of the world's largest botanical collections, with over half a million items, including books, illustrations, photographs, letters, manuscripts, periodicals and maps.

Marianne North Gallery: Opened in 1882 and recently refurbished, the Marianne North Gallery is the only permanent solo exhibition by a female artist in Britain. Marianne North (1830-1890) – naturalist and botanical artist – was a remarkable Victorian who travelled the world recording its flora with her paint brush. Although she had no formal training and was rather unconventional in her methods, North had a natural artistic talent and was very prolific. The gallery contains 833 paintings – depicting over 900 plant species – all completed in 13 years of world travel.

Museum No. 1: Near the Palm House is a building known simply as Museum No. 1 (despite being Kew's only museum), designed by Decimus Burton and opened in 1857. It houses Kew's economic (i.e. used by humans) botany collections, including tools, ornaments, clothing, food and medicines. The upper two floors comprise an education centre, while the ground floor houses the

'Plants+People' exhibition, which highlights the variety of plants and the ways we use them.

Nash Conservatory: Originally designed for Buckingham Palace, the Nash Conservatory was moved to Kew in 1836 by William IV. With an abundance of natural light, the building is used to house displays of photographs and educational exhibitions.

Shirley Sherwood Gallery of Botanic Art: Opened in April 2008, the gallery displays paintings owned by Kew and by botanical art collector Dr Shirley Sherwood, many of which have never been seen by the public before. It features works by artists and illustrators such as Georg Dionysius Ehret, the Bauer brothers and Walter Hood Fitch.

 FOOD & DRINK

Orangery Restaurant: Kew's self-service restaurant, operated by the acclaimed Peyton & Byrne.

Pavilion Restaurant: With its gorgeous vine-sheltered terrace, the Pavilion is a great spot for an al fresco summer lunch.

Cafés: If you're after a quick drink or snack, try the Victoria Gate or White Peaks cafés.

---

2 RICHMOND PARK

Address: Richmond, TW10 5HS (☎ 0300-061 2200, 💻 royalparks.org.uk/parks/richmond-park and frp.org.uk).

Opening hours: Unrestricted access for pedestrians and cyclists. Motor vehicles, 7am (7.30am in winter) to dusk; see website for seasonal closing times.

Cost: Free.

Transport: Richmond rail or tube then 371 or 65 bus to Petersham gate or car to Broomfield Hill car park.

Attractions & amenities: Gardens, horse and cycle paths, restaurant (Pembroke Lodge), café (Roehampton), refreshment points, playgrounds, kiting, bike hire, guided walks, stables, fishing, two golf courses, various other sports facilities, free parking.

Richmond Park is the largest royal park in London and the second largest urban park in Europe, extending to 2,360 acres (955ha). It's classified as a European Special Area of Conservation, a National Nature Reserve and a Site of Special Scientific Interest – with a plethora of flora and fauna – and is famous for its deer, which number around 650.

The park is enclosed by a high brick wall – Grade II listed and 8 miles (13km) long – with a dozen gates, allowing access to pedestrians and motor vehicles. Cars are only permitted during daylight hours, and no commercial vehicles apart from taxis are allowed entry. Pedestrians and cyclists have 24-hour access except when there's a deer cull, and the park also has designated bridleways for horse riders and cycle paths.

Legal action in 1758 by John Lewis, a public-spirited brewer from Richmond, frustrated attempts by Princess Amelia, daughter of George II and Richmond's 'park ranger', to close the park to all but her close friends, and confirmed the right of access for pedestrians at all times.

Despite its proximity to London and some of the capital's busiest roads, Richmond Park can still feel like a wilderness – especially under the canopy of one of the many woods and

spinneys, or on a misty morning when you glimpse a stag gazing back at you, antlers outlined against the sky.

History: The royal connections date back to Edward I (1272-1307), who established a royal palace at the Manor of Shene (Sheen). In the late 15th century Henry VII rebuilt Sheen and renamed it Richmond Palace after his lands in Yorkshire. In 1625, Charles I brought his court to Richmond to escape the plague in London and turned the area on the hill above the palace into a park for hunting deer. His decision, in 1637, to enclose the land was unpopular with local residents, but he did allow pedestrians the right of way and his boundary walls remain intact to this day, although they have been partially rebuilt over time. Apart from a period after the Civil War, the park remained in royal ownership until 1851.

In the 18th century, Richmond Park was a fashionable destination, and two vistas were created to showcase its best views. One looked down the grand avenue of Queen's Ride towards White Lodge, while the other looked out from King Henry's Mound – the park's highest point, said to have been used by Henry VIII to watch the hunt. The view from Henry's Mound to St Paul's Cathedral some 10mi (16km) to the east is protected by a 'dome and a half' width of sky on either side of St Paul's, where building isn't allowed to intrude.

Richmond Park has changed little over the centuries, despite the surrounding urbanisation. In 1746, Pen Ponds was dug and is now a haven for water birds, while in the 19th century several small woods were established. Modern sports amenities were added in the early 20th century and the park has also hosted Olympic events, most recently the men's and women's cycling road races in 2012.

Buildings: Richmond Park contains a number of notable buildings, ten of which are listed. Pembroke Lodge, set in 13 acres (5ha) of landscaped grounds, was built as a mole-catcher's cottage in the mid-1700s, but in 1788 was enlarged for George III. In 1847 the then prime minister, Lord John Russell, resided in the lodge, where he held cabinet meetings and was visited by dignitaries such as Giuseppe Garibaldi and Queen Victoria. Grade II listed, Pembroke Lodge now houses a restaurant.

Another house that stands within the park is the White Lodge, built in

Pembroke Lodge

1727-29 by Roger Morris for George II. Since 1995 it has been home to the Royal Ballet School, where young ballet students are trained. It also houses White Lodge Museum and the Ballet Resource Centre.

There are four other houses – plus several gate lodges – including Holly Lodge, Oak Lodge, Thatched House Lodge and White Ash Lodge. Holly Lodge contains a visitor centre (bookings only) and is also the park's administrative HQ.

> Houses backing on to the park pay a feudal fee, known euphemistically as 'Richmond Park Freebord', ranging from £2 to £200 per annum.

Landscape: Centuries of grazing by deer have helped maintain the park's special habitat as the most important area of lowland acid grassland in Greater London. There are around 50 species of grasses, rushes and sedge, along with a huge range of wildflowers that thrive on the acidic and nutrient-poor soil. These include harebell, heath bedstraw, germander speedwell, heath speedwell, bluebell, mouse-ear hawkweed and tormentil.

Richmond is also famous for its ancient trees – numbering around 1,200 – particularly oaks, which have great historic and ecological importance. The old English oaks were traditionally managed by pollarding, a way of cutting back the crown of the tree above the reach of the deer to stimulate the growth of foliage and timber for harvesting. The varied landscape of hills, woodland and grassland also includes numerous woods and copses, some created with donations by members of the public.

Highlights include the Isabella Plantation (see below), and Queen Mother's Copse, a small triangular enclosure on the wooded hill halfway between Robin Hood Gate and Roehampton Gate, established in memory of the late Queen Elizabeth, the Queen Mother. Other places of interest include Two Storms Wood (near Sheen Gate), containing some very old trees, and Sidmouth Wood which was added in the 19th century. An important development was the addition of the Queen's Ride created in the mid-18th century, providing an

Mandarin Duck

venue of oak and sweet chestnut linking White Lodge to Sawyers Hill.

The park's water features – which are its lifeblood – include Pen Ponds in the centre and Beverley Brook, which crosses the eastern corner. There are a number of other ponds, some created as a result of gravel digging in the late 17th century, including Ham Gate Pond and Ham Dip Pond, Martin's Pond and the Isabella Plantation ponds. A new Jubilee Pond was created in 2012 to commemorate Queen Elizabeth II's Diamond Jubilee. It joins other commemorative royal features in Richmond Park: two Coronation Plantations (for Edward VII in 1902 and the present Queen in 1953); King George V's Jubilee Plantation; the Queen Mother's Copse; and Prince Charles's Spinney.

Isabella Plantation: This is a stunning ornamental woodland garden created after the Second World War. The Plantation extends to 42 acres (17ha) south of Pen Ponds and has been open to the public since 1953. It's managed organically, resulting in rich flora and fauna – it's jam-packed with exotic plants and well worth visiting all year round. The name is thought to derive from the old English word 'isabel', meaning 'greyish-yellow' – the colour of the soil in this part of the park. In 1831, Lord Sidmouth (the park's deputy ranger) gave it the much more attractive name Isabella Plantation and fenced it in to protect the plants from the park's deer; he also planted oak, beech and sweet chestnut trees.

Today's garden of clearings, ponds and streams was established from the '50s onwards and is largely the work of George Thomson, the park's superintendent from 1951 to 1971. He removed invasive *Rhododendron ponticum* from large areas and replaced it with other rhododendron species, established evergreen Kurume azaleas around the Still Pond, and planted other exotic shrub and tree species. The three ponds are colonised by ferns, water plantains and brook lime.

Disabled Access

The park has disabled access and parking, and many gates also have toilet facilities for the disabled.

Isabella Plantation contains species that flower in different seasons, making it an all-year-round garden. In spring there are camellias, magnolias, daffodils and bluebells, then azaleas and rhododendrons in late April. These are followed by Japanese irises and day lilies in summer and then by Guelder rose, rowan and spindle trees in the autumn, when the Acer trees are a riot of colour. During the winter months there are early camellias and rhododendrons, as well as mahonia, winter-flowering heathers and stinking hellebore.

Wildlife: Richmond Park has changed little since its creation in the 17th century and its varied landscape

of hills, woodland and grasslands still abounds with wildlife. Most obvious are the herds of red and fallow deer that roam freely within much of the park. It's also an important refuge for other wildlife, including squirrels, rabbits, foxes, shrews, mice, voles, cardinal click and stag beetles and many other insects, plus numerous varieties of fungi.

As in other royal parks, the use of barbecues and lighting of fires is illegal. The playing of radios or other musical equipment is also prohibited. Dog owners are urged to keep their pets on a lead, both for the safety of the park's wildlife, e.g. deer and birdlife, and the dogs themselves (a number of dogs have been killed by deer).

The oldest, largest and most widespread inhabitants of the park – its trees – provide homes for a wide range of wildlife, from ants and beetles to birds and bats. Recorded wildlife includes around 140 spider species, over 500 butterfly and moth species and some 1,350 types of beetle, including one that lives on deer dung. Abundant insects and plentiful roosting sites in turn make the park an excellent habitat for bats, which include all three species of pipistrelle, plus noctule, serotine, brown long-eared

and Daubenton's. Birdlife is also hugely varied, with some 150 species recorded (over 60 breeding here), including all three native woodpeckers, kestrels, owls and a range of waterfowl.

The park provides a wide range of amenities for visitors, including two playgrounds (Kingston Gate and Petersham Gate) and educational facilities for those with special needs (Holly Lodge). During the 20th century various recreational facilities were created, including a golf course, sports pitches and a polo field. Picnics are a great way to enjoy the park, particularly during the summer months.

 FOOD & DRINK

Pembroke Lodge (9am to 5.30pm in winter or 30 minutes before the gates close in summer): A magnificent listed Georgian mansion, the Lodge tea rooms offers a wide variety of refreshments including hot lunches (with a carvery) and cream teas.
Roehampton Café (9am to 5pm): Serves a range of snacks, drinks and ice creams, with both indoor and outdoor seating areas.

HAMPTON COURT PALACE, PARK & GARDENS   3

Address: Hampton Court Road, East Molesey, KT8 9AU (☎ 0844-482 7777/020-3166 6000, 💻 hrp.org.uk/hamptoncourtpalace and fbhp.org.uk).

Opening hours: Park, 7am to 9pm (5.30pm winter). Informal Gardens, 7am to 8pm summer (6pm winter). Formal Gardens, 10am to 7pm summer (5.30pm winter). Palace, daily, Apr-Oct 10am to 6pm, Nov-Mar 10am to 4.30pm (dates and times may vary, so check website). The Formal Gardens can be visited separately from the palace, as can the maze. The palace and formal gardens are closed from 24-26th Dec.

Cost: Park and Informal Gardens, free. Formal Gardens: £5.72 adults, £4.84 concessions, children under 15 free. Maze: £4.40 adults, £2.75 children, £13.20 families (two adults, three children). Palace, Gardens & Maze: £17.60 (£16.50 online) adults, £14.85 (£13.65) concessions, £8.80 (£8.25) children aged 5 to 16, £45.19 (£41.80) families. Prices include a 'voluntary' donation.

Transport: Hampton Court rail.

Amenities: Palace, museum, three cafés, four shops.

H ampton Court Park (also called Home Park) covers 750 acres (304ha), including 60 acres (26ha) of formal palace gardens set within a loop of the River Thames. The huge park, while tranquil and unspoilt, isn't of particular interest. The real star is the spectacular gardens, with a feast of formal period features, sparkling fountains and glorious displays of over 200,000 flowering bulbs.

The Palace: This vast royal palace covers 6 acres (2.5ha) of prime riverside land at Hampton Court – a rightly regal location. It was built in 1514 for Cardinal Thomas Wolsey – then Lord Chancellor and favourite of Henry VIII – and was appropriated by the King in 1529 when Wolsey fell from favour. Henry made it his main London residence and greatly enlarged it. Further rebuilding by William III in the following century – he intended it to rival Versailles but lost interest after his wife Mary's death in 1694 – left

the palace in two distinct contrasting architectural styles: domestic Tudor and Baroque.

Now Grade I listed, Hampton Court is one of only two surviving royal palaces previously occupied by Henry VIII (the other is St James's), but it hasn't been inhabited by the British royal family since the 18th century, when George II was resident (his son, George III, never set foot there as king). It's maintained by an independent charity, Historic Royal Palaces, and is a major tourist attraction.

In July, some 24 acres (10ha) of Hampton Court Park becomes the venue for the RHS Hampton Court Palace Flower Show (💻 rhs.org. uk), the world's largest annual flower show.

The Park: The parkland of Hampton Court was enclosed in the

Privy Garden

early 16th century, when Sir Giles Daubeney, Lord Chamberlain to Henry VII, leased the property and enclosed it as a deer park. Following Sir Giles's death in 1508, Cardinal Wolsey (1475-1530), Archbishop of York and Henry VIII's chief minister, leased the property, and from 1515 onwards transformed it, building Hampton Court Palace and developing the sumptuous formal gardens.

👁 DON'T MISS!

The fascinating exhibition about the development of Hampton Court Palace's gardens, which trace the evolution of the gardens from their Tudor beginnings to the present day.

In 1528 it became the property of Henry VIII and both palace and gardens were developed from 1530 onwards, establishing Hampton Court as a showpiece for English garden design. Henry VIII made Wolsey's gardens into the Privy Orchard, added the Great Orchard in parkland to the north and the Tiltyard to the west. Henry's Privy Garden, to the south of the palace, extended to the Thames and included a mount and banqueting house.

Home Park, which surrounds the palace and gardens, consists of grassland scattered with large oak trees (one is believed to be over 750 years old), and has remained virtually unchanged since opening to the public in 1894. It's bordered by the formal palace gardens, Hampton Court Road which connects the palace with Kingston Bridge, and Barge Walk running along the curve of the River Thames. An outstanding feature of the park is its great avenues of some 550 lime trees (planted in the 1660s by Charles II) which radiate out from the palace

Flower Show garden

or around three-
quarters of a mile
(1km) towards the
east. In the centre
runs Long Water, with
the Jubilee Fountain
(2002) at its eastern
end.

The Gardens:
The gardens – as
they appear today
– date from the late
17th century. Nothing
remains of Henry
VIII's designs, save
a small knot garden
planted in 1924 which

Wilderness Garden

only hints at its 16th-century origins.
The dominating feature is the great
landscaping scheme constructed for
Sir Christopher Wren's intended new
palace and laid out in the 1690s for
William III and his wife Mary II. From
a semi-circular parterre, bounded by
water, which runs the length of the
east front, three avenues radiate out
in a crow's-foot pattern. The central
avenue contains not a walk or a drive,
but the great canal, known as the
Long Water, which was excavated in
1662 during the reign of Charles II.
The design, radical at the time, is an
immediately recognisable influence
from Versailles, and was indeed laid
out by pupils of André Le Nôtre, Louis
XIV's landscape gardener.

 ALLOW...

It's easy to spend the whole day at
Hampton Court Palace – and it's a
good way to justify the high cost of
admission! There's plenty to keep
children amused, whether getting lost
in the maze or following the ghost
trail in search of Catherine Howard
(Henry's fifth wife, who was arrested
at the palace and later beheaded) and
the 'Grey Lady'.

In the late 17th century, Hampton
Court Palace contained one of the
finest botanical collections in the world.
William and Mary were passionate
collectors of all sorts, from porcelain
and rare birds to plants. Their dramatic
plant collection encompassed over
2,000 different species, including 1,000
orange trees (the symbol of the House
of Orange dynasty) and was sourced
from as far afield as Ceylon (Sri Lanka),
the Cape of Good Hope, North America
and Barbados. Their 'Tender Exotics'
were displayed at Hampton Court,
protected from the English winter in hot
houses and orangeries, like the one to
the rear of the Lower Orangery garden.
In summer months the precious plants
– planted in wooden tubs and great

Tijou Screen

clay pots – were carried outside and exhibited in the garden.

 FOOD & DRINK

Tiltyard Café & Deli: Serves homemade hot dishes, beverages, cakes and organic ice cream – why not buy a picnic and eat it in the gardens?

The Privy Kitchen: Located in the heart of the Tudor palace, the Privy Kitchen café was originally Elizabeth I's private kitchen.

King's Arms Hotel: A 300-year-old inn perched on the Lions Gate of the palace, rich in atmosphere, décor and history.

Today, the Lower Orangery Exotics Garden has been faithfully restored using contemporary accounts, plant lists, maps, documents and pictures, plus more recent archaeological digs to confirm the exact layout. As with the original garden 300 years ago, the restored garden has different planting schemes for each season. In the winter, the beds are stark and sculptural, featuring carefully shaped trees such

as yew, juniper, holly and box, while in early spring, a riot of daffodils, primroses and polyanthus bloom beneath the trees. During the summer the exotics are displayed outside the Orangery in sculpted flower pots, while in colder weather they're moved inside (originally into the palace).

Other garden highlights include the Great Vine, Maze, Privy Garden, 20th Century Garden, Rose Garden, Great Fountain Gardens, Pond Gardens and the Wilderness, some of which are described below.

The Great Vine: Planted in 1768 by the celebrated gardener Lancelot 'Capability' Brown, the magnificent Great Vine still produces an annual crop of black, sweet grapes that are sold in the palace shops in early September.

The Maze: Hampton Court's maze was designed by George London and Henry Wise and commissioned around 1700 by William III as a form of courtly entertainment. Today it covers one-third of an acre and consists of half a mile of winding paths surrounded by towering

Flower Show garden

The Maze

ft (2m) yew tree (originally hornbeam) hedges. The maze is trapezoid in shape and it takes around 20 minutes to reach the centre.

The Privy Garden: On the south side of the palace is the Privy Garden, bounded by semi-circular wrought iron gates and railings designed by French iron-worker Jean Tijou (ca. 1660-1725), known as the Tijou Screen. Privy means private, and from Henry VIII's day until the 18th century, only the monarch and his or her closest advisors and confidantes would have been permitted to enter the garden. The Privy Garden was replanted in 1992 to reflect William III's private garden, with manicured holly and yew along a geometric system of paths. It has been accurately and painstakingly reconstructed, thanks to the wealth of information recorded about the original 1702 garden.

Wilderness: This area contains a remarkable variety of ornamental trees and shrubs. The Wilderness (the term suggests a place to wander, rather than an uncultivated area) is an English version of a French *bosquet* or small plantation,

Ice Skating at Hampton Court

and would have comprised 18ft (5.5m) high hornbeam hedges, with interstices planted with elm.

The 20th Century Garden: Contemporary style planting with trees and shrubs in an informal setting, creating a place of peace and tranquillity away from the busier parts of the palace.

Pond Gardens

4 BATTERSEA PARK

Address: Albert Bridge Road, SW11 4NJ (☎ 020-8871 7530, 💻 wandsworth.gov. uk > parks and open spaces and batterseapark.org).
Opening hours: Daily, 8am to dusk.
Cost: Free.
Transport: Battersea Park railway.
Attractions & amenities: Gardens, lake, fountains, statuary, gallery, two cafés, zoo, children's play area, bowling green, various sports facilities.

lake and Pumphouse Gallery

Battersea Park is a delightful 200-acre (83ha) public park – opened in 1858 by Queen Victoria – situated on the south bank of the River Thames opposite Chelsea. Rarely has an inner city park had so much variety, hidden secrets and simple enjoyment – it's considered by many to be the most interesting of all London's major parks. The park's success depended on the completion of the new Chelsea Bridge – also opened in 1858 – which allowed access from north of the Thames. Battersea Park quickly became a major attraction and continued to be a unique destination until the early years of the 20th century and beyond.

On 21st March 1829, the Duke of Wellington and the Earl of Winchilsea met on Battersea Fields to settle a matter of honour, although neither actually attempted to shoot the other and Winchilsea later made a grovelling apology.

Before 1846 the area was known as Battersea Fields (once a popular spot for duelling) and was a mixture of marshland reclaimed from the Thames and market gardens. Separated from the river by a narrow raised causeway, the fields consisted of low, but fertile, marshes intersected by streams and ditches where the chief crops

(1815-75) – had a perimeter gravelled carriage drive, well-planted with trees and shrubberies, a grand tree-lined avenue, winding walks and landscaped areas noted for their horticultural displays. It was bounded to the north by the Thames, where a promenade was laid out following the embankment of the river in 1877. The park was fenced on the east, west and south boundaries, with (four) lodges and ornamental gates built at the entrance points.

War memorial, Eric Kennington

🍴 FOOD & DRINK 🍴

La Gondola al Parco: By the lake, La Gondola serves home-style Italian food, coffee and ice-cream, which you can enjoy 'al fresco' while watching the ducks and boats.

The Tea Terrace kiosk: Hidden away between the fountains and the zoo, the Tea Terrace serves drinks and a selection of fresh sandwiches and other snacks.

---

vere carrots, melons, lavender and he famous 'Battersea Bunches' of asparagus.

In 1845, championed by both the ocal vicar and Thomas Cubitt, the builder and developer, whose yards were located across the river in the still marshy area of Pimlico, an application was made to Parliament to form a royal park, and the act was passed in 1846. Initial designs were laid out by Sir James Pennethorne (1801-71), although the end result varied somewhat from his vision. The park's original layout – designed by the first park superintendent, John Gibson

The 25-acre (10ha) serpentine lake in the southern part of the park was one of its main features, with rockwork features and cascades created in 1866 and 1870. An Italianate pump house (now a gallery) was built to pump water into the lake and its cascades.

Old English Garden

To the north and west of the lake were tree-clad earth mounds enclosing the famous Sub-tropical Garden created in 1863 by John Gibson (and recently restored), while to the south of the lake was a deer enclosure and to the north a smaller body of water, known as the Ladies' Pond.

New features added after the park opened included a woodland walk formed in around 1904, and the Old English garden laid out in 1912. From its early days the park was famous for its fine horticultural displays, but later there was a greater emphasis on sports provision. The early park also provided a bandstand, bowling green and children's gymnasium. A lakeside café was built by the landing stage for hired boats in 1939.

In 1951 the park was a venue for the Festival of Britain, when an area of 37 acres (15ha) was used to create the Festival Pleasure Gardens, from which the funfair remained an attraction until 1974. The Festival Gardens comprised a Grand Vista, plus upper and lower terraces linked by wide flights of steps

to the Fountain Lake, flanked by willows. A flower garden designed by the leading English landscape artist Russell Page (1906-1985) formed the central part of the gardens, which also contained a concrete amphitheatre. To the east was an aviary and children's zoo. Many of these features have been restored (see below), including the stunning Vista Fountains which

Peace Pagoda

Three Standing Figures, Henry Moore

comprise over 50 jets and form a beautiful focal point.

On the east side of the park, an open grassed area was originally provided for sports, enclosed to the north and east by the American Ground – so called because when the park was first laid out it was planted with a range of native American flora and fauna – which later became a nature reserve. The Peace Pagoda, created by the Nipponzan Myōhōji Order of Japanese Buddhist monks, was built in 1985 on the riverside.

Sculpture

There's a long and varied history of sculpture being exhibited in Battersea Park – both permanent and temporary – which is home to a number of fine permanent sculptures and war memorials, including Henry Moore's *Three Standing Figures*, Barbara Hepworth's *Single Form*, Eric Kennington's Memorial and the Brown Dog by Nicola Hicks.

Today, the park is home to a small aviary, a boating lake, a bandstand and several all-weather outdoor sporting facilities, including tennis courts, a running track and soccer pitches. The park also boasts the Pump House Gallery (🖥 pumphousegallery.org.uk)

and the Battersea Park Children's Zoo (see 🖥 batterseaparkzoo.co.uk for opening times and admission charges), plus two cafés.

In the service yard is an organic garden created by Thrive Battersea (🖥 thrive.org.uk), a national charity that uses gardening as therapeutic activity for people with disabilities. It was established in the early '80s and is designed like a physic garden with a large range of edible, medicinal, therapeutic and other plants that are designed, planted and tended by disabled people. A herb garden was created here in 2000, which has won London in Bloom awards since 2007. The park is also home to a wide variety of specimen trees, and attracts a host of wildlife, particularly water birds.

After much delay, the park's 19th-century landscape and Festival of Britain gardens were finally restored in the 21st century thanks largely to a Heritage Lottery Fund grant in 1998. Work commenced in 2000 and the park was reopened by HRH the Duke of Edinburgh on 4th June 2004. In 2011, the Winter Garden designed by Dan Pearson – initiated by the Friends of Battersea Park and funded by donations – was opened in the southwest corner of the park, the culmination of seven years' work.

5 BUSHY PARK

Address: Hampton Court Gate, Hampton Court Road, TW11 0EQ (☎ 0300-061 2250, 🖥 royalparks.org.uk/parks/bushy-park and fbhp.org.uk).

Opening hours: Unrestricted access for pedestrians and cyclists (except Sep and Nov, 8am to 10.30pm). Motor vehicles, 6.30am to dusk (opens 7am in winter, 8am in Sep and Nov); see website for seasonal closing times. Water Gardens, Tue-Sun, 9am to dusk, closed Mon except Bank Holidays. Woodlands Gardens, daily, 9am to dusk.

Cost: Free.

Transport: Teddington, Hampton Wick or Hampton Court rail, then 5-10 minute walk to Sandy Lane Gates.

Attractions & amenities: Gardens, café, refreshment points, cycling, horse-riding, swimming pool, playground, various sports facilities, free parking.

Bushy Park is the second-largest of London's Royal Parks (after **Richmond Park**, see page 204), covering a mighty 1,100 acres (445ha) and, like Richmond, is a traditional deer park. It lies immediately north of **Hampton Court Palace Gardens & Park** (see page 209) and strikes a balance between wilderness and formality, its rough grassland and plantations complemented by formal avenues of lime and chestnut trees. There are also woodland and water gardens, ponds and streams, sports facilities and a playground.

History: The name 'Bushy Park' was first recorded in 1604 and was probably a reference to the thorn bushes planted to protect the young oak trees (grown to provide timber for naval ships) from the deer. But the land has been settled for at least 4,000 years – a Bronze Age barrow

and burial mound has been excavated near Sandy Lane, the contents of which are now housed in the British Museum. There's also evidence of medieval field boundaries; just south of the Waterhouse Woodland Gardens, there are traces of the largest and most complete medieval field system in Middlesex.

The origins of the deer park date from 1491, when Giles d'Aubrey enclosed 400 acres (162ha) of farmland, known as Middle Park. By 1504, Cardinal Wolsey had enclosed more areas of farmland, as well as the Home Park of Hampton Court Palace. When Henry VIII took over the palace in 1529, he also assumed the three parks that make up the modern-day park: Hare Warren, Middle Park and Bushy Park. Henry created a deer chase and built a brick wall around the park, a section of which remains.

At one end he built a large round pond and installed the statue (from Hampton Court Palace) and fountain in the centre of it. Although known as the Diana Fountain after the Roman goddess of hunting, the statue – designed by Hubert Le Sueur in 1637 – actually represents Diana's nymph, Arethusa.

Houses were added to the park in the 17th and 18th centuries, as hunting lodges and homes for the park ranger, one of which, Bushy House (1663), is now the National Physical Laboratory.

Among those who served as keeper or ranger (an honorary position, which included residence at Bushy House) was William IV, when he was still Duke of Clarence (1797-1830). To ensure that his wife Queen Adelaide could remain at their long-time home after his death, he appointed her his successor as park ranger, a title she held until her death in 1849.

His successors, perhaps less interested in hunting, added a number of picturesque features, including Longford River, a 12-mile (19km) canal which brought water from the River Colne in Hertfordshire. It was built in 1638-9 by order of Charles I to provide water to Hampton Court Palace, as well as to the park's various ponds, and cuts a path across the north of the park between Hampton and Teddington. Oliver Cromwell lived in Hampton Court Palace during the Commonwealth period (and enjoyed hunting in Bushy Park) and extended the water supply to Heron and Leg of Mutton ponds to improve the fishing.

In 1712, Sir Christopher Wren redesigned the Chestnut Avenue (then the Great Avenue) to make a long, formal route through the middle of the park. Flanked on both sides by a row of horse chestnuts and four rows of limes, it marks the park's zenith in terms of royal ambitions and sophistication.

Gardens: Bushy Park's most important gardens include the Upper Lodge Water Gardens, built by the 1st Earl of Halifax in 1710. They comprise a Baroque-style collection of pools, cascades, basins and a canal, and have had some surprisingly practical uses, including as a hospital for Canadian troops during the First World War, then as swimming pools in an open-air school for East End Boys

Upper Lodge Water Gardens

suffering from respiratory diseases. After decades of neglect, they were restored and reopened in 2009.

> During the Second World War, General Dwight D Eisenhower planned the D-Day Landings from Supreme Headquarters Allied Expeditionary Force (SHAEF) at Camp Griffiss in the park. A memorial by Carlos Rey, dedicated to the Allied troops who fell on D-Day, marks the spot where Eisenhower's tent once stood.

The Waterhouse Woodland Gardens, extending to around 99 acres (40ha), and the Waterhouse Plantation (now combined) were developed around 1949 by J M Fisher, who was also responsible for the Isabella Plantation in **Richmond Park** (see page 204). Dogs and cyclists aren't allowed in this tranquil spot which is stunning in springtime when first snowdrops, then later daffodils and bluebells, raise their heads.

Flora & Fauna: Bushy Park is home to a plethora of wildlife and habitats, but remains essentially a deer park, where red and fallow deer roam freely. Currently numbering over 300, their grazing is essential to maintain the high wildlife value of the park's acid grasslands. They can be aggressive during rutting (Sep-Oct) and the birthing (May-Jul) seasons and dog owners, especially, should give them a wide berth.

The mix of woodland and grassland areas make the park ideal for many small mammals, including rabbits, voles, mice, shrews and hedgehogs. The varied habitat, good insect populations and the availability of tree roost sites also make it an ideal habitat for bats – no fewer than seven species were recorded in 2004 – while the wealth of birdlife includes all three native woodpeckers, kestrel, tawny owl,

Diana Fountain

heath bedstraw and others. Wetter areas sustain a variety of rushes and other species, including mudwort, a real rarity.

> The Pheasantry Welcome Centre, located in the Woodland Gardens, houses an information point, café, public toilets, and an education and community room.

Bushy Park is a popular venue for many sports, including cycling, soccer, rugby, field hockey (the modern game of field hockey was largely invented at Bushy during the late 19th century), cricket, horse-riding, tennis, fishing, model boating, kite flying and lawn bowls, while the Hampton heated open-air pool and fitness gym (🖥 www.hamptonpool.co.uk) is situated on the western boundary of the park.

kingfisher, and waterfowl along the river and ponds. Of particular importance are a number of ground-nesting birds such as skylark, reed bunting, meadow pipit and stonechat. Bushy Park's many ponds and streams are home to a range of fish including perch, roach, chub, bream, rudd and carp (weighing up to 40lb/18kg). Fishing, for which a permit is required, is permitted in three ponds.

The park is of national importance for its insects – particularly butterflies and moths – with over 100 nationally scarce or threatened species recorded. It's also an important site for solitary bees and wasps with over 150 species, while the ancient trees and decaying woodland habitats are nationally important for endangered invertebrates, including the rusty click beetle, the cardinal click beetle and the stag beetle.

A key feature of Bushy is its extensive area of acid grassland (around 320 acres/130ha) where dry, nutrient-poor soils support fine grasses and characteristic wildflowers, including sheep's sorrel, harebell, tormentil,

6 LONDON WETLAND CENTRE

Address: Queen Elizabeth's Walk, Barnes, SW13 9WT (☎ 020-8409 4400,
🖳 wwt.org.uk/visit-us/london).

Opening hours: Daily except for Dec 25th. Summer (Apr-Oct) 9.30am to 6pm;
winter (Nov-Mar) 9.30am to 5pm. Guided tours at 11.30am and 2.30pm; bird
feeding tour 3pm.

Cost: £11.65 adults, £8.70 concessions, £6.50 children aged 4-16, £32.50 families
(up to two adults and two children), under 4s free. Prices include a 'voluntary' Gift
Aid donation.

Transport: Barnes rail or 283 bus from Hammersmith.

Attractions & amenities: Gardens, visitor centre, café, free parking.

The London Wetland Centre covers an area of over 100 acres (40ha) in Barnes and is probably Europe's best urban wildlife-viewing area. It's slightly off the radar for many visitors to the capital, which is a pity as there's nothing quite like it in any other major city: an unexpectedly large wildlife habitat near the centre of a metropolis.

The area was once part of lands belonging to the Archbishop of Canterbury. There was a manor house on the site known as Barn Elms – once the mansion of Sir Francis Walsingham, Secretary of State to Elizabeth I – but it was destroyed by fire and demolished in 1949. Later the land was used for market gardens and allotments, before becoming Barn

Elms reservoirs, owned by Thames Water, and Barn Elms Playing Fields, now situated adjacent to the London Wetland Centre.

The Centre was created by the Wildfowl and Wetlands Trust (it's one of nine WWT centres throughout the UK) when four concrete reservoirs become redundant after the completion of the Thames Water Ring Main in the '90s. Thames Water wished to use the land sympathetically, while at the same time Sir Peter Scott (1909-1989, founder of the World Wide Fund for Nature and the WWT) was seeking a London site to create a wildlife centre. It took five years to establish the Wetland Centre – during which 300,000 plants and 27,000 trees were planted – which

opened in May 2000, and was declared a Site of Special Scientific Interest in 2002.

Outside the Peter Scott Visitor Centre is a bronze sculpture of Scott with two Bewick's Swans, by Nicola Godden.

The Wetland Centre was designed to maximise the feeding, roosting and breeding opportunities for water birds, including species that are rare and endangered in southern England. The emphasis on diversity led to the creation of a range of habitats, including grassland, mudflats and reed beds. In the World Wetlands area you can discover ducks, geese and swans from around the globe, and learn about their habitats and behaviour. It's home to beautiful American wood ducks, elegant smews and noisy white-face whistling ducks; you can also see some of the wildfowl that are the subject of WWT's current conservation efforts, such as red-breasted and barnacle geese and the iconic nene (Hawaiian goose).

At the heart of the centre are the diverse lakes. Reservoir Lagoon is a deep water lake with artificial fish reefs to attract diving ducks and fish-eating birds such as grey herons and cormorants, while the Main Lake and Sheltered Lagoon appeal to wintering and moulting ducks. The Reed Beds are grazing marshland meadow which is drained in summer to provide nesting sites for waders, while the Wader Scrape in the east has lower water levels to expose areas of mud as a feeding ground for probing waders.

In addition, there are three sustainable gardens, designed especially for the centre:

♦ The RBC (Royal Bank of Canada) Rain Garden focuses on rainwater management in a changing climate and provides an arresting vista with a wildflower meadow, a cascade of 'rain gardens', green roof planting, a stream with lush, bold vegetation along its edges and a rocky 'dry' stream.

♦ The Wildlife Garden is more natural, with log piles, trees and stretches of tall reeds and grasses running down to the edge of the stream, creating an ideal habitat for amphibians, insects and small mammals.

♦ The Slate Garden is a riot of colour, its bold swatches of brightly-hued flowers providing an eye-catching display from spring to autumn. Like all the gardens, it provides food and shelter for insects such as bees and butterflies.

A stunning display of orchids and snake's head fritillaries make Cricklade Meadow unmissable in spring and summer, while the Bog Garden is the place to go hunting for newts, spot dragonflies and damselflies flitting across the pond, and see lizards sunning themselves on a log. The Pond Zone is a new high-tech version of a village pond, where you can operate Pond Cam, an underwater camera, to see up close what's living in the pool. There are also children's activities and educational displays in a number of pavilions, including the Pond Zone and Duck Tales.

The London Wetland Centre isn't just an important site for birds – which number over 200 species, including many not found elsewhere in London – but also for small mammals, insects and amphibians, including bats, otters, water voles, frogs, snakes, slow worms, dragonflies and butterflies, to name just a few species. It's also a notably user-friendly environment, where you can borrow binoculars and children can obtain small fishing nets for 'pond-dipping'.

> The London Wetland Centre was voted Britain's Favourite Nature Reserve in 2012 in the BBC *Countryfile* Magazine Awards.

Free walks are available with expert guides or you can just wander off on your own and stroll along the walkways between the lakes and pools, stopping to watch the wildlife from a number of hides. There's also an impressive visitor centre, with a gift shop, café and cinema. The grounds have level access and hard-surfaced paths with tarmac on main routes and a free electric mobility scooter is available (must be booked in advance).

> We will leave the last words to the esteemed wildlife film-maker and television presenter, Sir David Attenborough: 'The London Wetland Centre is the ideal model for how mankind and the natural world may live side by side in the 21st century.' Praise indeed.

Sir Peter Scott statue

CANNIZARO PARK 7

Address: West Side Common, Wimbledon, SW19 4UE (☏ 020-8545 3678,
🖥 merton.gov.uk > parks and cannizaropark.com).
Opening hours: Daily, 8am to dusk (opens 9am at weekends).
Cost: Free.
Transport: Wimbledon tube/rail.
Attractions & amenities: Gardens, lake, historic house.

The lovely Cannizaro Park is a Grade II* listed park on the edge of Wimbledon Common, although it sounds as if it should be in Italy. It was a private garden for some 300 years before opening to the public in 1949, and combines great natural beauty with a unique collection of rare and exquisite trees and shrubs, including sassafras, camellia, rhododendron and other ericaceous plants. It's also noted for its rich wildlife.

The park has a long history of staging arts and musical events (including the Wimbledon Cannizaro Festival in summer), and contains a variety of sculptures, including a statue of Diana and the fawn, and a teapot-shaped fountain. There's also a bust of Emperor Haile Selassie who spent time in Wimbledon in the '30s when exiled from Ethiopia.

The 35-acre (14ha) park has a large variety of green areas, from expansive lawns and leisurely walks through woodlands to formal areas such as the sunken garden next to Cannizaro House and an Italian garden near the pond, expressing the changing face of garden design over the years.

The park has its origins in the 299-acre (121ha) Warren estate on the southern edge of Wimbledon Common that was purchased in 1705 by William Browne, a wealthy London merchant. The estate was formerly known as Old Park and had been created in the early 1570s by Sir Thomas Cecil, later Lord of Wimbledon Manor. William Browne built Warren House – now Cannizaro House – in the early 1700s. Between 1785 and 1806, the house was occupied by Henry Dundas, 1st Viscount Melville (1742-1811), then Home Secretary, and was a major social centre for royalty and senior politicians. In later years, visitors included Lord Tennyson, Oscar Wilde and Henry James.

Diana and the fawn

Cannizaro House

The name Cannizaro dates from 1832 when Count St Antonio leased the house. He later succeeded to the dukedom of Cannizzaro in Sicily and left England to live with his mistress in Milan, but his long-suffering wife Sophia retained her title as Duchess of Cannizzaro, and when she died in 1841 the estate was recorded under her name. Apart from losing a 'z', the name has stuck ever since.

The park is a joy at any time – thanks to the tireless efforts of the Friends of Cannizaro Park – and is particularly special in spring when the rhododendrons, azaleas and magnolias are in bloom. Or visit in autumn, when the birch, maple and horse chestnut trees create a spectacular riot of colour.

With the exception of Viscount Melville, who planted Lady Jane's Wood in 1793, the greatest private contributions to today's park were made by Mr and Mrs E Kenneth Wilson who lived there from 1920 to 1947 and laid out a new garden, much of which remains today. Their daughter Hilary married the 5th Earl of Munster in 1928, and in 1948 sold the estate to Wimbledon Corporation for £40,000. Cannizaro House is now a smart hotel, with a terrace overlooking the park (🖥 cannizarohouse.com) – and a splendid venue for afternoon tea!

The design of the park has evolved over the centuries but the plants remain the stars, many of which were sourced from around the world in the late 19th and first half of the 20th century. Today they're displayed in some exquisite individual gardens, such as the azalea dell, water garden, Mediterranean garden, rose garden, herb garden and tennis court garden. Other delights include lakes, fountains and woodland, where some of the trees date back several hundred years.

MORDEN HALL PARK 8

Address: Morden Hall Road, SM4 5JD (☎ 020-8545 6850, 🖥 nationaltrust.org. uk/morden-hall-park).
Opening hours: Daily, 8am to 6pm.
Cost: Free.
Transport: Morden tube.
Attractions & amenities: Gardens, cafés, mill, shop, visitor centre, garden centre, play area.

Morden Hall Park, owned by the National Trust, covers over 125 acres (50ha) of parkland in what was once rural Surrey. This tranquil former deer park is one of the few estates to survive from those that lined the River Wandle during its industrial heyday, and contains Morden Hall (closed to the public), a stable yard (now restored and containing a café and visitor centre), pretty Morden Cottage sited in the rose garden, and many old farm buildings, some of which house a garden centre and a city farm.

👁 DON'T MISS!

The beautiful rose garden contains some 2,000 roses, including 25 varieties of floribunda roses displayed across 38 flowerbeds. Visit between May and September to enjoy the rich aroma of the roses in full bloom.

The Snuff Mill – one of the original Grade II listed mills – is used as an education centre. Visitors can see the conserved waterwheel that, until 1922, turned the massive millstones used to crush tobacco into fine powder for use as snuff and, behind it, the modern equivalent, an Archimedes screw hydro-electric turbine which generates electricity for the park's visitor centre.

The estate was originally owned by Westminster Abbey, and there's evidence of an earlier manor house, although the current Morden Hall was built between 1750 and 1765 within a moated enclosure created from the Wandle. It was home to the Garth family for generations, until being sold

in 1873 to a tobacco merchant, Gilliat Hatfield (1827-1906).

Hatfield created much of the current park, removing field boundaries and cottages, and planting new trees, predominantly chestnuts and willows. Several new bridges were built across the existing watercourses and Hatfield also made changes to Morden Hall's garden – he replaced its boundaries to leave the lawns sloping down to the moat, but retained a fountain and formal walk. He also built a new stable block and lodges.

> The former walled kitchen garden – which once employed 14 gardeners – is now home to the Riverside Café and National Trust shop. There are also craft stalls and a demonstration kitchen garden.

His son, Gilliat Edward Hatfield (1864-1941), inherited the estate in 1906 and made few changes apart from planting a new rose garden in 1922 by Morden Cottage, where he lived in preference to the main house. A philanthropist, he allowed the hall to be used as a convalescent home. On his death, Hatfield left the estate to the National Trust, although the National Trust didn't directly manage it until 1980.

Morden Hall Park sits on the flood plain of the River Wandle and consists of three main habitats: meadowland, marshland and woodland. Water lies at the heart of the park, with the river, mill ponds and a lake. The lush wetlands, riverbanks and islands provide an ideal habitat for a variety of plants, mammals (such as voles and pipistrelle bats), insects and birdlife. Herons, kingfishers, ducks and swans are regularly seen along the river, and there's a heron colony in the wetlands, which is also visited by a little white egret. Rarer birds such as warblers shelter in the hedgerows, while woodpeckers and owls live in the woods.

The meadows are managed to provide a mixture of natural grasses and wildflowers during summer, while the marshes and river's edge provide wetland habitats for flowers such as yellow iris and marsh marigold. There's also an ornamental avenue of lime and horse chestnut trees, and a mulberry tree thought to have been planted by Huguenots in the 18th century. The park has other native trees such as oak, beech, ash, birch, and some lovely riverside willows and alders, plus one of the oldest yews in England.

SYON HOUSE & PARK 9

Address: Syon Park, Brentford, TW8 8JF (☎ 020-8560 0882, 🖥 www.syonpark. co.uk).

Opening hours: Gardens, Mar-Oct, daily, 10.30am to 5pm. House, Mar-Oct, Wed, Thu, Sat and Bank Holidays, 11am to 5pm. Dates vary so check the website before visiting.

Cost: Gardens & Great Conservatory: £6 adults, £4.50 concessions, £3 children (5-16), £13 families. House, Gardens & Great Conservatory: £11 adults, £9.50 concessions, £4.50 children, £25 families.

Transport: Gunnersbury or Ealing Broadway tube, then 237 or 267 bus to Brent Lea Gate bus stop or E2 or E8 bus to Brentford.

Attractions & amenities: Gardens, conservatory, garden centre, café, shop, trout fishery, art centre.

Syon House and its 200-acre (80ha) park – both Grade I listed – comprise one of England's finest estates. The name derives from Syon Abbey, a medieval monastery of the Bridgettine Order which was founded nearby in 1415 by Henry V. It moved to the site now occupied by Syon House in 1431 and was closed in 1539, during the Dissolution of the Monasteries. In 1594, Henry Percy, 9th Earl of Northumberland, acquired Syon House through his marriage to Dorothy Devereux, and the Percy family have lived there ever since.

Capability Brown's lake is a haven for wildlife (including terrapins) and the views across the Thameside water meadows, still grazed by cattle, give Syon a unique rural landscape, close to the heart of London.

In 1750, Sir Hugh Smithson inherited the Percy estates through his wife, Elizabeth Seymour; they revived the Percy name when Sir Hugh became Earl and then 1st Duke of Northumberland in 1766. In 1761, he commissioned architect and interior designer Robert Adam (1728-1792) and landscape architect Lancelot 'Capability' Brown (1716-1783) to redesign the house and estate. While Adam's architecture was inspired by classical Rome, Brown took the medieval deer park as his model.

Adam's plans for the interior of Syon House included a complete suite of rooms on the principal level, together with a rotunda in the main courtyard (which was never built). In the event, only five main rooms on the west, south and east sides of the house, from the Great Hall to the Long Gallery, were designed in the Neo-classical style. But Syon House is feted as Adam's early English masterpiece and is the finest surviving evidence of his revolutionary use of colour. Two rooms

Conservatory

sum up Adam's genius: the grand scale and splendour of the Great Hall, which resembles the Imperial Rome of a Hollywood epic, and the richly-decorated Ante Room or Vestibule, with its riot of coloured marble – one of Adam's most ingenious designs.

Syon Park – now a Site of Special Scientific Interest – is renowned for its rare trees, including wing nut, Turkish hazel, medlar and quince, and its 40 acres (16ha) of gardens and ornamental lake. The rose garden, which adjoins the south lawn by the side of the house, is dominated by old-fashioned varieties including damask, moss and albus roses (although modern varieties are constantly being introduced). This area is in brilliant contrast to the wilderness garden, where visitors can walk beside the lake under the shade of some of the park's 3,000 trees.

Syon House remains the London home of the Duke of Northumberland and is the last surviving ducal residence, complete with its country estate, in Greater London.

One of the more unusual objects in Syon Park is Flora's Column, a 55ft (16.7m) high pillar surmounted by a statue of Flora, goddess of flowers and spring. It was erected by the 1st Duke of Northumberland around 1758, when he converted a large orchard

into the 'Syon Pleasure Ground'. Flora now overlooks a lawn named after her, which includes herbaceous beds containing ornamental thistles, euphorbias, phlox, scabiosa, gypsophila and great clumps of Prince of Wales feathers.

The crowning glory of the gardens is the Great Conservatory – an architectural feat of magnificent proportions – designed by Charles Fowler (1792-1867) and completed in 1830. It was the first large-scale conservatory to be built from metal and glass, and was conceived as a show house for the Duke's exotic plants; it's said to have given Joseph Paxton inspiration when he designed the Crystal Palace (see page 256) and has featured in several films and music videos. Other features in the gardens include an ice house and a curving range of glasshouses containing ferns, vines, succulents and flowers, set off by a formal Italianate garden.

Duchess of Kent's bedroom

BARNES COMMON & OLD BARNES CEMETERY 10

> **Address: Vine Road, SW13 0NE** (☎ 08456-122660, 🖥 richmond.gov.uk > parks and open spaces and barnescommon.org.uk).
> **Opening hours:** Unrestricted access.
> **Cost:** Free.
> **Transport:** Barnes rail.
> **Attractions & amenities:** Nature reserve, sports pitches.

Barnes Common is a peaceful area of open grassland, trees and woodland and, at more than 124 acres (50ha), one of the largest areas of unenclosed common land within easy reach of the centre of London. Designated a Local Nature Reserve, it was owned by the church from the Middle Ages and is now managed by the borough of Richmond-upon-Thames. The common was used jointly by the people of Barnes and Putney until 1589 when a dispute arose and Barnes folk refused to allow people from Putney access!

Until it was drained in around 1880, the common was mainly marshland and almost entirely treeless. Today it's primarily woodland, coppice and heathland, with some open areas of grass where cricket and soccer are played. It's home to an abundance of flora (particularly grasses) and fauna, though there are few mammals due to its open nature.

> On the edge of the common, on Queen's Ride, is a memorial to the rock star Mark Bolan, who was killed in a car crash here in 1977.

The Old Barnes Cemetery within Barnes Common – adjacent to the boundary with Rocks Lane Recreation Ground – was established in 1854 on 2 acres (0.8ha) of land as an additional burial ground for Barnes parish churchyard. A number of distinguished Victorians are interred here and a wealth of monuments and statues erected to their memory. The cemetery closed in the '50s and in 1966 was acquired by the borough council with the intention of turning it into a lawn cemetery. The council demolished the chapel and lodge and removed the boundary railings to prepare it for its new role, but then abandoned their plans and the cemetery.

Today, it's one of London's forgotten corners, overgrown with trees and shrubs, with many of the monuments vandalised and statues decapitated. It's a sorry sight, but also an atmospheric and evocative place with an air of gentle decay and quiet seclusion.

11 CLAPHAM COMMON

Address: Windmill Drive, SW4 9DE (☎ 020-7926 9000, 🖥 www.lambeth.gov.uk > parks and green spaces and claphamcommon.org).
Opening hours: Unrestricted access.
Cost: Free.
Transport: Clapham Common or Clapham South tube.
Attractions & amenities: Gardens, cafés, playgrounds, ponds, bandstand, fishing, various sports facilities.

Clapham Common (220 acres/89ha) has existed for over 1,000 years (it's first mentioned in the *Domesday Book* of 1086) and is one of London's largest open spaces, performing an essential task as a green lung and a place for recreation. It consists mainly of grassland with trees and ponds, and was historically common land for the parishes of Battersea and Clapham, but was converted into parkland in the 19th century. Today it's almost equally split between the boroughs of Lambeth (who manage it) and Wandsworth.

The common contains three ponds which evolved from old gravel pits. Eagle Pond and Mount Pond are open for fishing between June 16th and March 14th, and contain a variety of species including bream, carp (weighing up to 20lb/9kg), roach and tench. Eagle Pond was refurbished in 2002, when it was completely drained, landscaped and replanted to provide a better fish habitat. Fishing is prohibited on Long Pond which has a century-old tradition of being used for model boating.

Sports are a big attraction on Clapham Common which has an all-weather games area, tennis courts, bowling green, skate park and pitches, as well as two playgrounds. There's also a historic bandstand (Grade II listed and recently restored), dating from 1890, said to be the oldest and largest in London, and three cafés. The common also has a number of ecological areas, including woodland and meadow grasslands, which are managed for the wildlife as well as the public.

The Friends of Clapham Common is an active community group that helps maintain the common, its buildings and facilities, and improve its biodiversity. During the winter the friends plant young trees to replace fallen and diseased stock and have sown a wildflower meadow, planted daffodils, crocuses, snowdrops and bluebells for the benefit of people, birds and insects.

CRANE PARK ISLAND 12

Address: Crane Park, Whitton, TW1 (☎ 020-8755 2339, 🖳 wildlondon.org.uk and richmond.gov.uk > parks).
Opening hours: Unrestricted access. The Shot Tower is open on the first and last Sun of each month.
Cost: Free.
Transport: Whitton rail.

Crane Park Island is a nature reserve – designated a Local Nature Reserve in 1990 and one of 60 managed by the London Wildlife Trust – situated on the north bank of the River Crane. The Island is part of the larger Crane Park, which runs between Hanworth Road to the west and Meadway to the east (the best places to access the reserve are via the footpath from Ellerman Avenue or Great Chertsey Road).

The River Crane is a short river that begins in Hayes, skirts Heathrow Airport and eventually meets the Thames at Isleworth. Crane Park Island was created to contain a pool of water from the river which was used to power mill machinery, remains of which can still be seen (including wheel pits and machine bases), along with various mill streams. The river was also called the 'Powder Mill River' after its most important industry – the Hounslow Gunpowder Mills, which operated until the early 20th century.

The Gunpowder Mills was a highly dangerous place to work and there were a number of explosions during its operation, many fatal. The large mounds that can still be seen throughout Crane Park were built to help absorb the impact of explosions.

After the closure of the Gunpowder Mills in 1927, the new owner sold part of the site for housing and part to Twickenham Council, who created a public park which opened in 1935. The site still contains important industrial archaeological remains, including the Shot Tower (Grade II listed) built in 1828 and used to make lead shot. It now houses a nature study and visitor centre.

Nowadays the island is a rich mosaic of woodland, scrub, meadow, reedbed and river bank, home to a rich variety of wildlife, from darting dragonflies to secretive foxes, stately herons to noisy marsh frogs. If you're lucky you may even see a rare water vole.

Shot tower

13 EAST SHEEN & RICHMOND CEMETERIES

Address: East Sheen Cemetery, Sheen Road, TW10 5BJ and Richmond
Cemetery, Grove Road, TW10 6HP (☎ 020-8876 4511, 🖥 richmond.gov.uk >
cemeteries).
Opening hours: Daily, 10am to 6.30pm (4.30pm, Nov-Mar).
Cost: Free.
Transport: North Sheen rail or Richmond tube and 493 bus.

East Sheen and
Richmond Cemeteries
are two beautiful
neighbouring cemeteries
which have existed side
by side for over a century,
although they're now
managed as a single entity.

East Sheen Cemetery
opened as Barnes Cemetery
in 1905 and was renamed
East Sheen in the '30s. It's
linked to Sheen Road to the
north by an avenue of plane
trees, with a lodge at the entrance and a
mortuary chapel on its southern boundary.
Although it now forms a continuous area
of graves with Richmond Cemetery, the
boundary is still clearly defined by a holly
hedge. The cemetery contains various
fine trees, clumps of pampas grass, with
yews behind the chapel and on either side
of the main roadway.

Interesting monuments include
those of actor Roy Kinnear, with a
moving tribute from his wife, the steps
and gate of the Mawhinney family
monument, and the seated soldier on
the grave of William Rennie-O'Mahony
of the King's African Rifles.

Richmond Cemetery opened in
1839, although it has its origin in a
small burial plot donated by George
III in 1786. The oldest part of the
cemetery contains many mature trees,
including yew and cypress, while the
more open grassed area is surrounded
by horse chestnuts, lime, false acacia
and ash, with yew and holly throughout.
There are two Gothic chapels: the
non-conformist ragstone chapel in Early
English Gothic style and a Church of
England chapel designed by Sir Arthur
Blomfield in 1875.

The cemetery is rural and
picturesque, not unlike Highgate
Cemetery albeit on a smaller scale. The
old part is dominated by war graves,
particularly the South African section,
with a Cenotaph-like memorial by
Lutyens.

The East Sheen Lancaster family
tomb (1920) has a striking bronze,
Angel of Death, by Sydney March. It's
described by Hugh Meller (in his book
London Cemeteries) as 'arguably
the most dramatic sculpture in any of
London's cemeteries'.

HAM HOUSE & GARDENS 14

Address: Ham Street, Ham, Richmond-upon-Thames, TW10 7RS (☎ 020-8940 1950, 🖥 nationaltrust.org.uk/ham-house).
Opening hours: Gardens, shop and café, Mar-Oct, daily from 11am to between 4 and 6pm; closed Fri except for mid-Jul to early Sep. See website for house opening times and winter opening times for both the house and garden.
Cost: Garden only, £4.50 (includes Gift Aid) adults, £2.25 children, £11.25 families. House and garden, £11 adults, £5.50 children, £27.50 families. Garden tours are cheaper during the winter months (see website). Free to National Trust members.
Transport: Richmond or Twickenham rail and 15-minute walk.
Attractions & amenities: Guided tours, café, shop.

Ham House – the name comes from an old English word for 'a place in the bend in the river' – is one of London's architectural and garden gems. The house – now owned by the National Trust – was built in 1610 for Sir Thomas Vavasour, Knight Marshal to James I, and was extended and refurbished as a palatial villa under the ownership of Lord and Lady Dysart. It was mainly the vision of Lady Dysart (1626-98) – Elizabeth Maitland, Duchess of Lauderdale – who's variously described as ambitious, beautiful, greedy and sharp-witted.

The ghost of Lady Elizabeth Dysart, and that of her dog, are said to still walk the corridors of Ham House, which is – allegedly – a very haunted property.

The meticulously restored Ham House has rooms of sumptuous splendour, including walls hung with tapestries, rich fabrics and rococo mirrors, with spectacular collections of furniture, textiles and paintings and a notable group of Coade Stone statues; the River God statue outside the front of the house is one of the largest pieces ever made.

The faithfully restored 17th-century formal garden (17 acres/7ha), which includes a kitchen garden, is a remarkable survivor. Most 17th-century gardens were replaced in the following two centuries by the then-fashionable English landscape garden, but these are little changed. The strong architectural nature of the wilderness, gravel terraces and parterres of lavender add to the charm and interest of this year-round riverside garden.

You can also see Britain's oldest orangery (dating from the 1670s), now the tea room. The tea room terrace is reputed to have the oldest Christ's thorn bush in the country, while walnut and chestnut trees in the outer courtyard act as roosts and nesting sites for a flock of green parakeets. There's also a lovely, trellised cherry garden, while the formal avenues are lined by over 250 mature trees. Ham House garden is an important habitat for wildflowers, mammals, insects and birds.

15 MARBLE HILL HOUSE & PARK

Address: Richmond Road, Twickenham TW1 2NL (☎ 020-8892 5115, 🖥 www.english-heritage.org.uk/daysout/properties/marble-hill-house and marblehillsociety.org.uk).

Opening hours: Park, daily, dawn to dusk. House, Apr-Nov, Sat-Sun, guided tours only (see website for details and time).

Cost: Park, free. House, £5.70 adults, £5.10 concessions, £3.40 children (5-15), £14.80 families. Free to English Heritage members.

Transport: Richmond rail/tube. The house can be reached via a scenic walk along the Thames footpath.

Attractions & amenities: Gardens, museum, grotto, café, picnic area, shop.

Marble Hill Park (66 acres/27ha) surrounds Marble Hill House, a beautiful Palladian villa on the north bank of the Thames. It's the last complete survivor of the lovely villas and gardens that bordered the Thames between Richmond and Hampton Court in the 18th century – a romantic reminder of a lost world.

Marble Hill House was built between 1724 and 1729 for Henrietta Howard, Countess of Suffolk and mistress to George II (when he was Prince of Wales), by the architect Roger Morris. The house – now managed by English Heritage – has tightly controlled elevations, which became a standard model for villas in southern England and much further afield, including plantation houses in the American colonies. Its grand interiors have been beautifully restored and conjure up the atmosphere of fashionable Georgian life, with a collection of early Georgian furniture and some fine paintings, as well as the Lazenby Bequest Chinoiserie collection.

The grounds (open to the public since 1903), sloping gently down to the Thames, were laid out in the early 18th century – with advice from Alexander Pope and Charles Bridgeman – with terraced lawns, avenues of chestnuts and scattered trees, plus an ice house and two grottos, one of which

remains. Today there are small areas of woodland to the east and west of the house, with broad lawns to the north and south flanked by trees along the approach drives, and lawn borders overlooking the Thames. A notable black walnut from the mid-18th century stands in an enclosure 650ft (200m) southeast of the house.

Marble Hill Park is linked to **Ham House** (see page 235) just across the Thames by Hammerton's Ferry, a ferry service for pedestrians and cyclists. One of only four remaining ferry routes in London, it operates at weekends and on weekdays between April and October.

OSTERLEY PARK & OSTERLEY HOUSE GARDENS

16

Address: Jersey Road, Isleworth TW7 4RB (☎ 020-8232 5050, 🖵 www.hounslow.gov.uk/osterley_park.pdf and nationaltrust.org.uk/osterley-park).

Opening hours: Park, summer, 8am to 7.30pm, winter, 8am to 6pm. House & garden, Apr-Oct, Wed-Sun, 11am to 5pm; Mar and Nov, noon to 6pm; see website for exact dates and winter opening times.

Cost: Park, free. Garden, £4.35 (includes Gift Aid) adults, £2.25 children. House and garden, £9.95 adults, £5 children, £24.75 families. Free to National Trust members.

Transport: Osterley tube.

Attractions & amenities: Gardens, children's activities, concerts, exhibitions, café, shops (gift, farm, books), car park.

Osterley Park and its surrounding gardens, park and farmland make up one of the last surviving country estates in London, covering an area of 357 acres (144ha) – one of west London's largest open spaces. It isn't, however, the most tranquil, as the M4 motorway cuts through the middle and you can also hear aircraft at nearby Heathrow. However, it's a stunning landscape with some lovely planting, notably in the Pleasure Gardens where the floral displays are at their best between June and September, and a fine collection of trees, particularly oak and cedars of Lebanon on the Cedar Lawn which are believed to be over 200 years old. The grounds also boast three lakes which are important wildfowl habitats.

Osterley Park House – once dubbed 'the palace of palaces' – is an original Tudor (1576) redbrick house, built for Sir Thomas Gresham (1519-79), an Elizabethan tycoon (who, among other things, was financial adviser to Queen Elizabeth I and founder of the Royal Exchange). The house wasn't just somewhere for him to relax away from the city, but also a source of income. The land was fertile and well-watered, ideal for wheat, and he also established one of England's first paper mills here.

The property was remodelled for the Child family by the fashionable architect and designer Robert Adam between 1760 and 1780. The interiors are one of the most complete surviving examples of Adam's work, with beautiful plasterwork, splendid carpets and fine furniture, all designed specifically by Adam for the house.

Outside, the beautiful gardens, carefully restored to their 18th-century glory, are a delightful retreat, while the park is perfect for picnics and leisurely walks. Don't miss the walled gardens and the newly-created winter garden – and lunch or afternoon tea in the tea garden.

Osterley's shopping options include a gift shop, a secondhand bookshop and a farm shop, where you can buy locally-produced fruit and vegetables at reasonable prices.

17 STRAWBERRY HILL HOUSE & GARDENS

Address: 268 Waldegrave Road, Twickenham TW1 4ST (☎ 020-8744 1241, 🖥 strawberryhillhouse.org.uk).

Opening hours: Gardens, daily, 10am to 6pm. House, Mar-Oct, Mon-Wed, Sat-Sun 2-5.30pm (weekends from noon), closed Thu-Fri. Early Bird guided tours (2 hours) Mar-Sep, Sat 10.30am; twilight tours at 8pm on selected days. See the website for winter opening times, exact dates and tour information.

Cost: House and gardens, £8.40 (with Gift Aid) adults, £7.40 concessions, £5.25 students and children aged 5-15, £21 families. Early Bird guided tours, £13 adult (£8.40 child); twilight tours £20 (adults).

Transport: Strawberry Hill rail.

Attractions & amenities: Historic house, café, shop, guided tours.

The Strawberry Hill website claims the house is a 'truly theatrical experience', which certainly isn't understating the case with regard to this Gothic 'castle' of undoubted charm and originality. Many claim it to be Britain's finest example of Georgian Gothic architecture and interior decoration.

Built in 1698, the house was originally modest, but from 1747 it was transformed by Horace Walpole (1717-1797), the son of Sir Robert, Britain's first Prime Minister. The garden inspired Walpole – an art historian, antiquarian and man of letters – to pen *On Modern Gardening*, one of the most famous and influential essays ever written on garden design and history, He was also a dedicated collector, and Strawberry Hill was created to house his huge collection of 'treasures'.

Walpole created the first landscape garden to be associated with a picturesque house. In contrast with the fashion of the time, Walpole's designs were a riot of informality, featuring winding paths, groves of trees, and lilacs and honeysuckles 'hanging down in festoons'. The 9 acres (3.64ha) of garden contained a lawn with a meadow beyond, flanked by trees and an open terrace with views of the Thames. Unfortunately the expansive views have been lost to housing and the growth of woodland, but the grassed areas and the layout of the tree planting survive.

In 2002, the Strawberry Hill Trust was formed to restore the house and open it to a wider public. The Trust secured £9m in funding (largely through a Heritage Lottery Fund grant) to restore the house – completed in 2011 – and garden. The garden is (as far as possible) being restored to its original appearance; Walpole's extraordinary Shell Bench has been recreated and the lime grove is being replanted.

Walpole inspired a new fashion for the Gothic, in both architecture and literature, and Strawberry Hill was something of a sensation in its day.

STREATHAM COMMON & THE ROOKERY 18

Address: Streatham Common/Streatham High Road, SW16 and The Rookery, Covington Way, SW16 3BX (☎ 020-7926 9000, 🖵 lambeth.gov.uk > parks and green spaces).
Opening hours: Common, unrestricted access. Rookery, daily, 7.30am to dusk.
Cost: Free.
Transport: Streatham rail, various buses or car.
Attractions & amenities: Two cafés, playground, various events, sports facilities.

Streatham Common (64 acres/26ha) is a large open space at the southern tip of Lambeth with areas of woodland, grassland, wildflower meadows, a nature trail and the Rookery, a small and enchanting formal garden (see below). The common has a rich history stretching back to the Norman Conquest and the *Domesday Book*, and boasts spectacular views across south London and to the North Downs of Surrey. It has been used and recognised as a common for centuries, and in 1883 an Act of Parliament ensured its protection as a public open space in perpetuity.

Streatham Common includes a popular café, playground and a paddling pool, and is a popular venue for fairs and other events, including a kite festival.

The Rookery (9.5 acres/3.8ha) is an attractive, formally landscaped area with an ornamental pond, flower and herbaceous beds, and a rock garden with streams, encircled by Streatham Common. It's in an area formerly known as Streatham Spa, where in the 18th century people would drink water from local springs for its medicinal properties. Streatham Spa and its formal gardens were in the grounds of a large house called the Rookery. When the popularity of the spa declined, local residents successfully campaigned to buy the Rookery and save it and the surrounding woodland as a public open space. The Rookery (Grade II listed) became a public garden and was formally opened on 23rd July 1913 – it celebrated its centenary in 2013 with talks, walks, music and drama.

The Rookery is noted for its old cedar trees and for its White Garden, which echoes the one at Sissinghurst Castle (Kent). Its areas of woodland are important for biodiversity and environmental education, and bristle with birdsong and wildlife. The gardens have a café. In summer the lawns become an open-air theatre.

19   TOOTING COMMON

Address: Tooting Bec Road, SW16 1RU (☎ 020-8871 6347, 🖥 wandsworth.gov.
uk > parks information > the commons and friendsoftootingcommon.org.uk).
Opening hours: Unrestricted access.
Cost: Free.
Transport: Streatham rail.
Attractions & amenities: Lake, lido, horse-riding, fishing, athletics track, various
sports facilities.

Tooting Common consists of two adjacent areas, Tooting Bec Common and Tooting Graveney Common, with a combined area of 221 acres (92ha). The two are now a single entity and treated as such by Wandsworth Council, which has administered the common since 1971. It's the last remnant of common land that once stretched as far as Mitcham to the southwest and its landscape – now criss-crossed by busy roads – comprises some largely natural areas and sections that have been more formally landscaped for recreation use or sports activities.

The old western boundary between Bec and Graveney commons is marked by an avenue of oak trees along Dr Johnson Avenue – planted in the late 16th century to commemorate a visit by Elizabeth I. At the end of the avenue is the old keeper's lodge, built in 1879. The road gets its name from Dr Samuel Johnson (1709-84), a friend of the Thrale family who lived nearby in Streatham Park.

Tooting Common's acid grassland, secondary woodland, scrub and ponds is classified as a Site of Metropolitan Importance and includes a number of rare wildlife habitats, supporting a wide variety of woodland birds for an inner London site. It also contains important trees, including a line of oaks planted in the 17th century to the east of the common by Garrard's Road, and a row of elms which marked the southern boundary along Tooting Bec Road.

The lake, originally created by gravel excavation, became a focal point and ornamental feature in 1895. There's also an old yachting pond and nearby, sculptures created from trees felled during the Great Storm of 1987.

Tooting Bec Lido

The common has a famous outdoor swimming pool, Tooting Bec Lido, which opened in 1906 and is the largest swimming pool by surface area in the UK. Open from late May to late September.

WANDSWORTH COMMON 20

Address: Bolingbroke Grove/Bellevue Road, SW11 (☎ 020-8871 6347, 🖥 wandsworth.gov.uk > parks information > the commons).
Opening hours: Unrestricted access.
Cost: Free.
Transport: Wandsworth Common rail.
Attractions & amenities: Lakes, nature study centre, café/bar, playground, fishing, tennis courts, bowling green, sports pitches.

Wandsworth Common (175 acres/73ha) is an important historic common, the remains of more extensive common land that was part of the manor of Battersea and Wandsworth in the 11th century. By the 19th century it had been sub-divided by the railway and encroached upon by building as London became more developed. In 1887 it was transferred to the Metropolitan Board of Works (later London County Council) who carried out improvements including planting, paths and the creation of the ornamental lakes from old gravel pits, as well as the smaller Three Island Pond just off Bolingbroke Grove.

Despite being divided into two strips by the railway, crossed by a footbridge and criss-crossed by roads, the common is home to a wide variety of urban wildlife including foxes, squirrels, and numerous bird and invertebrate species. Habitats include a mosaic of secondary oak and birch woodland, acid and neutral grassland, and scattered gorse scrub. The acid grassland contains typical species such as tormentil and purple moor grass, while the three lakes (recently restored) support common waterfowl and a range of fish, and are popular with anglers.

Part of the common is known as the Scope (25 acres/10ha) and is managed specifically for wildlife, designed to create an ecologically rich environment.

> Wandsworth Common contains a wide range of amenities, including sports pitches, tennis courts, a bowling green, a lake (fishing in season), a trim trail, playground and a café/bar.

The name is derived from an enormous refracting telescope (once the largest in the world), constructed here in 1852 by the Rev John Craig. The expansion of London resulted in poorer air quality, making the telescope useless, and it was removed in the 1870s. The Scope contains young oak and silver birch woodland, various types of grassland and scrub habitats. A nature study centre is based here and provides support for ecological and educational work in the borough.

21 WIMBLEDON COMMON & PUTNEY HEATH

Address: Windmill Road, Wimbledon, SW19 5NR (☎ 020-8788 7655,
🖥 www.wpcc.org.uk).
Opening hours: Unrestricted access.
Cost: Free.
Transport: Wimbledon rail, tube and tramlink.
Attractions & amenities: Information centre, windmill and museum, playgrounds,
golf, horse-riding, guided walks, various sports facilities.

Wimbledon Common, together with Putney Heath and Putney Lower Common, is the largest expanse of heathland (1,136 acres/460ha) in the London area. Legally protected from development by the Wimbledon and Putney Commons Act of 1871, and funded by local residents' council tax, it was created for public recreation and the preservation of flora and fauna, and provides an oasis of calm in the midst of urban southwest London.

Putney Heath is a northern extension of Wimbledon Common, but Putney Lower Common is an entirely separate area, some 1.5mi/2.5km to the north. It's divided from Barnes Common by Lower Richmond Road with the nearest public transport Barnes rail.

The three commons consist of woodland, scrubland, heathland and nine ponds, plus mown areas set aside for recreation. They are the home to a wide variety of flora, including around one million trees, as well as mammals, amphibians, reptiles, fish and insects (it's a flagship site for stag beetles). Birds are well represented with some 100 species observed annually, of which around 50 breed here. The commons are also an important site for dragonflies and damselflies, and six species of bat are found here: Daubenton's, common and soprano pipistrelle, brown long-eared, serotine and noctule (bat walks are led by the London Bat Group – see 🖥 londonbats.org.uk). Some 900 acres (360ha) of the commons are designated a Site of Special Scientific Interest (SSSI) and Special Area of Conservation (SAC).

Recreational attractions are mainly located on Wimbledon Common and include an 18-hole golf course (and two golf clubs), cricket pitches, 16 miles (26km) of bridleways and the Richardson Evans Memorial Playing Fields covering 48 acres (20ha), providing soccer and rugby pitches in winter and athletics' facilities in summer. There's also a large pavilion with changing rooms, showers and toilets. Other buildings include 16 staff cottages, a café, pavilion, maintenance centre, stables, the ranger's office, information centre and a windmill, which is now a museum
(🖥 wimbledonwindmill.org.uk).

YORK HOUSE GARDENS 22

Address: Sion Road, Twickenham, TW1 3DD (☎ 08456-122 660, 🖳 richmond. gov.uk > parks and yorkhousesociety.org.uk).
Opening hours: Daily, dawn to dusk.
Cost: Free.
Transport: Twickenham rail.
Attractions & amenities: Historic house, tennis courts.

York House (Grade II listed) is a fine 17th-century building – now the HQ of the London borough of Richmond – with a fascinating history, set in beautiful grounds on the banks of the River Thames. The gardens were commissioned by Sir Ratan Tata (1871-1918), a Parsee industrialist from Mumbai who purchased York House in 1906.

Tata, whose family still runs one of the largest companies in India, installed a group of striking statues of naked female figures in the gardens. The figures represent the Oceanides (or sea nymphs) of Greek mythology, and include two winged horses with a female charioteer in a shell chariot, plunging through the water at the top of a cascade and pool, while seven other figures are sitting on rocks or clambering up them. Some of Tata's 'naked ladies' are in posed in unusual attitudes and can come as a surprise to the unsuspecting visitor!

Now Grade II listed, the sculptures are carved from Italian white Carrera marble, and it's thought they may have come from the Roman studio of Orazio Andreoni at the end of the 19th century. After decades of neglect, they were restored in 1988 thanks to Elizabeth Bell-Wright, who encouraged

the York House Society and the Twickenham Society to save them.

> The York House Garden statues were originally commissioned to adorn Lea Park (now Witley Park) near Godalming, Surrey, by the financier Whitaker Wright, but were sold in 1904 after he was found guilty of fraud and committed suicide (by swallowing cyanide) at the Royal Courts of Justice.

York House Gardens comprise a diverse range of areas, including tennis courts, formal planting, amenity grass and woodland. Around the recently restored cascades, planting has been designed to harmonise with the statues, with greens, pinks and whites predominating. Some unusual specimen trees and shrubs have been added to enliven the landscaping, including several types of magnolia, wedding cake tree and tulip trees, and there's also a beautifully restored Japanese garden.

23 BUDDHAPADIPA TEMPLE GARDENS

Address: 14 Calonne Road, Wimbledon Parkside, SW19 5HJ (☎ 020-8946 1357, 🖳 buddhapadipa.org).
Opening hours: Daily, 9am to 6pm. Group and school bookings by appointment (see website).
Cost: Free.
Transport: Wimbledon rail or tube, then 93 bus towards Putney and alight at the Common.
Attractions & amenities: Temple, meditation classes and courses.

This is Europe's only Thai temple, established by the London Buddhist Temple Foundation to create a centre for the dissemination of theoretical and practical Buddhist teachings. Now one of Europe's most important Buddhist training centres, its Thai name is Wat Buddhapadipa, a *wat* being a Buddhist sacred precinct consisting of monks' quarters, the temple proper, an edifice housing a large image of Buddha and a structure for lessons.

The grounds of the *wat* cover approximately 4 acres (1.6ha) in which the Uposatha Hall (temple) – a beautiful building with traditional white walls contrasting with the red and gold of the roof, windows and doors – is situated on an ornamental lake, with a small grove of trees, flower garden and orchard. The temple also has a house where the monks live and a cottage.

Although the temple is home to monks and nuns, it welcomes visitors of any faith to view the grounds and temple, and offers a wide range of Buddhism and meditation courses.

24 HAM COMMON & WOODS

Address: Upper Ham Road, Richmond, TW10 5LA (☎ 08456-122660, 🖳 richmond.gov.uk > parks).
Opening hours: Unrestricted access.
Cost: Free.
Transport: Richmond rail/tube.
Attractions & amenities: Pond, cricket pitch.

Ham Common and woods (120 acres/48ha) is a lovely wild area just to the west of Richmond Park beyond Ham Gate. In 1635 the local inhabitants were granted certain rights on the common by Charles I, in return for the 483 acres (195ha) he took when creating his New Park, later called **Richmond Park** (see page 204).

The avenue that leads south from **Ham House** (see page 235)

extends onto Ham Common which is open grassland crossed by paths, its perimeter planted with trees. The focal point is Ham Pond, surrounded by willows and once used to water horses. Across the main road, Ham Gate Avenue takes you straight through Ham Common Woods, thickly planted trees between which winds a network of paths and horse tracks.

Designated a Local Nature Reserve in 2001, the common is the venue for the annual Ham Fair and is also used for cricket, picnics and other recreational pursuits.

HUGUENOT BURIAL GROUND 25

Address: Huguenot Place, Wandsworth, SW18 2QZ (☎ 020-8871 6000, 🖥 wandsworth.gov.uk).
Opening hours: Unrestricted access.
Cost: Free.
Transport: Wandsworth Town rail.

The Huguenot Burial Ground (also known as Mount Nod) is a historic burial ground that opened in around 1687 as the cemetery for the French Church. The church was used by Huguenot refugees who had fled France after the Edict of Nantes in 1685 (which declared Protestantism illegal) and settled in Wandsworth during the 17th and 18th centuries. Burials ceased in 1854 and the ground was later reopened as a public garden.

The burial site is next to St Mary Magdalen Roman Catholic Church and, despite being sandwiched between two busy roads, is a peaceful place, mainly consisting of grass with trees and shrubs around the periphery. It contains a number of historic tombs, including five Grade II listed tombs and

over 100 other monuments. In 1911, a memorial was erected to the memory of the Huguenots who had found in Wandsworth 'freedom to worship God after their own manner' and 'added to the credit and prosperity of the town of their adoption'.

26 ORLEANS HOUSE & GARDEN

Address: Riverside, Twickenham, TW1 3DJ (☎ 08456-122 660 and 020-8831 6000, 🖳 richmond.gov.uk > parks and richmond.gov.uk/orleans_house_gallery).
Opening hours: Orleans Gardens, Mon-Sat, 7.30am to dusk (Sun and Bank Holidays, 9am). Orleans House Gallery, Tue-Sun and Bank Holidays (see website for times).
Cost: Free.
Transport: St Margarets rail.
Attractions & amenities: Two galleries, café, shop, playground, free parking.

O rleans House was built in 1710 and takes its name from its most famous resident, Louis Phillipe I, Duc d'Orleans (1773-1850), who lived there from 1815 to 1817 during his exile from Napoleonic France. Most of the house was demolished in 1926 but the Octagon (designed by James Gibbs) and two wings were saved and it now houses one of Greater London's finest small galleries (with a café), set in shady woodland gardens. In the early 18th century the gardens were described as among the finest in the country and were noted for their vines.

Octogan

Across the road from Orleans House is Orleans Gardens, on the banks of the Thames. The gardens were originally linked to those of Orleans House – the two extend to 3.8 acres (1.5ha) – by a tunnel passing under the road. It has a grassed area with an excellent playground with equipment suitable for disabled children, a café and toilet.

27 PUTNEY VALE CEMETERY

Address: Stag Lane, Kingston Vale, SW15 3DZ (🖳 wandsworth.gov.uk > cemeteries and crematorium).
Opening hours: Mon-Sat, 8am to 5pm, Sun 10am to 5pm; closes 4pm Nov-Feb.
Cost: Free.
Transport: Putney Bridge tube and 265 bus.

P utney Vale Cemetery – surrounded by Putney Heath and Wimbledon Common – opened in 1891 in 47 acres (19ha) of beautiful parkland, and has two chapels (one converted to a crematorium in 1938) and an extensive Garden of Remembrance. It's one of London's most striking cemeteries: in the small area of paths behind the chapel there are more fascinating monuments than you'll see in the whole of most cemeteries. Among the notable memorials is the tomb of J Bruce Ismay (featuring shipping scenes), ship owner and chairman of the White Star Line, who survived the sinking of the Titanic physically if not professionally.

Among the many household names interred here are comedian Arthur Askey, actor Sir Stanley Baker, author Enid Blyton, Olympian Lillian Board, archaeologist Howard Carter (who discovered the tomb of Tutankhamen), singer Sandy Denny, sculptor Sir Jacob Epstein, motor racing driver James Hunt, actress Hattie Jacques, footballer Bobby Moore, and actors Kenneth More, Jon Pertwee and Nyree Dawn Porter. There are also many war graves from both World Wars, including several Victoria Cross recipients.

RICHMOND GREEN   28

> **Address:** The Green, Richmond, TW9 1LX (☎ 08456-122660, 🖥 richmond.gov.uk > parks).
> **Opening hours:** Unrestricted.
> **Cost:** Free.
> **Transport:** Richmond tube/rail.
> **Attractions & amenities:** Cricket pitch.

Richmond Green (12 acres/4.8ha) has been an important open space since medieval times when jousting tournaments and pageants took place; as common land, it was also used for grazing sheep. From around the 14th century the Lord of the Manor was the King (it's still owned by the Crown Estate) and the Green was overlooked by Richmond Palace – then Sheen Palace

– which was occupied by monarchs until the late 17th century (the gatehouse remains). The royal connection led to the early growth of Richmond, which continued to develop as a fashionable town. Many fine old houses, the central library and Richmond Theatre (1899) surround Richmond Green, which is also a venue for festivities such as the May Fair and the Victorian Evening at Christmas time.

The Green – essentially square in shape and consisting of open grassland bordered by fine mature trees – was described by Nikolaus Pevsner as 'one of the most beautiful urban greens surviving anywhere in England'. It has been a famous and popular venue for cricket matches since the 17th century and is currently home to two village teams.

29 SOUTHSIDE HOUSE & GARDENS

> **Address:** 3-4 Woodhayes Road, Wimbledon, SW19 4RJ (☎ 020-8946 7643, 🖥 southsidehouse.com).
> **Opening hours:** Guided tours (1hr 15mins), Wed, 2pm and 4pm, Sat, Sun and Bank Holidays, 2pm, 3pm and 4pm, from Easter Sat to the last Sun of September. Tours (which must be booked – see website) include the gardens, which are also open under the National Gardens Scheme in the spring.
> **Cost:** £9 adults, £6 students, £15 families (maximum four).
> **Transport:** Wimbledon rail, then 93 bus to Wimbledon Village and a 10-minute walk.
> **Attractions & amenities:** Historic house, museum, tours, lectures, concerts.

Southside House is a 17th-century property situated on the south side of Wimbledon Common. It was built for Robert Pennington, who commissioned Dutch architects to construct it, incorporating an existing farmhouse into the design (Pennington had shared Charles II's exile in Holland). The house was passed down through the Pennington-Mellor-Munthe family whose descendants still own it today.

While the house is a period treasure and living museum, the gardens are a delightful hotchpotch of wilderness, woodland, orchard and wildflower meadow. Set out over 2 acres (0.8ha), they comprise a series of 'rooms' with secret pathways, sculptures, temples, grottos and a canal, all of which combine to create a garden full of surprises. Most gardening is organic, which encourages wildlife, particularly birds – regular visitors include great tits, blue tits, hedge sparrows, dunnocks, green and bull finches, greater-spotted woodpeckers, tawny owls and jays.

While you explore, look out for the poignant pet cemetery.

30 THE WATERGARDENS

> **Address:** Warren Road, off Kingston Hill, KT2 7LF (☎ 01483-211535, 🖥 ngs.org.uk).
> **Opening hours:** Open under the National Gardens Scheme in spring and autumn, otherwise private. See website for dates.
> **Cost:** See NGS website above.
> **Transport:** Kingston rail, then 57/485 bus.

This delightful Japanese landscaped garden of 9 acres (3.6ha) was originally part of Coombe Wood Nursery. The gardens were created by horticulturalist James Veitch Jnr in the 1860s – apparently inspired by the Willow pattern on Chinese plates – who transformed former gravel workings in the south of the nursery into a charming Japanese watergarden (the first of its kind in Britain) with plants brought back from Japan. The gardens were later incorporated into the grounds of the adjacent Warren House until 1985, when they were included in a parcel of land sold for a private housing scheme.

Today, the gardens have been restored and although private, can be visited on certain days. They're a patchwork of ponds, streams and waterfalls – criss-crossed by bridges – with many rare trees providing stunning colour in spring and autumn. They're a haven for both wildlife and people; the real delight of the gardens is simply to wander the myriad pathways and let them take you to unexpected places.

WIMBLEDON PARK 31

Address: Wimbledon Park Road, SW18 5NR (☎ 020-8545 3655, 🖳 merton.gov. uk > parks).
Opening hours: Daily, Mon-Fri, 8am to dusk (Sat-Sun and Bank Holidays, 9am).
Cost: Free.
Transport: Wimbledon Park tube.
Attractions & amenities: Lake, formal gardens, café, pavilion, crazy golf, play areas, paddling pool, bowling green, watersports centre, athletics track, tennis courts, soccer pitches, toilets, car park.

The second-largest park in Merton at 66 acres (27ha), Wimbledon Park is situated to the east of the All England Lawn Tennis and Croquet Club. It's a remnant of an 18th-century park that English landscape architect Lancelot 'Capability' Brown laid out for Earl Spencer of Wimbledon House. The lake – one of the largest in south London – was formed as a focal point for the house and is located to the south of the current park.

The estate was broken up in the late 19th century and in 1914 Wimbledon Borough Council purchased the northern part and opened Wimbledon Park. Land to the west was purchased for Wimbledon golf course and in around 1930 the All England Tennis Club was established.

Today, the park contains an old woodland area (Horse Close Wood), comprising mostly ash and oak, that predates Brown's landscaping, plus a range of amenities including sports pitches, bowling greens, tennis courts and playgrounds. Municipal planting includes a lime avenue, formal and ornamental gardens, a rockery, plus ponds and other water features.

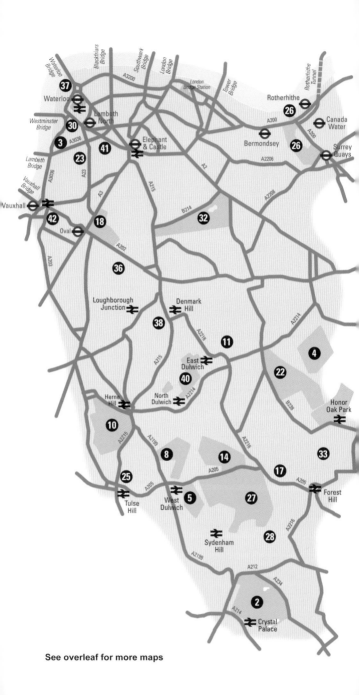

See overleaf for more maps

CHAPTER 6

SOUTHEAST LONDON

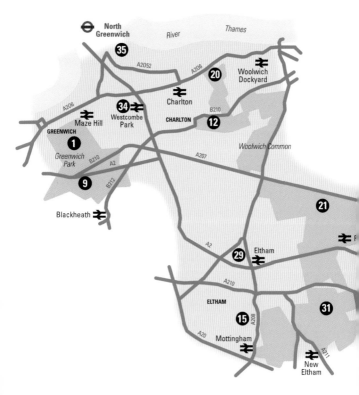

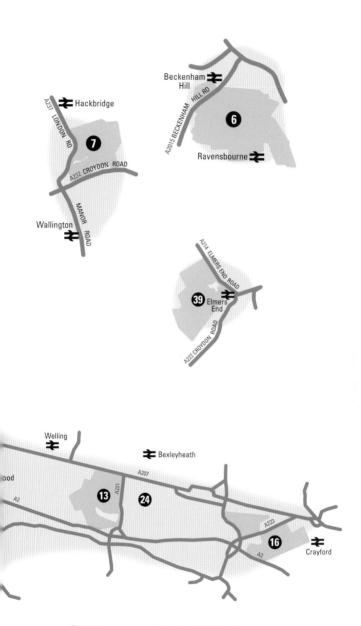

See previous page for key and main map

1 GREENWICH PARK

Address: Greenwich, SE10 8QY (☎ 0300-061 2380, 🖥 royalparks.gov.uk/
greenwich-park.aspx and friendsofgreenwichpark.org.uk).
Opening hours: 6am to between 6pm (Nov-Feb) and 9.30pm (Jun-Jul),
depending on the time of the year (see website).
Cost: Free.
Transport: Cutty Sark DLR or Maze Hill rail.
Attractions & amenities: Formal gardens, ponds, wilderness area, guided walks,
museum, gallery, observatory, historic buildings, four cafés, refreshment points,
various sports facilities.

Queen's House and Old Royal Naval College with Canary Wharf in the background

Greenwich Park (Grade I listed) is London's most interesting and varied royal park, rich in historic buildings, museums, galleries, monuments, gardens and wildlife. It extends to 183 acres (73ha) – one of the largest green spaces in southeast London – and has been open to the general public since 1830. Greenwich is London's oldest royal park and has some of the capital's most impressive views across the Thames towards Docklands and the City.

The park is part of the Greenwich World Heritage Site, which provides a setting for several historic buildings, including the Old Royal Observatory, the Royal Naval College, the National Maritime Museum and the Queen's House.

History: There has been a settlement on this site since Roman times. It was first owned by the Abbey of St Peter at Ghent, but reverted to the Crown in 1427 when Greenwich began its long association with royalty. It was given by Henry VI to his uncle Humphrey, Duke of Gloucester, who built a house by the river, Bella Court, as well as a small castle (Greenwich Castle) and Duke Humphrey's Tower. Bella Court evolved into the Tudor Palace of Placentia and later into Greenwich Hospital and the Royal Naval College. In 1675, Charles chose Greenwich Castle, by then in disrepair, as the site for his Royal Observatory.

Greenwich was the birthplace of Henry VIII – who introduced deer to the park – and his two daughters Mary I and Elizabeth I were also born there, while his son Edward VI died in Greenwich (aged 15). In the early 1600s, the park was laid out in the French style with many trees, some of which remain today. James I enclosed it within brick walls 12ft (3.7m) high and 2mi (3km) in length – much of which remains and defines the park's modern boundary – and gave both the

Boating Lake

...ark and palace to his wife, Queen Anne. She commissioned Inigo Jones to design a home, which became today's Queen's House (she died before it was completed). Charles II was fascinated by science, and in 1675 he commissioned Sir Christopher Wren to build the first Royal Observatory. It was named Flamsteed House after the first Royal Astronomer, John Flamsteed 1646-1719).

the 18th century the park was opened to pensioners. During the Georgian era, relatives of the king often became park rangers, but its appearance changed little. In 1873 the Royal Naval Hospital became the Royal Naval College (until 1998) and the National Maritime Museum was established within the park in 1934.

Buildings, Monuments & Attractions: Greenwich Park is rich in buildings, monuments and historic sites. In addition to the royal buildings, in the park 'proper' are the Royal Observatory, Conduit (or Standard) House, the Pavilion Tea House, the Bandstand, McCartney House, Ranger's House and Blackheath Gate Lodge. There are also a number of statues, which include those of Captain Cook, William IV and General Wolfe, and a sculpture by Henry Moore.

The park also contains Roman remains, the Wilderness deer park, a wildlife centre, various gardens, an ornamental fountain, a boating pond, a playground, tennis courts and a sports pavilion. It also provides visitors with

---

🍴 FOOD & DRINK 🍸

Astronomy Café: Serves a range of cakes, pastries and hot and cold drinks, and has a sun terrace with panoramic views over Greenwich Park.

The Pavilion Tea House: With large gardens at the front and rear, the nearby licensed Pavilion is a great place to have an alfresco drink, snack or lunch.

Cow and Coffee Bean café: Located near the St Mary's Gate entrance, the Cow and Coffee Bean serves farm-made, dairy ice cream, milkshakes, cream scones, sandwiches and treats.

The Honest Sausage: Serves free range sausages and bacon rolls/sandwiches and hot drinks, with a large outdoor seating area.

The last monarch to use Greenwich was James II, whose daughter Mary donated the palace site as a hospital for sailors and in the early years of

Shepherd Gate Clock

Royal Observatory

the opportunity to stand astride time, as the Prime Meridian Line, which marks zero degrees longitude and Greenwich Mean Time, is clearly marked where it cuts directly through the park.

> In 2012, Greenwich Park hosted the 2012 London Olympics' equestrian events and elements of the Modern Pentathlon.

Landscaping: The park was first landscaped in the 17th century, possibly by André Le Nôtre (Louis XIV's landscape gardener), who's known to have designed plans for it. A series of grass terraces were cut into the slope, known as the Great Steps, lined with hawthorn hedges; today the terraces are almost invisible but you can still see evidence of hawthorn. The scheme included a formal avenue of chestnut trees – now called Blackheath Avenue – and a large semicircle of chestnuts inside Blackheath Gate, known as The Rounds. Small woodlands were also planted in the Wilderness and Ranger's Field. Some of the trees

still survive and work is underway to restore many of the avenues.

Flora & Fauna: Greenwich Park is a Site of Metropolitan Importance for Nature Conservation and a haven for wildlife. At the time of its enclosure as a deer park in 1433, it was largely covered by common land with scrub oak, thorns, birch, gorse, broom and heath. Today it's a rich location for biodiversity, including the ancient grazed grassland in the deer enclosure, the acid grassland on Crooms Hill, and its regiment of ancient and veteran trees. The park contains

Bandstand

ver 4,000 trees, including a number eemed 'ancient', including 52 sweet hestnuts – relics of the formal avenues reated in the 1660s – eight oaks, one ycamore and a cedar. It has a number f themed gardens, including a flower arden, herb garden and rose garden, ne latter planted with 100 varieties of olourful, scented blooms.

Two small herds of wild red and allow deer live and breed in the Wilderness and can be seen from everal viewing points. One of these, ocated in the Secret Garden Wildlife Centre (an educational facility created n 2002), has one-way glass and backs nto the enclosure, so deer practically ouch the glass. The Wilderness is also a sanctuary for nesting birds, roosting ats (common pipistrelles), foxes, vood mice and many other species. Greenwich Park is a good site for bird vatching, with up to 70 species, some 0 of which breed here, including woodpeckers, tawny owls, thrushes and warblers. Standing and lying dead wood is left to decay naturally, providing an important habitat for invertebrates such as stag beetles, spiders, fungi, lichen, and an abundance of butterflies and moths.

Amenities: Greenwich Park offers a wealth of amenities and facilities for entertainment, recreation and sport. On the lower level of the park there's a popular playground (in the northeast corner, close to Maze Hill railway station) – with entertainment such as puppet shows and workshops during summer school holidays – and a bandstand offering Sunday concerts in summer. The park hosts a range of formal and informal sports, including cricket, rugby, tennis, a putting green, cycling routes, running and rollerblading – not to mention model boating, kite-flying and frisbee throwing.

Equestrian events, Olympics 2012

2 CRYSTAL PALACE PARK & DINOSAURS

Address: Crystal Palace Park Road, SE20 8DT (☎ 020-3236 0078, 🖥 bromley.
gov.uk > parks and open spaces, sydenham.org.uk/crystal_palace_park.html and
crystalpalacepark.org.uk).
Opening hours: Daily, dawn to dusk.
Cost: Free.
Transport: Crystal Palace rail.
Attractions & amenities: Formal gardens, lakes, boating pond, children's play
area, athletics track, fishing, city farm, sports centre, parking.

Crystal Palace Park is a historic pleasure ground used for a wide variety of cultural and sporting events. Managed by the borough of Bromley, it gets its name from the Crystal Palace, a cast-iron and glass building originally erected in Hyde Park by Sir Joseph Paxton (1803-1865) to house the Great Exhibition of 1851.

Following the exhibition, the palace was dismantled, and then redesigned and reconstructed in Penge Place estate at Sydenham Hill (one of the highest points in London, 357ft/109m above sea level). The grand opening by Queen Victoria took place on 10th June 1854 in the presence of 40,000 spectators and a choir of 1,000, and the palace and park became the setting for numerous events, including firework displays, exhibitions and sports. Sadly, the palace suffered a number of fires

and the entire structure burnt down in spectacular fashion in November 1936. Remnants of its splendour can still be seen in the ruins of the old Grand Terraces (Grade II listed) still standing in the park.

The pleasure grounds that surrounded the palace, now named Crystal Palace Park, were also designed by Paxton and included gardens, gravel walks, hundreds of statues and an awesome array of fountains (fed by three lakes) which for grand displays had '11,788 jets... pumping 120,000 gallons per minute and consuming six million gallons of water'. Working under Paxton was landscape gardener Edward Milner (1819-1884), who became superintendent of works in 1852 and was responsible for the Italian garden, the maze and the English landscape garden.

The park once had a football ground that was the base for Crystal Palace FC and hosted the FA Cup Final from 1895 to 1914, as well as staging London County Cricket games from 1900 to 1908 (WG Grace played here).

In 1852, Benjamin Waterhouse Hawkins (1807-1894) was commissioned to build the first ever fe-sized models of extinct animals, which he did under the guidance of Sir Richard Owen (1804-1892), celebrated palaeontologist and the man who invented the word 'dinosaur'. Hawkins' creatures were the first attempt to interpret what full-scale prehistoric animals would have looked like, based on the best scientific evidence available at the time. Around 30 models, representing 15 species, can be seen today, positioned around the lower lake, and all Grade I listed.

Unveiled in 1854, Hawkins' models were the first-ever depictions of dinosaurs in the world, pre-dating the publication of Charles Darwin's *On the Origin of Species* by five years.

As further discoveries of dinosaurs were made, the reputation of the Crystal Palace dinosaurs declined, and by 1895 experts looked on them with scorn, although they continue to capture the imagination of the public. They were extensively restored in 2003, when anatomical errors were retained to maintain their Victorian authenticity.

In 1981, the Crystal Palace Foundation was formed to restore and care for the park, and in 2001 restoration works comprised a new farm complex and woodland garden, a remodelled tidal lake, the creation of new parkland, planting enhancements to Paxton's English landscape garden, new public viewing areas and a restored rhododendron dell.

In September 2006, Capel Manor College opened a centre at the park, leasing the model farm to provide education for children, as well as training in animal care, horticulture and arboriculture. The farm (noon to 4pm daily, except Wed) has pigs, goats, rabbits, rodents, poultry and exotica in the form of lizards, snakes and spiders.

Crystal Palace Park is also home to the adjacent National Sports Centre (built in 1964), a circular maze (London's largest labyrinth), museum, pool with flamingos, playground, concert area, café and the Crystal Palace TV transmitting station, at 720ft (219m) the fourth-tallest structure in London.

Iguanodon

3 GARDEN MUSEUM

Address: St Mary-at-Lambeth, Lambeth Palace Road, SE1 7LB (☎ 020-7401 8865, 🖳 gardenmuseum.org.uk).

Opening hours: Sun-Fri, 10.30am to 5pm; Sat, 10.30am to 4pm. Closed first Mon of the month (except Bank Holidays) and over Christmas and New Year (see website for details).

Cost: £7.50 adults, £6.50 seniors, £3 students, free for under-16s, jobseekers and carers; includes entrance to temporary exhibitions. Free guided tours on the last Tue of the month at 2pm.

Transport: Lambeth North tube or Waterloo tube/rail.

Amenities: Café, shop, library.

Despite being described by the *Daily Telegraph* as 'one of London's best small museums', the Garden Museum – which used to be called the Museum of Garden History but was revamped and renamed in 2008 – is sometimes overlooked. Ironically, this is partly due to its splendid riverside location, next to Lambeth Palace and almost directly opposite the Houses of Parliament.

> Anne Boleyn's mother, Elizabeth, rests in the old churchyard, as does William Bligh, captain of the *Bounty*.

The museum is the world's first museum dedicated to the history of gardening, and celebrates British gardens and gardening through its collection, temporary exhibitions, events, symposia and garden. Three exhibitions each year explore the making of British gardens, and a programme of over 30 talks and interviews celebrate horticultural heroes and heroines, from forgotten plant-hunters and gardeners of the past to designers and writers in vogue today.

The museum cares for a unique collection of around 10,000 objects, amassed over the last three decades and continuing to grow. Exhibits span 400 years of gardening in Britain, from tools to artists' impressions, each representing the history, culture and design of gardens in some way. Grand country house gardens and small back yards are all represented; rare and precious objects are displayed alongside the most familiar and everyday ephemera. The collection paints a broad and revealing picture of the changing ideas, technologies and passions of British gardens and gardeners.

The permanent collection comprises three main categories: tools, ephemera (including prints, photographs and catalogues, giving an insight into the social as well as practical history of gardening) and a library. The tools range from Neolithic implements to a Victorian cucumber straightener, while one of the more unusual plants is the Vegetable Lamb of Tartary, thought until the 18th century to be a cross between an animal and a vegetable (it's actually the stem of a variety of fern).

🍴 **FOOD & DRINK** 🍷

Garden Café: This highly-rated oasis (number 6 in *Gourmet* magazine's top ten best museum restaurants in 2012!) specialises in vegetarian food – soups, tarts and splendid cakes – making the most of the museum's kitchen garden. Lunch is served from noon to 3pm and on Suns the emphasis is on all-day afternoon tea. **Free access.**

The museum is based in the deconsecrated church of St Mary-at-Lambeth, dating from the 14th century (restored in 1850), which by 1971 was threatened with demolition, its churchyard neglected and unkempt. Following the discovery there of the graves of two 17th-century royal gardeners and plant hunters, John Tradescant the Elder (ca.1570-1638) and Younger (1608-1662), the Tradescant Trust was formed in 1976. It campaigned to save the church and churchyard for conversion into a museum of garden history.

The tomb of John Tradescant the Elder stands at the heart of a lovely, recreated 17th-century knot garden – designed by the Garden Museum's President, the Dowager Marchioness of Salisbury (owner of Hatfield House) – in a formal, geometric style, with authentic period planting and brick paths. The garden is surrounded by clipped box hedges, with a topiary spiral in the centre of old golden holly, and planted with columbines, old-fashioned roses, foxgloves, scarlet runner bean, red maple, tulip tree, and other plants, herbs and bulbs which were grown by the Tradescants in their Lambeth garden. The garden has other examples of topiary and includes a mature strawberry tree and a large climbing musk rose, reputedly the largest in the country.

Today, the museum's gardens are surrounded by mature plane trees, and in 2007 a wild garden was created in the former churchyard in front of St Mary's. It's an inspiring place to visit, for gardeners and non-gardeners alike.

4 NUNHEAD CEMETERY

Address: Linden Grove, Southwark, London SE15 3LP (☎ 020-7732 9535/7525 2000, 🖥 southwark.gov.uk > parks and open spaces and www.fonc.org.uk).
Opening hours: Daily, Apr-Sep, 8.30am to 7pm; Oct-Mar, 8.30am to 4 or 5pm (see website for exact dates and closing times). The Friends of Nunhead Cemetery (FONC) organise tours on the last Sun of each month (2.15pm from Linden Grove gates) and there are special interest tours on other Suns (see Friends' website).
Cost: Free, but donations welcome.
Transport: Nunhead rail.
Attractions & amenities: Chapel, guided tours.

The Magnificent Seven were built in response to a massive surge in London's population in the first half of the 19th century, when it more than doubled, from 1m to 2.3m. The city's small parish churchyards became dangerously overcrowded, with grim consequences: decaying corpses got into the water supply, causing a number of epidemics. As a result, seven large cemeteries were built between 1832 and 1841 at Abney Park, Brompton, Highgate, Kensal Green, Nunhead, Tower Hamlets and West Norwood – all of which are included in this book (see **Index**).

Consecrated in 1840, Nunhead Cemetery (originally called All Saints' Cemetery) is one of seven large Victorian cemeteries – known as the Magnificent Seven (see below) – built in a ring around London's outskirts. According to the Friends of Nunhead Cemetery, it's 'perhaps the least known, but most attractive, of the great Victorian cemeteries of London', while Southwark Council regards it as 'one of Southwark's hidden treasures'.

The new cemeteries appealed to the growing middle classes, who were eager to distance themselves from the working classes and demonstrate their status. Graves – or, more importantly, elaborate monuments and tombs – were regarded as a visible display of a family's wealth and status.

Nunhead – named after the Old Nun's Head Tavern – was laid out on former farmland, with curving paths and planting which took advantage of its elevated site on Nunhead Hill. It's

visit. At its highest point, it's around 200ft (60m) above sea level and commands vistas stretching from the towers of Canary Wharf westwards as far as the London Eye. Much of the cemetery is mysterious and overgrown, which many people see as fundamental to its charm, with weathered gravestones and tumbling statuary peaking through extravagant under- and overgrowth and weed-choked paths.

Nunhead Cemetery has become an important haven for flora and fauna, including trees from the original planting, such as holm oak, lime, plane, yew, ginkgo and swamp cypress. Part of the cemetery has been designated a Local Nature Reserve and a Site of Metropolitan Importance for wildlife, populated with songbirds, woodpeckers and tawny owls, plus many species of butterflies and moths.

he second-largest of the Magnificent 5even, covering 52 acres (21ha), ind was laid out by James Bunstone Bunning, who also designed the monumental entrance and lodges. There were also catacombs (now ealed) and two Gothic chapels Anglican and non-conformist), designed y Thomas Little, of which only the Anglican chapel remains (now restored).

One of the most intriguing monuments is the Martyrs' Memorial, an obelisk erected in 1851 to commemorate five Scottish nationalists who campaigned for Parliamentary Reform and were transported to Australia in 1793.

During the 20th century the once vell-kept cemetery deteriorated and it closed in 1969, badly neglected and vandalised. Purchased by Southwark Council in 1975, it was restored with funding from the Heritage Lottery Fund and the council, and the active participation of the Friends of Nunhead Cemetery, re-opening in 2001.

Nunhead Cemetery's history, architecture and stunning views make it a fascinating and beautiful place to

The cemetery is full of interesting contrasts, for example, between the magnificent monuments in memory of the era's most eminent citizens and the modest, small headstones erected for common people; and between the formal, elegant avenue of tall lime trees and the many smaller pathways, some of which resemble country lanes.

Among those laid to rest or commemorated at Nunhead Cemetery are Frederick Cotton, co-inventor of cordite, music hall star Jenny Hill, and nine boys (aged 11 to 14) who died in the Leysdown Tragedy, when a boat carrying a troupe of Sea Scouts went down off the Isle of Sheppey in 1912.

5 WEST NORWOOD CEMETERY

Address: Norwood Road, West Norwood, SE27 9JU (☎ 020-7926 7999,
📧 lambeth.gov.uk > cemeteries and crematoria, westnorwoodcemetery.com and
fownc.org).
Opening hours: Daily, weekdays 8am to 6pm, weekends and Bank Holidays,
10am to 6pm (closes 4pm, Nov-Mar).
Cost: Free.
Transport: West Norwood rail.
Attractions & amenities: Catacombs, guided walks.

West Norwood Cemetery is a site of major historical, architectural and ecological interest, yet many people have never heard of it. It was built by the South Metropolitan Cemetery Company and opened in 1837, the second of London's Magnificent Seven cemeteries (see **Nunhead Cemetery** on page 262), which were created in the 1830s and 1840s to solve London's chronic shortage of burial grounds. The cemetery, now owned by Lambeth Borough Council, covers 40 acres (16ha). It was the first and only British cemetery designed in the Gothic Revival style, in both its landscaping and original architecture, and is one of the most significant examples of this style in Europe.

👁 DON'T MISS!

Among the most famous monuments is the mausoleum for Sir Henry Doulton's family, constructed appropriately of pottery and terracotta. Other notable memorials include Mrs Beeton (cookery book writer), Dr William Marsden (surgeon), Sir Hiram Stevens Maxim (inventor of the Maxim gun), Baron Julius de Reuter (founder of the Reuters news agency), Charles Spurgeon (preacher) and Sir Henry Tate (Tate Gallery).

Norwood, once part of the Great North Wood, was a rural landscape in the 1830s when the cemetery was surrounded by open countryside. Designed by Sir William Tite, its layout of gently winding paths leading to two chapels on the upper slopes, was that of a rural park. It was planted in the style advocated by John Claudius Loudon (a celebrated cemetery designer) with numerous evergreen and deciduous trees, such as copper beech, weeping willow and London plane. Catacombs were constructed beneath the Anglican chapel with space for 2,000 coffins, a hydraulic pump lowering coffins from the chapel to the vaults below.

In 1842, a section of the cemetery was acquired by London's Greek community for a Greek Orthodox necropolis, which was soon filled with grand monuments and large mausoleums (18 of which are listed), memorialising the history of Anglo-Hellenic families.

West Norwood Cemetery's design and location attracted wealthy Victorians, who commissioned fine mausoleums and memorials for their burial plots and vaults. Today, its grounds are a mixture of historic monumental cemetery and modern lawn cemetery, but it also contains catacombs, cremation plots and a columbarium for cinerary ashes. The two chapels which stood here (the Dissenters Chapel and the Episcopal Chapel, both with catacombs beneath them) were damaged in the Second World War and later demolished. In 1915 the non-conformist chapel was rebuilt to provide a crematorium (the first in a London cemetery), and there's a memorial garden where the Episcopal Chapel once stood.

Considered to house the best collection of sepulchral monuments in London, West Norwood contains over 65 Grade II and Grade II* listed buildings and structures (more than any other cemetery), including the entrance arch and railings..

By the '60s, the cemetery had become neglected and overgrown, and in 1966 it was purchased by Lambeth Council, which maintained the cremation service and turned the grounds into a memorial park. The cemetery contains a wide variety of trees (including many rare species) and shrubs (bramble, ivy, rose and hawthorn), while in the spring there are daffodils, wild primroses and bluebells.

> The grounds are a wonderful place for wildlife such as foxes, squirrels and numerous bird species, including willow warblers, kestrels and tawny owls. It's a delightful spot in which to relax and commune with nature.

6 BECKENHAM PLACE PARK

Address: Beckenham Hill Road, Beckenham, BR3 1UL (☎ 020-8314 2047, 🖥 lewisham.gov.uk > parks and open spaces > local parks and beckenhamplaceparkfriends.org.uk).
Opening hours: Daily, 8am to dusk.
Cost: Free.
Transport: Beckenham Hill and Ravensbourne rail.
Attractions & amenities: Gardens, water feature, visitor centre, guided walks, café, playground, public golf course, tennis, cycle paths, sports pitches.

Beckenham Place Park is the largest green space in the borough of Lewisham, covering 237 acres (96 hectares) of grassland and woodland, bisected by a railway line. The park is an important wildlife site and is both a Local Nature Reserve and a Site of Metropolitan Importance. It lies on the routes of the Green Chain Walk and the Capital Ring (circular walk).

> Bursting with wildlife and stunning greenery, Beckenham Place is one of London's best-kept secrets.

Beckenham Manor has medieval origins and in the 17th century was owned by Walter St John, in whose family it remained until 1773, when John Cator of Bromley purchased the manorial rights and built Beckenham Place Mansion. Cator was a friend of Swedish botanist Carl Linnaeus and son-in-law of the landscape architect Peter Collinson; Collinson approved Cator's planting and may have influenced his introduction of exotic trees and a lake. The estate was purchased by the London County Council in 1927 and the lake drained to build a golf course; the Palladian-style mansion (Grade II* Listed) became the clubhouse.

The park retains much of the form of a landscape park and includes grassland, ancient woodland and water habitats (including the Ravensbourne river in the east), which support a wide range of wildlife. The woodland contains some 60 species of tree, including oak (some of which are very old), turkey oak, ash, sweet chestnut, mature lime, horse chestnut, London plane, pedunculate oak, wild service tree, sycamore, elm, hazel, holly, mulberry and many more.

Breeding birds include sparrow hawk, stock dove, ring-necked parakeet, tawny owl, all three native woodpeckers, blackcap, chiffchaff, goldcrest, spotted flycatcher, nuthatch and treecreeper, while little egrets are regular visitors. The park's mammals include badgers, foxes, grey squirrels, hedgehogs and bats (pipistrelle), plus many smaller creatures such as woodmouse, bank vole and common shrew. The park is also rich in invertebrates, including rare beetles and spiders, and a host of butterflies (including the rare purple hairstreak) and moths.

BEDDINGTON PARK & THE GRANGE   7

Address: Croydon Road, Wallington, SM6 7LF (☎ 020-8770 5000, 🖥 sutton.gov.uk > beautiful Sutton > open spaces and friendsofbeddingtonpark.co.uk).
Opening hours: Park/Grange, unrestricted access. Carew Manor, occasional tours of the great hall and dovecote (booking necessary – see Sutton Council's website or call ☎ 020-8770 4781).
Cost: Free. Tours £4.50.
Transport: Hackbridge rail or car.
Attractions & amenities: Lake, gardens, historic manor house, café, playground, tennis courts, soccer pitches, ball courts, changing rooms, toilets.

Carew Manor

Shortly after, the park was acquired by Canon Alexander Henry Bridges, the wealthy rector of Beddington, who filled in the long lake and replaced the avenue of trees. He carried out a great deal of planting and is responsible for most of the older trees in the park.

Beddington Park (94 acres/38ha) was originally part of the deer park attached to Carew Manor (Grade I listed), a major country house. The *Domesday Book* of 1086 mentions two Beddington estates, which were united by Nicholas Carew to form Carew Manor in 1381. The family reached its zenith in the Tudor period, when the park occupied most of the land between today's Mitcham Common, Beddington Lane, Croydon Road and London Road.

At the beginning of the 18th century, a long canal-like lake was created in front of the manor, with avenues of trees along either side. But by the mid-18th century the fortunes of the Carew family had declined and most of the northern part of the park had been converted into fields. The southern part survived as a deer park until the estate was sold in 1859.

Adjacent to Beddington Park is **The Grange** (44 acres/18ha), which contains an ornamental garden created on the north side of Mill Pond by Alfred Smee FRS, surgeon to the Bank of England, who purchased the site in the 1860s. In 1935, the house and grounds were acquired by the borough of Beddington & Wallington and turned into a public park. The garden has been considerably altered over the years, but the little stone bridge by the lake (originally a mill pond), the adjacent rockery and many trees date from Smee's time.

Carew Manor's banqueting hall survives from the original house and boasts a splendid hammerbeam roof, a collection of fine period furniture, antiques and works of art.

8   BELAIR PARK

Address: Gallery Road, West Dulwich, SE21 7AB (☎ 020-7525 2000, 🖥 southwark.gov.uk > parks and open spaces and belairpark.org.uk).
Opening hours: Daily, 7.30am to dusk.
Cost: Free.
Transport: West Dulwich rail.
Attractions & amenities: Gardens, lake, wildlife area, restaurant/bar, tennis courts (free), skate park, play area, sport pitches.

Belair Park (26 acres/10.6ha) is a beautiful park in West Dulwich – Southwark's only Grade II* listed landscape – formerly the grounds of Belair House, a country villa built in 1785 in the style of, or possibly by, Richard Adam. Belair House (now a restaurant), its lodge, entrance gates and an old stable building are all Grade II listed.

Belair is a typical late 18th-century 'pocket estate' with a mansion, home farm and landscaped grounds, including a lake created by damming the River Effra. It was originally called College Place and was renamed Belair in around 1829. The estate was in private ownership until 1938, but after the war was acquired by the borough of Southwark as a quasi-country club facility accessible to Southwark residents, and the house was restored. When the new borough of Southwark was formed in 1965, the grounds were opened as a public park and the mansion leased.

The park contains some fine trees, including willow and alder around the lake, and some beautiful mature oaks; poplars were planted in the late '40s to hide the railway embankment, which runs alongside the park. Resident wildlife comprises numerous species of animals and plants, including water birds and bats which can be seen at dusk in the summer feeding over the lake. Alongside the lake is a wildlife area, maintained by the Friends of Belair Park, containing native lakeside wildflowers (such as ragged robin, sedges and irises), and log piles and small ditches to provide a habitat for invertebrates and small mammals. 'Bird islands' have been built on rafts in the lake to provide protected nesting areas for waterfowl.

The restored Belair House is now an upmarket restaurant, bar and wedding venue – named Beauberry House (🖥 beauberryhouse.co.uk) – with a terraces for alfresco dining with spectacular views.

BLACKHEATH 9

Address: Shooters Hill Road, SE3 (☎ 020-8314 2047, 🖥 lewisham.gov.uk >
parks and open spaces > local parks).
Opening hours: Unrestricted access.
Cost: Free.
Transport: Blackheath rail.
Attractions & amenities: Tea hut, soccer pitch, bowling green, tennis courts,
various annual events including a fair and circus.

Blackheath (300 acres/121ha) is common land and the name is thought to arise from the colour of the soil or possibly 'bleak heath' – although it's also claimed that the area was a burial ground for victims of the Black Death in the 14th century. It has been in public use since 1871 and is now jointly managed by the boroughs of Lewisham and Greenwich.

The heath has played host to more than its fair share of events, including rebel gatherings, military encampments, royal meetings, religious festivals, celebrations, battles, hold ups by highwaymen, fairs, circuses and a variety of other activities. It has many sporting associations, including its early use as a venue for golf, cricket and soccer, is a popular spot for kite flying and the starting point for the London Marathon.

Blackheath was a massing point for Wat Tyler's Peasants Revolt of 1381, a protest against taxes, when 100,000 'rebels' gathered on the heath before their doomed assault on London.

Despite being crossed by one of London's busiest roads, the A2 (old Watling Street), Blackheath is an important spot for wildlife. Its grasses and shrubs such as gorse and broom, which once covered much of the heath, are still abundant, along with occasional young oak and silver birch trees. Its four ponds are home to greater spearwort and water mint, sticklebacks and even the occasional toad.

The process of landfill has created some contrasting habitats. Gravel, sand and the underlying chalk were extracted from large areas of the heath during the 18th and early 19th centuries, leaving large pits. The Vanbrugh Pits in the northeast part of the heath, long reclaimed by nature, now form one of the more attractive parts of the generally rather flat heath, and is particularly striking in spring when gorse and harebells are in bloom. The pits are named after Sir John Vanbrugh, architect of Blenheim Palace and Castle Howard, who lived nearby in Vanbrugh Castle.

10 BROCKWELL PARK

Address: Norwood Road, SE24 9BJ (☎ 020-7926 9000, 🖳 lambeth.gov.uk > parks and green spaces, brockwellpark.com and madforbrockwellpark.com).
Opening hours: Daily, 7.30am to dusk.
Cost: Free.
Transport: Brixton tube or Herne Hill rail.
Attractions & amenities: Gardens, green houses, café, lido, children's play area, paddling pool, miniature railway, toilets, sports facilities.

Brockwell Park (125 acres/51ha) is one of south London's best and most diverse public parks, with the late Georgian Brockwell Hall (Grade II* listed) at its heart. Designed by DR Roper in a style loosely termed 'free Grecian', the house was built between 1811 and 1813 for John Blades, a wealthy Ludgate Hill glass merchant, who also created Brockwell Hall Park Estate.

On the death of Blades in 1829, the hall and estate passed by marriage to the Blackburn family who lived there until 1888, when the property was acquired by the London County Council (LCC) as a public park. The purchase followed a campaign led by Thomas Lynn Bristowe, the first MP for Norwood, who was instrumental in raising funds from public, church, charity and private subscription. Tragically, the man who did so much to create the park died of a heart attack on the steps of Brockwell Hall shortly after taking part in the opening ceremony in 1892. In 1901 the LCC acquired a further 43 acres (17ha) of land north of the original park.

The park incorporates a wide range of facilities and green areas, including ornamental ponds, wetlands, a wild meadow, open grassland, community greenhouses, formal flower beds, a tranquil walled rose garden (the former kitchen garden of the hall) with benches, and a charming 19th-century clock tower. Sports facilities include tennis courts, a bowling green, a purpose-built BMX track, basketball, soccer, cricket, tennis courts and the magnificent Brockwell Lido (Grade II listed – see 🖳 brockwelllido.com), opened in July 1937 and recently restored to its former glory (with a gym). The park also has a children's play area, a paddling pool and miniature railway, plus a café in Brockwell Hall.

Brockwell Park is the venue for various community events, including the Lambeth Country Show, an impressive Guy Fawkes' firework display, open-air theatre and concerts.

CENTRE FOR WILDLIFE GARDENING 11

Address: 28 Marsden Road, SE15 4EE (☎ 020-7252 9186, 🖳 wildlondon.org.uk).
Opening hours: Tue-Thu and Sun, 10.30am to 4:30pm.
Cost: Free.
Transport: East Dulwich rail or car.
Attractions & amenities: Nursery, garden shop, workshops/talks.

The Centre for Wildlife Gardening is an idyllic spot in Peckham, developed in the late '80s and run by the London Wildlife Trust. The Trust manages over 40 London-wide reserves and is the only charity dedicated solely to protecting the capital's wildlife and wild spaces. It campaigns to save important wildlife habitats, engaging London's diverse communities through access to nature reserves, volunteering programmes and education work.

The Centre for Wildlife Gardening was previously a council depot, but has developed beyond all recognition over the past 20 years and is now a Green Flag winner and home to an award-winning visitor centre demonstrating innovative environmental building techniques. The Centre offers practical advice to city gardeners and is the perfect place to learn new skills and obtain ideas and inspiration.

It has a demonstration wildlife garden with a range of mini habitats showing how you can help wildlife however little space you have available, including the mini-beast village, summer meadow, woodland copse, stag beetle sanctuary, wildlife pond, bog garden and flowery chalk bank. There's also a wildflower nursery and some well used community raised beds.

Species you may spot include frogs and newts, grasshoppers and stag beetles, foxes and a wide variety of songbirds. Children are well catered for with a toddlers' sand-pit area, a nature trail and picnic facilities. The plant nursery supplies British wildflowers, herbs, cottage-garden plants and pond plants, as well as native trees, shrubs and climbers in season. It also sells delicious 'Peckham' honey from its hives.

The Centre organises school visits and works with the Southwark Adult Learning Service, particularly with regard to adults with learning disabilities. It also organises a wide range of talks and workshops.

The Wildlife Trusts (🖳 wildlifetrusts.org) is the UK's largest voluntary organisation dedicated to conserving the country's wildlife habitats and species, whether they be in the countryside, in cities or at sea.

12 CHARLTON PARK & CHARLTON HOUSE GARDENS

> **Address:** Charlton Road, Charlton, SE7 8RE (☎ park. 020-8921 6885, house, 020-8856 3951, 🖳 royalgreenwich.gov.uk > parks and gardens > all parks and charlton-house.org).
> **Opening hours:** Park, unrestricted access. Gardens, 10am to 5pm in summer (dusk in winter). Mulberry Tea Rooms, weekdays 9am to 4pm.
> **Cost:** Free.
> **Transport:** Charlton rail.
> **Attractions & amenities:** Tea rooms (Charlton House), playground, sports pitches.

Charlton House

Charlton House is a little-known architectural gem; it's regarded as Greater London's best-preserved Jacobean house and is one of England's finest examples of Jacobean domestic architecture. It's closed to the public but can be visited as part of Open House London and during special events (see website).

Charlton Park (53 acres/21ha) is the former parkland of the manor of Charlton. The estate was given to Greenwich council by the Maryon Wilson family in 1929 and opened as a public recreation ground, separated from Charlton House gardens by a brick ha-ha dating from 1847. The park's northern boundary wall dates mainly from the 17th century and there's a notable lime walk aligned with Charlton House. Charlton Park is dominated by sports pitches but there are also a number of recently redesigned gardens, including a Japanese-style herb garden and an adjoining pond garden. There's a special focus on the sensory nature of these gardens for visitors with visual or physical disabilities. The park is surrounded by railings with a perimeter planting of limes.

The walled gardens have recently been planted as a series of gardens. The peace garden was opened in July 2006 with harmony as its central theme, with planting based on cool, soft, reflective colours, in order to create a relaxed and tranquil environment. The central bed is planted with Russian sage, and there are two large pomegranate shrubs either side of the gateway. There's also a pond garden with a geometric path design and an abundance of grasses and flax, an adjoining sensory garden within a secluded courtyard lined with plants that stimulate the senses, and an herbaceous garden that attracts dragonflies and butterflies in summer.

> In the gardens of Charlton House is a mulberry tree, said to be the oldest of its species (*Morus nigra*) in the country, thought to have been planted in 1608 at the behest of James I.

DANSON PARK & HOUSE 13

> **Address:** Danson Park, Bexleyheath, DA6 8HL (☎ park. 020-8303 7777, house, 01322-526574, 🖳 bexley.gov.uk > parks and open spaces and bexleyheritagetrust.org.uk/dansonhouse).
>
> **Opening hours:** Park, Mon-Fri, from 7.30am, Sat-Sun and Bank Holidays from 9am; closing time is dusk or 4.30pm in winter (Nov-Jan). House, Apr-Oct, Sun-Thu, 10am to 5pm (☎ 020-8303 6699 to confirm).
>
> **Cost:** Free entry to park. House, £7 adults, £6 concessions, children under 16 free when accompanied by an adult; discount for English Heritage members.
>
> **Transport:** Bexleyheath rail.
>
> **Attractions & amenities:** Gardens, lake, restaurant/pub, café, kiosk, water park, playground, shop, tennis courts, bowling greens, pitch and putt, sports pitches, car park.

Danson House (Grade I listed) is a Georgian mansion in Danson Park (Grade II listed) situated to the west of Bexleyheath. Originally called Danson Hill, the Palladian villa was designed by Sir Robert Taylor, architect to the Bank of England, and constructed in 1764-67 for sugar merchant and vice-chairman of the British East India Company, Sir John Boyd (1718-1800). The estate was acquired by Bexley Urban District Council in 1924 and opened to the public a year later. However, the house remained uninhabited and was allowed to deteriorate badly until being acquired by English Heritage in 1995, faithfully restored and re-opened in 2005.

> The Charter Oak in Danson Park is one of the Great Trees of London. Thought to be over 200 years old, it has pride of place on Bexley's borough Coat of Arms.

Danson House – described by architectural expert Nikolaus Pevsner as 'crystalline' in its architecture – reflects the Georgians' preoccupation with the golden age of antiquity and is packed with the symbolism of classical mythology. The principal floor is sumptuous after painstaking reconstruction, with a fine entrance hall, a stunning dining room with the original 18th-century wall paintings, an elegant salon and an opulent library containing the Danson organ (still played at recitals).

Danson Park originally extended to over 600 acres (243ha) of pleasure grounds and agricultural estate. Today's park still covers some 180 acres (73ha) and is the largest in the borough of Bexley. The landscape was designed and laid out by Nathaniel Richmond, assistant to 'Capability' Brown, from 1761 to 1763. At its centre is a large and picturesque 12-acre (4.9ha) lake with fishing, boating, sailing and other watersports. The park also contains three ornamental gardens – an old English garden near the house, a rock garden at the western end and a peace garden in the southeast corner – as well as a nature reserve.

14 DULWICH PARK

Address: College Road, Dulwich, SE21 7BQ (☎ 020-7525 2000, 💻 southwark. gov.uk > parks and open spaces and dulwichparkfriends.org.uk).
Opening hours: Daily, 8am to dusk.
Cost: Free.
Transport: North Dulwich or West Dulwich rail.
Attractions & amenities: Café, community centre, playground, boating lake, bicycle hire (including recumbent bikes), free tennis courts, bowling green, outdoor gym, table tennis, sports pitches, organised walks, toilets, free car park.

Dulwich Park (72 acres/29ha) was formerly part of the Manor of Dulwich, first mentioned in 967 and owned by Bermondsey Abbey until the Dissolution of the Monasteries in the 1530s. In the early 17th century, actor/impresario Edward Alleyn purchased the estate and in 1619 founded his College of God's Gift as a school and almshouses for the poor – now Dulwich College.

Dulwich Park was opened in 1890 by Lord Roseberry, after whom one of the park gates is named. The land was donated in 1885 by the Dulwich Estates' Board of Governors who gave 'five fields' of the Dulwich College estate to the Metropolitan Board of Works for a public park. It was laid out by the newly formed London County Council in 1889/90 – and is considered by many to have been the forerunner of modern country parks. It was restored in 2004-6 and much of its original layout is still intact.

features, facilities, a beautiful lake, gardens and an expansive lawned area for picnics. It contains a number of historic and rare trees including ancient oaks which mark its boundary, a bay laurel, swamp cypress, cypress oak and Indian bean. Among its many gardens is the American garden, famous for its rhododendrons and azaleas, which are spectacular when in bloom in May. Other highlights include a dry garden, which aims to demonstrate the wide range of plants that can be successfully grown with little water, a winter garden specially planted for winter colour, and the vegetable garden community gardening project, with vegetable beds in constant rotation throughout the year.

👁 DON'T MISS!

The nearby Dulwich Picture Gallery, opposite the College Gate entrance to the park, is one of the best (designed by Sir John Soane) galleries in Greater London (💻 dulwichpicturegallery. org.uk).

A Green Flag holder since 2007, Dulwich Park is packed with historic

ELTHAM PALACE & GARDENS 15

Address: Court Yard, Eltham, SE9 5QE (☎ 020-8294 2548 or 0870-333 1181, 🖥 www.english-heritage.org.uk/daysout/properties/eltham-palace-and-gardens).
Opening hours: Palace, 1st Apr to 31st Oct, Mon-Wed, Sun and Bank Holidays, 10am to 5pm. Gardens open Suns in winter (see website for times).
Cost: Palace and gardens, £9.60 adults, £8.60 concessions, £5.80 children (5-15), £25 families. Gardens only, £6.20 adults, £5.60 concessions, £3.70 children. Free to English Heritage members.
Transport: Eltham or Mottingham rail.
Attractions & amenities: Historic palace with Art Deco interiors, café, gift shop.

Eltham Palace is one of the few important medieval royal palaces in England to survive with substantial remains intact, although nowadays it's perhaps more famous for its remarkable interior. It was acquired by English Heritage in 1995, and major repairs and restoration of the palace and gardens were completed four years later.

Initially a moated manor house set in extensive parkland, the original palace was given to Edward II in 1305 and was a royal residence from the 14th to 16th centuries, including Henry VIII in his younger days. The estate – retained for deer hunting after the royals moved to Greenwich – was almost stripped of trees and deer during the English Civil War (1642-1651), while the palace and its chapel were badly damaged.

The current building – incorporating parts of the medieval palace – was largely created when Sir Stephen and Lady Courtauld were granted a lease in the '30s. They restored the Great Hall, which boasts England's third-largest hammer-beam roof, created a minstrels' gallery, and incorporated it into a sumptuous home with a variety of Art Deco styles. Among many notable features are Lady Courtauld's gold-plated mosaic bathroom and the stunning circular entrance hall, the work of the Swedish designer Rolf Engströmer.

> The Courtaulds reinstated the moat and created seven new garden areas, retaining most of the trees south and east of the moat, while adding ornamental plantations, shrubberies and specimen trees.

Eltham Palace is set in 19 acres (7.7ha) of beautiful Art Deco-influenced gardens dotted with medieval ruins and features, including the 14th-century moat (and 15th-century bridge). The outer gardens are laid out as a series of 'rooms', filled with shade-loving and winter flowering plants, leading around the palace to a sunken rose garden with hybrid tea and musk roses, pergola and loggia. Beyond it is the dry south moat, where award-winning garden designer Isabelle Van Groeningen has created herbaceous borders reflecting the spirit and era of the Courtaulds.

16 HALL PLACE & GARDENS

Address: Bourne Road, Bexley, DA5 1PQ (☎ 01322-526574, ✉ bexley.gov.uk > parks and open spaces and hallplace.org.uk).
Opening hours: Gardens, daily, 9am to dusk. House, daily, 10am to 5pm.
Cost: Gardens free. House, £7 adults, £5 under-16s/concessions, £20 families (two adults and up to three children).
Transport: Bexley rail.
Attractions & amenities: Historic house/museum, parkland, river, plant nursery, visitor centre, café, restaurant/pub, shop, sports pitches, car park, events and activities.

Hall Place (Grade I listed) is a former stately home set in a beautiful 160-acre (65ha) estate, sitting beside the River Cray on the outskirts of Crayford (Bexley). The house dates from around 1537 when wealthy merchant Sir John Champneys, former Lord Mayor of London, used stone recycled from nearby **Lesnes Abbey** (see page 279) to build a country house. The house was owned by wealthy merchant Sir Robert Austen (1587-1666) and his family until being purchased in around 1772 by his brother-in-law, Sir Francis Dashwood (1708-1781), founder of the notorious Hellfire Club. For much of the 19th and early 20th centuries it was let to various tenants, although it remained in the Dashwood family until 1926. The borough of Bexley became the owners of the estate and Hall Place in 1935.

Hall Place is surrounded by magnificent, award-winning formal gardens and landscaped parkland. The gardens are one of only a handful in the UK to have won a Green Flag award for 11 successive years and also have coveted Green Heritage Site status. They include enclosed gardens, rose and herb gardens, inspirational herbaceous borders and a stunning topiary lawn, including chess pieces and topiary versions of the Queen's Beasts, planted for the coronation of Queen Elizabeth II.

The former walled gardens contain a plant nursery (with shop), display gardens, model gardens and a sub-tropical plant house with a wide range of exotic plants. The parkland, through which the River Cray flows, contains an exceptional variety of trees and a host of wildlife.

Much of the house that Sir John Champneys built still survives, with outer walls of a distinctive checkerboard design made of flint and rubble masonry – a beautiful example of the Tudor love of pattern. Seventeenth-century additions and improvements by Sir Robert Austen include a vaulted long gallery and a spectacular great chamber with a fine plaster ceiling.

HORNIMAN MUSEUM GARDENS 17

Address: 100 London Road, Forest Hill, SE23 3PQ (☎ 020-8699 1872, 🖳 horniman.ac.uk).
Opening hours: Gardens, Mon-Sat, 7.15am to sunset (Sun and Bank Holidays opens 8am). Museum, daily, 10.30am to 5.30pm; closed 24-26th Dec.
Cost: Free.
Transport: Forest Hill rail.
Attractions & amenities: Museum, aquarium, animal enclosures, conservatory, nature trail, café, bandstand.

Opened in 1901, the Horniman Museum is housed in a lovely Arts and Crafts and Art Nouveau-style building designed by Charles Harrison Townsend. It was founded by the Victorian tea trader Frederick John Horniman to house his vast collection of over 350,000 items, including cultural artefacts, ethnography, natural history and musical instruments, some collected personally on his travels, but most accumulated by his tea merchants.

The Horniman's exhibits aren't dusty or static, and the collection is constantly being extended, researched and brought into public view. The music and ethnography collections, especially, are of national importance; the latter is the third most significant in the UK after the British Museum and the Pitt-Rivers Museum (Oxford). The detailed website contains comprehensive information about the various objects on display.

> The Horniman Museum is set in 16 acres (6.5ha) of unique, award-winning gardens offering stunning views across London.

The beautifully maintained formal gardens and natural landscapes include delightful rose gardens, herbaceous borders, ethno-botanical planting, enchanting wildflower displays and a number of unique sundials. There's also a Grade II listed conservatory, a 1903 bandstand from a design by Charles Harrison Townsend, a 20ft (6m) totem pole and a nature trail. An Animal Walk (opening in 2013) features rabbits, guinea pigs, chickens, ferrets, sheep, goats and alpacas.

The extensively-restored display gardens are designed to complement the museum's collections. For example, the Materials Garden contains plants used to make things, from textiles to musical instruments, such as the giant reeds used in clarinets, while the Sound Garden encourages visitors to 'play' outdoor musical instruments. The Sunken Garden has a reflection pool and is surrounded by plants used to create natural dyes, while the Medicinal Garden contains plants used to treat illness in different areas of the body. The Food Garden is a beautiful allotment, and there's also a Wildlife Garden packed with ideas on how to attract wildlife to gardens and green spaces.

18 KENNINGTON PARK

Address: Kennington Park Road, SE11 4BE (☎ 020-7926 9000, 🖥 lambeth.gov.uk > parks and green spaces and kenningtonpark.org).
Opening hours: Daily, 7.30am to dusk.
Cost: Free.
Transport: Oval tube.
Attractions & amenities: Nature trail, café, information centre, playground/adventure playground, tennis courts, basketball/netball, skateboarding, fitness trail, sports pitches,

Kennington Park opened in 1854 on land that was previously Kennington Common, first recorded in 1600. The common was a site of public executions (the south London equivalent of Tyburn) from around 1678 until 1799, as well as a venue for public speaking and political rallies. Illustrious orators included Methodist founders George Whitefield and John Wesley, who's reputed to have attracted a crowd of 30,000 in 1739, while on 10th April 1848 thousands attended a rally organised by the Chartists, the working-class movement for political reform. The common was also one of London's earliest cricket grounds and the venue for major matches in the 18th century (the Oval, Surrey's County Cricket ground, is close by).

This much-loved open space (35 acres/14ha) consists of two parts: the Victorian Grade II listed park and an extension to the east, created in the '60s. With its abundance of trees, plants, shrubs and formal flower beds, the park is a magnet for both people and wildlife. It was one of the first public parks to provide free access to mass displays of flowers – its unique 19th-century flower beds are still a treat – and boasts many mature and historic trees. There are also open areas for wildlife and biodiversity, an 'old English' flower garden, rose beds and a new 'Green Link', which connects the older Victorian park to the '60s extension. The park was awarded its first Green Flag in 2011.

> Kennington Park is home to the Prince Consort Lodge, aka Prince Albert's Model Cottages, built for the Great Exhibition of 1851 as a 'model dwelling' to house four families. It was relocated here in 1853 and is now home to the charity Trees for Cities (🖥 treesforcities.org).

There's also a beautiful Arts and Crafts style café (1897), one of London's few surviving Victorian 'refreshment houses' still in use. As well as being a popular meeting place, the café hosts regular art and photographic exhibitions, and acts as an information centre.

LESNES ABBEY WOODS 19

Address: Abbey Road, Belvedere, DA17 5DY (☎ 020-8303 7777, 🖥 bexley.gov.
uk > parks and open spaces).
Opening hours: Unrestricted access.
Cost: Free.
Transport: Abbey Wood rail.
Attractions & amenities: Formal gardens, 12th-century abbey ruins.

One of southeast London's unexpectedly rich sites, Lesnes Abbey is a ruined Norman monastery in Abbey Wood, an area named after the 217 acres (88ha) of woods adjacent to the ruins. The abbey is a scheduled monument of national importance, while the surrounding ancient woodland, park and heathland (one of Greater London's few remaining heaths) is a Local Nature Reserve and a Site of Special Scientific Interest.

The Abbey of St Mary and St Thomas the Martyr was founded in 1178 by Richard de Luci, Chief Justiciar of England, perhaps as penance for his involvement in the murder of Thomas Becket. It was a poor monastery and one of the first to be disbanded after the Dissolution of the Monasteries.

The abbey grounds and woods were acquired by London County Council in 1930 as a public park. Gardens laid out after a 1951 excavation comprise three formal lawns with flower beds divided by large herbaceous borders, the whole enclosed with yew hedges and a terrace along the south side. There are specimen trees on the lawn to the west, including gingko, flowering cherry, horse chestnut, larch, swamp cypress, copper beech, hornbeam, zelkova and rhododendron beds. To the south is ancient woodland, chiefly sessile oak and sweet chestnut.

A series of trails wind through Lesnes Abbey Woods, which is rich in flora and fauna, particularly wildflowers, which include bluebell, violet, wood anemone, foxglove, heather, willow herb, red campion, figwort, dogs mercury, ramson, St John's wort, yellow archangel and yellow iris. Birdlife includes all three native woodpeckers and other woodland species, such as jay, magpie, robin, song thrush, blackbird, wren, collared dove and various tits. You may also see kestrel, pheasant and ring-necked parakeet.

One of the curiosities of Lesnes Abbey Wood is its fossil bed, which lies southeast of the ruins and contains fossils from the Eocene epoch (about 54m years ago), including sharks' teeth and seashells.

20 MARYON PARK & MARYON WILSON PARK

Address: Maryon Park, Maryon Road and Maryon Wilson Park, Thorntree Road, SE7 (☎ 020-8921 6885, 🖳 royalgreenwich.gov.uk > parks and gardens > all parks and friendsofmaryonparks.org).

Opening hours: Maryon Park, daily, 9am to dusk. Maryon Wilson Park, unrestricted access.

Cost: Free.

Transport: Charlton rail then bus.

Attractions & amenities: Playground, tennis courts, basketball court, children's farm, deer enclosure.

Maryon Park and Maryon Wilson Park are two beautiful parks in Charlton, created in the late 19th and early 20th centuries respectively. The land was given to the London County Council (LCC) by the Maryon-Wilson family and named in honour of them. There are also two associated green spaces, Gilbert's Pit and Barrier Gardens, in the north of Charlton.

Maryon Park (15 acres/6ha) was donated to the LCC in 1890 by Sir Spencer Maryon-Wilson, Lord of the Manor of Charlton, and opened to the public the following year. It's laid out on a hilly site that was once ancient woodland known as Hanging Wood, used for sand and chalk quarrying from the early 18th century until 1870. One former quarry, Gilbert's Pit – a Site of Special Scientific Interest – adjoins the park. Cox's Mount is a tree-lined grass hilltop at the Thames end of the park, affording panoramic views over London, the Thames and the Thames Barrier.

Maryon Wilson Park (32 acres/13ha) opened in 1926 and, like Maryon Park, was created out of Hanging Wood, owned by the Maryon-Wilson family from 1767 to 1925. In the 18th and 19th centuries it was a wild wooded area frequented by highwaymen who robbed travellers on Blackheath and Shooters Hill – those apprehended were hanged here (hence the name of the wood).

The park is more informal than Maryon Park, beautifully landscaped with open grassland and woodlands, set in a valley with streams running through the woods. The wood is predominantly native scrub, containing birch, thorn and willow, with some rhododendron and other shrubs along the brook. The park contains a small (children's) farm with sheep, ducks, geese, chickens, goats and pigs, and a deer enclosure.

Maryon Park also has a large sheltered green space used for recreation, a playground, tennis courts and an outdoor basketball court.

OXLEAS WOOD 21

> **Address:** Crown Woods Lane, Shooters Hill, SE18 3JA (☎ 020-8921 6885,
> 🖳 royalgreenwich.gov.uk > parks and gardens > all parks and oxleaswood.com).
> **Opening hours:** Unrestricted access.
> **Cost:** Free.
> **Transport:** Falconwood rail.
> **Attractions & amenities:** Guided walks (see council website), café, toilet, car park.

Oxleas Wood (190 acres/77ha) is part of a large continuous area of woodland and parkland on the south side of Shooters Hill. The wood also includes Oxleas Meadows, Jack Wood, Castle Wood, Shepherdleas Wood, Falconwood and Eltham Park North. It's the remains of a much larger area of forest, estimated to be at least 8,000 years old, where a complex ecosystem of plants and animals developed and evolved together.

The woods were part of the Royal Manor of Eltham, established in 1311, which were leased to Sir John Snow, 2nd Baronet, from crown occupation in 1679. His family managed them until 1811, when they were taken over by the War Department. The woods were acquired by the London County Council in 1930 and opened to the public in 1934.

Today, Oxleas is an area of atmospheric ancient woodland – a Site of Special Scientific Interest – dominated by tall oak trees with an understorey of hazel and sweet chestnut. The woods contain many other species, including silver birch, hornbeam, ash, coppice hazel, crack willow, alder and many wild service trees, plus beech, birch, holly, hawthorn, sycamore, yew, holm oak and turkey oak. In spring there are drifts of bluebells with wood anemone and wood sorrel, and in autumn a wide variety of fungi, while in summer the grassland of Oxleas Meadows is bright with buttercups, ox-eye daisies, yarrow, and red and white clover, and humming with bees, grasshoppers, ladybirds and butterflies.

The wood is reckoned by ecologists to be one of the most important for wildlife in the whole of London, home to a wealth of fauna, particularly breeding birds such as tree creepers, nuthatches, woodpeckers, chiffchaffs, long tailed tits and relative newcomers such as ring-necked parakeets.

> The woodland contains a famous folly called Severndroog Castle (🖳 severndroogcastle.org.uk), a Gothic tower built in 1784 as a memorial to William James of the East India Company.

Oxleas Wood café

22 PECKHAM RYE PARK & COMMON

Address: Strakers Road, Peckham, SE15 3UA (☎ 020-7525 2000,
🖳 southwark.gov.uk > parks and open spaces and foprp.org.uk).
Opening hours: Unrestricted access.
Cost: Free.
Transport: Peckham Rye rail.
Attractions & amenities: Formal gardens, arboretum, lake, nature garden, adventure play area, café, soccer pitches, skate park, bowling green, outdoor gym.

Victorian Peckham Rye Park (49 acres/20ha) and historic Peckham Common (64 acres/26ha) to its north comprise one of the most attractive green spaces in south London. Peckham Rye has a long history and is recorded as being cultivated before the Norman Conquest. 'Pecheham' – which may have been 'Peche's Home' – was referred to in the *Domesday Book* of 1086, when it was owned by Bishop Odo of Bayeux. By around the 14th century the area was known as Peckham Rye, which originally only referred to the River Peck, 'rye' meaning watercourse in Old English. Peckham Rye Common was used as a deer park for centuries, although local people had common rights.

When the Lord of the Manor of Camberwell Friern proposed to develop the land in 1868, Peckham Rye Common was purchased by Camberwell Vestry to ensure that it remained a public open space. The land that makes up the park was in turn purchased by the Metropolitan Board of Works in 1882, and in 1890 the adjacent Homestall Farm was purchased and added to the park, which opened in 1894. The park had an artificial lake with an island and lakeside walks, rock and water gardens, an American garden, a Japanese garden and an ornamental old English garden, later renamed the Sexby Garden after Colonel JJ Sexby, London County Council's first Chief Officer of Parks. The park was redeveloped in 1936 and the paths re-laid with York stone paving.

As with many London parks, Peckham Rye was rundown and neglected after the Second World War and wasn't restored to its former splendour until 2004-5. The formal Sexby Garden remains at its centre, containing a wide variety of plants and shrubs, rose-planted pergolas, fountains and benches. Peckham Rye Park has been awarded a Green Flag annually since 2007.

The delightful Japanese garden features a series of stream-fed ponds, with Japanese plants and shrubs, and a Japanese bridge and shelter.

ROOTS & SHOOTS GARDEN 23

Address: Walnut Tree Walk, off Kennington Road, SE11 6DN (☎ 020-7587 1131, 🖥 rootsandshoots.org.uk).
Opening hours: Mon-Fri, 10am to 4pm (but check during school term periods). Also evening and weekend events (see website for information).
Cost: Free.
Transport: Lambeth North tube.
Attractions & amenities: Eco-training centre, nursery, shop, wildlife study centre and wild garden.

The Roots and Shoots Garden (RSG) – full name 'Roots and Shoots Wildlife Garden and Study Centre' – is an outstanding, award-winning centre in Kennington, providing vocational training for urban youngsters. Established in 1982 by the Lady Margaret Hall Settlement, a charity working in North Lambeth since 1897, it allows young people who find it difficult to cope with traditional educational systems to spend a year in the garden acquiring the necessary skills and self-confidence to find and retain employment.

The Roots and Shoots Garden is also the base for the London Beekeepers' Association (🖥 lbka.org.uk), which holds meetings and courses here; its honey – some of the best in London – is sold in the RSG shop.

The project began in a derelict 1-acre (0.4ha) site donated by Lambeth Council. It now contains an eco-training centre, plant nursery, shop, wildlife study centre and wild garden, which provides environmental education for schools and the community. Diverse habitats have been developed to increase and promote the biodiversity of insect, plant and bird life. There's a summer meadow, lush with wildflowers and buzzing with insects; a pond that's hopping with frogs, newts and

all manner of insects, and flower beds designed to provide shelter and food for wildlife, rather than neat herbaceous borders. Surrounded by high buildings, it's a lush inner-city oasis, where plants from warm temperate and Mediterranean climates flourish.

An eco-building – clad in wood with sustainable energy and other environmental features – is the hub of Roots and Shoots' activities. Completed in 2005, it has a large photovoltaic roof (for solar energy), which provides around half the garden's electricity needs, solar water heating, rainwater collection for WCs and plants, and built-in insect and bird boxes.

The RSG has won a number of awards for its work on biodiversity and education for local communities, and for excellence in the provision of horticultural and environmental education.

24 THE RED HOUSE & GARDEN

> **Address:** Red House Lane, Bexleyheath, DA6 8JF (☎ 020-8304 9878, 🖳 nationaltrust.org.uk/redhouse and friends-red-house.co.uk).
> **Opening hours:** Mar-Oct, Wed-Sun, 11am to 5pm; Nov to mid-Dec, Fri-Sun, 11am to 5pm; closed Jan-Feb. Until 1.30pm visits are only by pre-booked guided tours (every 30 minutes between 11am and 1pm). See National Trust website for exact opening dates and details.
> **Cost:** Garden, £2.20 (incl. Gift Aid) adults, £1.10 children, £5.50 families. House and garden, £8 adults, £4 children, £20 families. Free to National Trust members.
> **Transport:** Bexleyheath rail.
> **Attractions & amenities:** Museum, tea room, shop.

Although situated in one of London's outer suburbs, it's well worth the journey to see this architectural and horticultural gem and shrine to William Morris, described by the Pre-Raphaelite painter Dante Gabriel Rossetti as 'more a poem than a house' and by the designer and artist Edward Burne-Jones as 'the beautifullest place on earth'.

The Red House (Grade I listed) was designed by the architect Philip Webb and William Morris, founder of the Arts and Crafts movement, an international design movement instigated by Morris and inspired by the writings of the critic John Ruskin.

The house is a large elegant building made of warm red bricks with substantial chimneys, a steep tiled roof, diverse window styles and a beautiful stairway – it's striking both externally and internally. It retains plenty of Arts and Crafts features – original and restored – including furniture designed by Morris and Webb, and stained glass and paintings by Burne-Jones. Morris and his family lived in the Red House for five years from 1860, only giving it up for financial reasons.

The garden is also magnificent, designed to harmonise with the house, or 'to clothe it'. In fact, the house and garden were planned together, even to the extent that plant names (such as white jasmine, roses, and passion flowers) were included in Webb's architectural drawings. It was one of the first gardens designed as a series of rooms that were extensions of the house; originally these were a herb garden, a vegetable garden, and two gardens of traditional British flowers and fruit trees.

For many, the Red House garden represents the start of the Arts and Crafts garden movement, which was later exemplified in the work of William Robinson and Gertrude Jekyll.

> The Red House was a private home until 2003, when it was acquired by the National Trust and opened to the public.

UTH LONDON BOTANICAL INSTITUTE GARDEN 25

> **Address:** 323 Norwood Road, SE24 9AQ (☎ 020-8674 5787, 🖳 slbi.org.uk).
> **Opening hours:** Thu, 10am to 4pm; other times by appointment. Closed in Aug.
> **Cost:** Free.
> **Transport:** Tulse Hill rail.

The South London Botanical Institute (SLBI) provides facilities for the study of plants, including ecology and conservation, and aims to encourage interest in all aspects of plant life. Since its foundation in 1910 by botanist and ornithologist Allan Octavian Hume (1829-1912), it has provided an environment where anyone interested in plants, be they amateur or professional, can meet and develop their knowledge.

Originally a civil servant, Hume spent 45 years in India before returning to England in 1894 and turning his attention to horticulture, embarking on an intensive study of British flora. His dream was to make the study of plants accessible to the working classes: he recognised the difficulty in identifying alien plant species and began growing and pressing plants to create a herbarium. This led him to purchase a Victorian house in Tulse Hill in 1909, which a year later became the South London Botanical Institute.

> Several generations of botanists have benefited from (and contributed to) the facilities at the Institute; today's members enjoy evening lectures and field trips, plus access to the library, garden and herbaria.

The Institute's garden – London's smallest public garden at just 4,130ft² (384m²) – fell into decline after Hume's death in 1912, but was restored in 1975 under the Institute's director Frank Brightman. Twenty numbered beds containing rare and unusual plants were created, including plants from John Gerard's *Herball* (1597) such as *Mirabilis jalapa* (the four o'clock plant). The garden now contains over 500 labelled species in themed borders, with traditional medicinal herbs alongside plants used in current pharmaceutical research. British natives, ferns, scented plants, drought-tolerant plants and unusual vegetables flourish alongside rare trees and shrubs from the southern hemisphere. At the heart of the garden is a pond supporting native wetland plants, which is also home to frogs and newts.

26 SOUTHWARK PARK & KING'S STAIRS GARDEN

Address: Southwark Park, Gomm Road, SE16 2TY and **King's Stairs Gardens**, Jamaica Road, SE16 4RS (☎ 020-7525 2000, ▢ southwark.gov.uk > parks and open spaces and friendsofsouthwarkpark.co.uk).

Opening hours: Park, 7.30am to dusk. Gardens, unrestricted access.

Cost: Free.

Transport: Bermondsey tube, Canada Water DLR/rail, Rotherhithe rail.

Attractions & amenities: Formal rose garden, wildlife garden, boating lake, visitor centre, café/gallery, bandstand, athletics track, bowling green, tennis courts, soccer pitches.

Southwark Park is a splendid public park in Rotherhithe of 63 acres (25ha), managed by the borough of Southwark. Designed by Alexander McKenzie, it was opened in 1869 by the Metropolitan Board of Works (later the London County Council) and was London's first municipal park. The original layout had a wide carriage drive around the perimeter, part of which survives; various facilities were added by 1885, including a lake and a bandstand, while further additions in the early 20th century included a lido (closed in the '80s) and the Ada Salter rose garden (named for the wife of a local MP).

The park underwent a major restoration in 2001, which included a new bandstand (a replica of the original 1833 model), bowling pavilion and children's play area. The lake and the main gates were also restored. As with many parks in London, the plane tree is dominant in Southwark Park, particularly in the northernmost section around the bandstand, although there are also rarer trees such as walnut, red oak, silver maple and swamp cypress.

King's Stairs Gardens (11.5 acres/4.5ha) – to the north of Southwark Park – were opened in 1962 and were added to Southwark's public open space in the '80s. It's one of the last remaining riverside parks in London and gets its name from Edward III, who used the stairs to access his manor house on Bermondsey Wall East. The park contains mature trees, lawns and steep, undulating hillocks, with fine views over the river; the gardens have a new children's play area, although the entire park is a playground in a sense as it's situated in an area where few homes have gardens.

King's Stairs has been designated a Site of Importance for Nature Conservation and provides an important habitat for local wildlife.

SYDENHAM HILL WOOD & DULWICH WOODS   27

Address: Crescent Wood Road, off Sydenham Hill, SE26 (☎ 020-7525 2000/020-7252 9186, 🖥 southwark.gov.uk > parks and open spaces and wildlondon.org.uk).
Opening hours: Unrestricted access.
Cost: Free.
Transport: Sydenham Hill and Forest Hill rail.

Sydenham Hill Wood & Dulwich Woods (62 acres/25ha) are the last surviving fragments of the Great North Wood, which once covered large tracts of land, a chain of oak woods and wooded commons that extended from Deptford to just north of Croydon. Sydenham Hill Wood belonged to the Abbey of Bermondsey and is the last of the Dulwich coppices. In the 17th century, the woods were acquired by Edward Alleyn and devolved to Dulwich College, which still owns them.

The woods, along with Cox's Walk, have been managed by the London Wildlife Trust since 1982 and are a valuable reserve for both wildlife and the public. Cox's Walk (5 acres/2ha) – named after its creator John Cox – is a rare survival of an 18th-century public path. This oak-lined avenue has been owned by Southwark since 1965, and links the wood to the junction of Lordship Lane and Dulwich Common.

In the 1870s a number of large Victorian garden villas were established on Sydenham Hill; they were later demolished, and the woods are now scattered with the remnants of Victorian gardens. There are over 200 species of trees and flowering plants, including wild garlic, early dog violet and bugle, and it's also home to a multitude of fungi, rare insects, birds and elusive woodland mammals. Oak and hornbeam confirm the site's ancient woodland heritage, and in the eastern part of the wood there are relics from former domestic gardens such as a cedar of Lebanon (one of the largest trees in the wood) and a monkey puzzle. There's also a Victorian folly, once a proudly displayed garden ornament or conversation piece, now hidden deep among the trees.

The Nunhead to Crystal Palace railway line (closed in 1954) once passed through the woods, and you can still follow the trackbed up to a disused tunnel, now used as a roost by bats.

28 SYDENHAM WELLS PARK

Address: Wells Park Road, Sydenham, SE26 (☎ 020-8314 2047, 🖳 lewisham.
gov.uk > parks and open spaces > local parks).
Opening hours: Daily, 8am to dusk.
Cost: Free.
Transport: Sydenham rail.
Attractions & amenities: Formal gardens, playgrounds, water play area, tennis
and ball courts, putting green (summer), nature reserve, toilets.

Sydenham Wells Park (20 acres/8ha) is situated near the former site of mineral springs that were discovered in the 17th century. It became a popular spa whose numerous visitors included George III, and its success led to the building of large houses as wealthy patrons settled in the area.

Sydenham Wells opened as a public park in 1901 following a successful campaign to save the land from housing development. It was laid out with broad paths, ornamental plantations, a miniature watercourse and a variety of sports facilities. Springs have since emerged in several places and have been channelled into drains, while a bog garden and bamboo walk have also been created.

Today, this Green Flag park is one of the most attractive in Lewisham with its fine water features, formal gardens, and array of mature trees (including some pedunculate oaks that may be relics of the Great North Wood) and shrubs, with lovely rhododendron, hornbeam and bedding displays. There's a wooden shelter and kiosk beside the bowling green and a '60s paddling pool. A serpentine path runs around the upper part of the stream that flows through an area of lawn planted with willow and other ornamental trees and shrubs.

In 1995, the gardens of two Victorian houses were added to the park and used to create a 'wild' area on the western edge with bark-chip footpaths. The park also has a sensory garden with a wide range of vibrant and colourful plants designed to stimulate all five senses. It features a rock with recycled (solar powered) water trickling over it, symbolising the underground springs that first put Sydenham Wells Park on the map.

The park has a range of facilities including an under-fives playground, a large playground for older children with a water play area, a multi-surface court with basketball and soccer facilities, two tennis courts, ponds and toilets.

WELL HALL PLEASAUNCE | 29

Address: Well Hall Road, Eltham, SE9 6SZ (park: ☎ 020-8921 6885, Tudor Barn restaurant: 0845-459 2351, 🖥 royalgreenwich.gov.uk > parks and gardens > all parks, wellhall.org.uk and tudorbarneltham.com).
Opening hours: Daily, 8am to dusk, excluding Christmas Day, Boxing Day and New Year's Day. Guided walks on the first Wed of the month at 10.30am and the second Sun at 2pm.
Cost: Free.
Transport: Eltham rail.
Attractions & amenities: Formal gardens, Tudor barn, bar/restaurant, moat, art gallery.

Well Hall Pleasaunce is a beautiful 11-acre (4.5ha) park of landscaped gardens, dating back to the 13th century. It contains many lovingly-restored historical elements, including an original Tudor barn, a moat with a 16th-century bridge and a variety of water features. Formal gardens, including an Italian garden displaying glorious colour, sit adjacent to natural gardens designed to attract wildlife. The Pleasaunce has been extensively restored (funded by the Heritage Lottery Fund) and is a focal point for the local community, hosting events throughout the year.

The history of the site can be traced back to 1253, when it was owned by Mathew de Hegham. During the Tudor period the estate was inherited by John Roper in 1488 through his marriage to Sir John Tattersall's daughter Margery. William Roper (1496-1578) – who built the Tudor Barn in around 1525 – was married to Margaret, the daughter of Sir Thomas More, Lord Chancellor to Henry VIII.

In 1930, Well Hall was purchased by Woolwich borough council for use as a public park. The Tudor Barn (Grade II* listed) was restored, while the surrounding outbuildings were demolished, as was Well Hall itself. The gardens were redeveloped in an Arts and Crafts style, while the ground floor of the barn became a restaurant, with the first floor used as an art gallery. The second floor, which was extensively dilapidated, was removed to reveal the stunning oak roof construction, the outstanding feature of the Tudor Barn. In the upstairs west end of the barn are stained glass windows depicting paintings of Sir Thomas More's family by Holbein.

Today, Well Hall Pleasaunce offers a tranquil respite from the bustle and stresses of life, while the historic barn is an atmospheric bar and fine restaurant.

The park is a haven for nature and wildlife, and home to a variety of mammals and a wealth of insects and bird species.

30 ARCHBISHOP'S PARK

Address: Carlisle Lane, Lambeth, SE1 7LE (☎ 020-7926 9000, 🖥 lambeth.gov. uk > parks and green spaces and archbishopspark.org).
Opening hours: Daily, 7.30am to dusk.
Cost: Free.
Transport: Lambeth North tube or Waterloo tube/rail.
Attractions & amenities: Guided tours, playground, toilets, sports facilities.

Archbishop's Park is a historic park adjacent to Lambeth Palace. It was once part of the grounds of the palace, the official London residence of the Archbishop of Canterbury since the 13th century. The Victorian Archbishop Tait (1868-82), concerned about the wellbeing of poor and underprivileged Londoners, opened up the grounds of the palace to local families, which enabled 'scores of pale children to play in the fresh air'. A section of the grounds, known as Lambeth Palace Field, was put aside for children to play in long after Archbishop Tait's death in 1882.

In 1901, Lambeth Palace Field became a public park, while remaining under the ownership of the Church Commissioners, and a playground was built there, along with courts for ball games. Today, Archbishop's Park has earned a Green Flag but the emphasis is still very much on play, with facilities that include an all-weather games area, tennis and netball courts and a children's play area. Wildlife-friendly zones include a community orchard, planted in 2010 in the northwest corner of the park.

31 AVERY HILL PARK & WINTER GARDENS

Address: Bexley Road, Eltham, SE9 2PQ (☎ 020-8921 6885, 🖥 royalgreenwich. gov.uk > parks and gardens > all parks).
Opening hours: Park, unrestricted access. Winter garden, daily, 10am to noon and 1-4pm.
Cost: Free.
Transport: New Eltham or Falconwood rail.
Attractions & amenities: Formal gardens, conservatory, playground, café, toilets, sports pitches.

Avery Hill Park (89 acres/36ha) was once the grounds of a mansion owned by Colonel North, a 19th-century entrepreneur who made his fortune exporting fertiliser from Chile. The house, built in 1890, is now part of the University of Greenwich and is noted for its superb domed conservatory, known as the Winter Garden, one of London's best surviving examples of this kind of steel-and-glass Victorian extravaganza. The tropical house contains banana, coffee, breadfruit and pineapple plants, as well as an impressive collection of palms and some striking statues.

The park also encompasses Pippenhall Meadows, a group of hedge-lined fields on gently sloping terraces, with a small stream (the River Shuttle) rising in the central part, flowing south through the park. These wet meadows are rare, particularly so close to London. The ancient hedges are completely overgrown in places and contain a large number of shrub

and tree species, some of which are estimated to be over 600 years old.

The well-used sports fields include 11 soccer and two rugby pitches.

Galatea, Leopoldo Ansiglioni

BURGESS PARK & CHUMLEIGH GARDENS 32

> **Address:** Albany Road, SE5 0RJ (☏ 020-7525 2000, 🖥 southwark.gov.uk > parks and open spaces and friendsofburgesspark.org.uk).
> **Opening hours**: Unrestricted, except for the area around the lake, 7.30am to sunset.
> **Cost:** Free.
> **Transport:** Elephant and Castle tube.
> **Attractions & amenities:** Formal gardens, lake, café, barbecue area, playground, BMX track, toilets, tennis, fishing, sports centre, events, various sports pitches, car park.

Unlike most London parks, Burgess Park – named after Councillor Jessie Burgess, Camberwell's first female Mayor – was carved out of a highly built-up area of the city. Virtually all the land it's built on was previously used for housing, industry and transport infrastructure, and the park has been gradually assembled and landscaped over decades. Today it comprises 114 acres (46ha) and is one of south London's largest parks.

It's been completely refurbished and redeveloped in recent years, with new gardens – including thousands of plants – over 150 new trees, man-made hills affording panoramic views across

London, an expanse of open parkland, wetland habitats and a stunning extended lake with two 30ft (9m) fountains.

One of the highlights is **Chumleigh Gardens**, a group of world gardens reflecting styles and planting from different parts of the world, including Oriental, African, Caribbean, Mediterranean and Islamic gardens. There are also raised beds where community gardeners and school groups can grow their own plants. Chumleigh Gardens also offers conference facilities in former almshouses (Grade II listed), which are home to an excellent café.

33 DEVONSHIRE ROAD NATURE RESERVE

Address: 170 Devonshire Road, Forest Hill, SE23 (☎ 020-8314 2047,
🖥 lewisham.gov.uk > nature reserves and www.devonshireroadnaturereserve.org).
Opening hours: Last Sun of the month, 1-5.30pm, plus special events and
activities (see website).
Cost: Free.
Transport: Forest Hill or Honor Oak Park rail.

Devonshire Road Wildlife Reserve is part of the Forest Hill to New Cross Gate railway cutting, originally part of the Great North Wood. It's now a Site of Metropolitan Importance for Nature Conservation and contains one of the finest rail-side wildlife habitats in London. There are three separate sections to the 2.5m/4km-long cutting, which includes woodland, meadow, a pond and a beehive. All three are managed as nature reserves, with the emphasis on organic and wildlife gardening; Devonshire Road, first established in 1981, is the oldest.

Woodland and scrub of various types cover the majority of the reserve, with a canopy of sycamore and ash, plus the occasional oak, and a variable under-storey of hawthorn and elder. Other trees and shrubs include hazel, blackthorn, sessile oak, yew, wild cherry, holly, holm oak and silver birch, while in springtime there's a colony of wild garlic. The cutting is also home to a plethora of animal life, particularly birds, which include tawny owl, great and lesser spotted woodpeckers, bullfinch, blackcap, chiffchaff, willow warbler and garden warbler, plus most common songbirds.

34 EAST GREENWICH PLEASAUNCE

Address: Chevening Road, SE10 0LB (☎ 020-8291 6885, 🖥 royalgreenwich.gov.
uk > parks and gardens > all parks and fegp.typepad.com).
Opening hours: Daily, dawn to dusk.
Cost: Free.
Transport: Cutty Sark DLR or Greenwich rail.

East Greenwich Pleasaunce – the word derives from French and means 'a secluded garden' or 'enclosed plantation' – is the former walled burial ground for Royal Navy pensioners from the old Royal Hospital at Greenwich (founded in 1694). It's a haven of peace and calm, as befits a former cemetery, and a real 'secret' garden, tucked away behind busy Woolwich Road. In 1926, the burial ground was purchased by Greenwich borough council as a public park, although the Admiralty reserved the right to make further burials (which continued until 1981).

The park contains a number of beautiful trees, including holm oak, silver birch, ash, mock orange, hawthorn, variegated holly, walnut, poplar, weeping birch, and an espaliered lime walk around the 19th-century boundary walls. Today, it's a much-loved community resource, with a playground, a mother-and-toddler drop-in centre (the One O'clock Club) run by Greenwich council, a caféteria and a small war memorial. It's also a haven for wildlife and home to a variety of bird species, including woodpeckers, finches and tits.

GREENWICH PENINSULA ECOLOGY PARK   35

Address: The Ecology Park Gatehouse, Thames Path, John Harrison Way, Greenwich Peninsula, London SE10 0QZ (☎ 020-8293 1904, 🖥 urbanecology. org.uk and greenwichecology.co.uk/index.html).
Opening hours: Wed-Sun, 10am to 5pm or dusk. Children under 8 must be accompanied by an adult.
Cost: Free.
Transport: North Greenwich tube.

The Greenwich Peninsula Ecology Park – run by the Trust for Urban Ecology – is the result of a major regeneration project in the late '90s to bring a wide tract of neglected land back to life. Once the site of chemical works and shipbuilding, this part of North Greenwich lost much of its industry in the '70s and the land began to revert to its original state – as a section of Greenwich Marsh.

Set in over 4 acres (1.6ha) just a short walk from the iconic Millennium Dome (now the O2), the park is a hidden gem, offering marshland, lakes, streams, wetland, woodland and a meadow: a wide variety of habitats to enjoy. It also presents a rare opportunity for a close look at the banks of an urban stretch of

the Thames. The park also has two lakes – the outer of which is always accessible, the inner only during opening times – where wildlife thrives, notably amphibians, birds and insects. Hides allow visitors a great view of the fauna and flora, which changes with the seasons – spring and summer are particularly colourful.

36 MYATT'S FIELDS PARK

Address: Cormont Road, SE5 9RA (☎ 020-7926 9000, 🖵 lambeth.gov.uk > parks and green spaces and myattsfieldspark.info).
Opening times: Daily, 7.30am to sunset.
Cost: Free.
Transport: Oval tube.
Attractions & amenities: Formal gardens, wildlife area, bandstand, café (summer), children's centre & playground, toilets, tennis courts, sports facilities.

Myatt's Fields Park (12.5 acres/5ha) is a handsome Victorian park which underwent a £3m renovation in 2010. First opened in May 1889, the park was originally part of a large estate purchased by Huguenot Hughes Minet in 1770, consisting of meadows, orchards and farmland. In 1882, his descendent William Minet – founder of the Huguenot Society – donated some of the land to create a new public park.

The Green Flag park, which lies at the heart of the Minet Conservation Area, is named after Joseph Myatt, a tenant market gardener who grew strawberries and rhubarb here in the 19th century. It retains many of its original features including the layout of serpentine paths, flowerbeds, mature trees, bandstand and summerhouse. More recent additions include a nature conservation area and a new playground with a wet play area. There are expanses of annual bedding and rosebeds in the northeast section, foliage displays around the summerhouse and a heather garden in the southern section. Mature trees include two avenues of planes, groups of silver birch and individual acacia, weeping ash, thorn, catalpa, oak and chestnut.

37 QUEEN ELIZABETH HALL ROOF GARDEN

Address: Southbank Centre, Belvedere Road, SE1 8XX (☎ 020-7960 4200, 🖵 southbankcentre.co.uk/venues/queen-elizabeth-hall).
Opening hours: Apr-Sep, 10am to dusk (see website for dates and times).
Cost: Free.
Transport: Waterloo tube/rail.
Attractions & amenities: Café/bar, great views.

The roof garden on top of Queen Elizabeth Hall is one of London's best-kept secrets. It's an oasis at the heart of the Southbank Centre offering stunning riverside views, a café/bar (run by the celebrated Company of Cooks) and a lovely place to relax.

Created through a partnership between the Southbank Centre and Cornwall's Eden Project, the garden is an annual enterprise. It was built from scratch in 2011 by the Grounded gardening team from the Providence Row Housing Association (PRHA), working with experts from Eden. In 2012 it hosted a wildflower garden – with over 90 varieties – celebrating of the diversity of British flora, attracting hordes of insects and butterflies while providing nectar for bees from the hives on the Royal Festival Hall's roof. The 2012 garden also contained lush lawns and a patchwork of vegetable plots, fruit trees in brightly coloured pots and a rustic pergola, clothed with sweet-scented climbers crowning a bridge to the Hayward Gallery. There was even a scarecrow!

It's well worth visiting the roof garden to see what the new summer brings.

RUSKIN PARK　38

Address: Denmark Hill, SE5 8EL (☎ 020-7926 9000, ▯ lambeth.gov.uk > Parks and green spaces and friendsruskinpark.org.uk).
Opening hours: Daily, 7am to dusk.
Cost: Free.
Transport: Brixton tube or Denmark Hill rail.
Attractions & amenities: Formal gardens, two ponds, bandstand, children's play area, paddling pool, toilets, tennis courts, sports pitches.

Ruskin Park (36 acres/15ha) is an Edwardian park named for John Ruskin (1819-1900) – artist, writer and social campaigner – who lived nearby. The land was previously the private gardens of demolished houses and was purchased in 1906 by the London County Council (LCC), which opened the park in 1907 and extended it in 1910.

The Green Flag park was laid out by the LCC's Chief Officer of Parks, Colonel JJ Sexby, and included an Old English garden, an oval duck pond with a central nesting island, and a delightful wooden bandstand in the centre of the park (restored in 2006). Among the splendid collection of trees are London plane, weeping willow, deodar, cedar of Lebanon, thorn, copper beech, holm oak, whitebeam, sycamore, lime and ash. The southern area of the park is separated by lines of lime and ash, and contains grass and sports areas. A late 18th-century entrance colonnade and flanking walls, retained from one of the demolished houses, provide a shelter near one of the entrances.

39 SOUTH NORWOOD COUNTRY PARK

Address: Albert Road, South Norwood, SE25 4BH (☎ 020-8726 6900,
🖳 croydon.gov.uk > parks and open spaces).
Opening hours: Unrestricted access for pedestrians and cyclists; car park closes
30 minutes before dusk.
Cost: Free.
Transport: Elmers End rail and Harrington Road Tramlink.
Attractions & amenities: Lake, visitor centre (weekends), playground, pitch and
putt, cycle path, toilets, car park.

Covering 125 acres (51ha), this sweeping country park in northeast Croydon opened in 1989. Originally part of the Great North Wood, the site has a long and chequered history, having been home to an ancient moated house (long since demolished), farmland and allotments, a brickworks, army manoeuvres (it was a civil defence training area during the Second World War), and a sewage works and refuse dump.

The park is now a Local Nature Reserve and has a wide range of contrasting habitats. The dragonfly pond was built to encourage dragonflies and damselflies – the emperor dragonfly, the largest in Britain, can be found here – as well as other creatures such as frogs, toads and newts. More than 20 varieties of butterflies have also been recorded and several moth species.

South Norwood Country Park has an excellent bird record with over 100 different resident and visiting species, including mallard, kestrel, pheasant, gulls, skylark, warblers, tits, finches and linnets, while the large wetlands and lake attract a wide variety of water fowl.

40 SUNRAY GARDENS

Address: Red Post Hill, SE24 9PL (☎ 020-7525 2000, 🖳 southwark.gov.uk >
parks and open spaces).
Opening hours: Daily, 7.30am to sunset.
Cost: Free.
Transport: North Dulwich rail.
Attractions & amenities: Lake, children's play area, multi-use games area.

Sunray Gardens (4 acres/1.8ha) are the former water gardens of the grounds of 'Casina' – a late 18th-century house built by John Nash – which were laid out by Humphry Repton. By 1920 the house had been abandoned and the Dulwich Estate donated the land to Camberwell Borough Council for much-needed social housing (Lloyd George's 'Homes

Fit for Heroes'). The plans allowed for an area of open space to be preserved for recreational purposes and the area around the lake – the sole survivor from Repton's landscape – was chosen and laid out in 1923.

This well-used Green Flag park retains many of its original landscape characteristics – dominated by the lake which occupies a quarter of the site and is important for wildlife – with mature trees, winding paths, flowerbeds and grass areas. Other facilities include a playground and a multi-use games area. The Friends of Sunray Gardens was formed in 1997 to preserve the park, which was refurbished in 2001.

TIBETAN PEACE GARDEN 41

Address: Geraldine Mary Harmsworth Park, St George's Road, SE1 6ER (📖 tibet-foundation.org/page/peace_garden).
Opening hours: Unrestricted access.
Cost: Free.
Transport: Lambeth North or Elephant & Castle tube.

The Tibetan Peace Garden is a beautiful, tranquil garden situated in Geraldine Mary Harmsworth Park in Southwark; it's a simple, poignant plea for peace, incongruously sited in the shadow of the Imperial War Museum. Commissioned by the Tibet Foundation and created by designer/sculptor Hamish Horsley, the garden was opened and consecrated in 1999 by His Holiness the Dalai Lama and honours one of his principal teachings: the need to create understanding between different cultures and to establish places of peace and harmony in the world.

At its heart is the Kalachakra Mandala, associated with world peace, here for the first time cast in bronze. It forms the central focus of the garden, while contemporary western sculptures represent the four elements of air, fire, earth and water (the open arena represents the fifth element, space). Near the garden's entrance is the Language Pillar, containing a peace message for the new Millennium from the Dalai Lama.

The inner gardens are planted with herbs and plants from Tibet and the Himalayan region, while the pergola is covered with climbing plants, including jasmine, honeysuckle and scented roses.

42 VAUXHALL PARK

> **Address:** Fentiman Road, London SW8 1PU (☎ 020-7926 9000, 🖳 lambeth.gov.uk > parks and green spaces and www.vauxhallpark.org.uk).
> **Opening hours:** Daily, 7.30am to sunset.
> **Cost:** Free.
> **Transport:** Vauxhall tube.
> **Attractions & amenities:** Formal gardens, model village, café, children's play area, toilet, tennis courts.

Vauxhall Park (7.5 acres/3ha) was laid out as a public park by Fanny Rollo Wilkinson for the Kyrle Society, a Victorian reforming organisation which aimed to 'bring beauty home to the people' – its treasurer was Octavia Hill, one of the founders of the National Trust. The park opened in 1890, and by 1914 had a bandstand, tennis court, drinking fountain and toilets; later additions included an open-air theatre, bowling greens and refreshment facilities.

One of Lambeth's Green Flag parks (since 2007), it's a charming Victorian park with a rich history, serving a diverse and vibrant community. It retains a number of original features together with some new ones which serve modern users of all ages and interests. These include formal gardens, a new lavender garden (laid out on the site of an old bowling green), a splendid model village and a café near the southwest entrance. There's also a popular playground, a Montessori Nursery and a One O'clock Club.

43 SMALL PARKS, GARDENS & SQUARES

Southeast London is blessed with a wealth of small parks, gardens and squares, many of which were created in the 19th century to provide the poor with somewhere to enjoy some green space and recreation facilities, and escape the city's pollution. A selection is described below:

A: All Hallows Church Garden (SE1, unrestricted, London Bridge tube) is the grounds of a former church destroyed in the Second World War, with lawn surrounded by flower beds and shrubberies. Steps lead up to a crucifix in the garden. This walled garden, just off Copperfield Street, has been developed over 40 years and includes old trees and plantings, much of which is overhung with decades-old ivy that's a haven for wildlife. It's a unique natural habitat in the city, home to bats, squirrels, and resident birds, including wrens, robins, tits, blackbirds, magpies and wood pigeons.

B: Bonnington Square Pleasure Garden (SW8, daylight hours, Vauxhall tube) is one of the finest community gardens in London. In 1994, local residents (funded by grants and sponsorship) purchased

derelict land on the square from Lambeth council with the aim of transforming it into a 'Pleasure Garden', in homage to the glorious Vauxhall Pleasure Gardens, a major entertainment venue in south London between the mid-17th and mid-19th centuries. It's now 'a unique mix of classic English and exotic tropical, of gentle textures and bold architectural,' with planting that includes a walnut tree, banana and bamboo. At night the garden is illuminated with uplighters and fairy lights that transform it into a place of serene magic.

C: Choumert Square (SE15, unrestricted, Peckham Rye rail), built in the latter half of the 19th century, presents visitors not with a square but a passageway of 46 tiny cottages – described as a 'floral canyon' – leading to a communal 'walled' garden. The tiny secret gardens of this Southwark lane, accessed via wrought iron gates off Choumert Grove, have evolved over some 20 years, triggered by a few

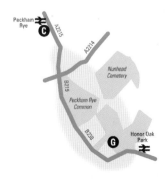

neighbours' gardening passions that infected the others with enthusiasm – a unique demonstration of how gardening can unite a community. Key features include a wide variety of roses, trees such as birch, willow, eucalyptus, and acer, and a colourful array of perennial border plants and annuals.

D: Christ Church Garden (SE1, unrestricted, Southwark tube) was opened in 1900 as a public garden and is now officially a Southwark park. It's a green retreat off Blackfriars Road, with beds and borders of shrubs and flowers and holly hedging, all under a lush canopy of London plane and lime trees. A church has stood on the site since 1671 – the current one is the third, dating from 1959.

The previous incarnation of Christ Church was destroyed in the Blitz, when its cross fell into the churchyard scorching the ground. The fiery imprint it left is now marked by a stone cross in the grass.

Leathermarket Gardens

E: Leathermarket Gardens (SE1, unrestricted, London Bridge tube/rail) were laid out in the '30s and derive their name from the leather market and tanneries that thrived here in the 19th century. To the east end of the garden is a rectangular sunken area with formal beds, while the central area,

Mint Street Park

lands belonging to the Honour of Gloucester; Elizabeth I was said to have rested here in 1602. The current oak tree that crowns the hill's summit was planted in 1905 after One Tree Hill became a public park. The park – which offers expansive views over London – is a haven for flora and fauna, including a wide variety of birds, moths and bats, plus a range of trees, fungi and other woodland flora.

H: Red Cross Garden (SE1, 7.30am to sunset, Borough tube) is a delightful small garden (just one-third of an acre) on Red Cross Way that formed part of Octavia Hill's pioneering social housing scheme in Southwark. Red Cross Garden, which predated the buildings, was designed by Miss Emmeline Sieveking of the Kyrle Society and officially opened in 1888. The garden had an elaborate layout of curved lawns, flower beds and serpentine paths, an ornamental pond with a fountain, a bandstand and a covered children's play area, plus two mosaics, of which one, The Sower, remains. In 2005, the Bankside Open Spaces Trust (📖 bost.org.uk) restored the garden to its former glory, complete with pond, bridge, fountain,

separated by a low brick wall, has a raised circular rose garden surrounded by lawn with ornamental trees, behind which is a quiet garden planted with trees and grass, shielded by privet. The gardens are accessed off Weston Street, in the shadow of The Shard.

F: Mint Street Park (SE1, unrestricted, Borough tube) is laid out on a site previously occupied by the Evelina Hospital for Sick Children, which was demolished after closure in 1976, when the site became green space. The park is the largest green park in Bankside and very much focused on young people, with an adventure playground, a community stage, and a renewed play area with a great rocky climbing wall and a ball court. The gorgeous raised beds were created and planted by the local gardening club working with Putting Down Roots, a project run by St Mungo's that works with homeless people.

G: One Tree Hill (SE23, unrestricted, Honor Oak Park rail) is a designated Local Nature Reserve five miles south of London Bridge, between Brenchley Gardens and Honor Oak Park, in an area that was once part of the famous Great North Wood. One Tree Hill is named after the Oak of Honor that marked the boundary of

Red Cross Garden

Southwark Cathedrral Gardens

flower beds, winding paths, lawn and benches.

I: St George's Gardens (SE1, 7.30am to sunset, Borough tube) at the end of traffic-ridden Borough High Street are a lovely quiet walled garden with a surprising history. Opened in 1882 on the site of an old graveyard serving the historic church of Saint George the Martyr, its northern boundary was the original wall of Marshalsea Prison (where Charles Dickens's father was incarcerated and which forms the backdrop for much of his novel *Little Dorrit*). The garden has a number of mature trees, including a fine London plane with seating around the trunk. It was re-landscaped in recent years by a local gardening club and now has a series of hooped arches, a hedged garden, gravelled paths and seats.

J: Southwark Cathedral Gardens (SE1, 8am to 6pm, London Bridge tube/rail) provide a tranquil and serene retreat from the surrounding urban landscape. Designed by Elizabeth Banks Associates and completed in 2001, the gardens and surrounds of Southwark Cathedral (the oldest Gothic church in London) were redesigned with improved disabled access after major extensions were made to the buildings. Three areas of the precinct were redesigned to the south, east and north of the cathedral with railings, straight and meandering paths, lawns and trees. A new courtyard space on the south and east sides was created, enclosed on the west side by planters containing a row of liquidambar trees, under-planted with aromatic shrubs, and paved with reclaimed York stone. Look out for a sculpture of the Holy Family by Kenneth Hughes.

In the south churchyard of Southwark Cathedral is an unusual granite boulder which commemorates Mahomet Weyonomon. A native American Indian, he came to London from Connecticut in 1735 to petition George II for restoration of his people's lands, but he and his companions died of smallpox before they even saw the king.

APPENDICES

APPENDIX A: USEFUL WEBSITES

Bankside Open Spaces Trust (bost.org.uk). BOST works with local residents to develop parks and gardens so that people can relax, kick a ball, grow plants or just hang out.

Department for Environment, Food and Rural Affairs (defra.gov.uk). The Government department concerned with everything from general environmental issues to wildlife and animal welfare.

English Heritage (english-heritage.org.uk). Protects and promotes England's spectacular historic environment. English Heritage maintains the 'Register of Historic Parks and Gardens of special historic interest in England' (established in 1983), which identifies over 1,600 sites assessed to be of national importance, including many in Greater London.

Environment Agency (environment-agency.gov.uk). Government agency charged with protecting and improving the environment.

Forestry Commission (www.forestry.gov.uk). The guardian of over 1m hectares of woodland in England, Scotland and Wales.

Garden History Society (gardenhistorysociety.org). The GHS is the oldest society in the world dedicated to the conservation and study of historic designed gardens and landscapes.

Garden Visit (gardenvisit.com/gardens/in/england/greater_london). A comprehensive website containing information about thousands of gardens, in the UK – including over 100 in London – and worldwide.

Gardens of the City of London (gardensofthecityoflondon.co.uk). Information about the many small gardens in the Square Mile, and suggestions for walks around them.

Gardens Guide (gardens-guide.com). Britain's premier open gardens directory.

Green Chain (greenchain.com). Website of the Green Chain walk, which loops around southeast London from Dulwich to Erith.

Green Flag (greenflag.keepbritaintidy.org). Discover which parks in London have earned this prestigious award, that recognises and rewards the UK's best green spaces.

Green Space (green-space.org.uk). A charity that works to improve parks and green spaces by raising awareness, involving communities and creating skilled professionals.

Historic Royal Palaces (hrp.org.uk). An independent charity that manages Hampton Court Palace, Kensington Palace and Kew Palace – all featured in this book.

London in Bloom (londoninbloom.co.uk). A campaign and competition, in which Londoners work together to improve their environment and make the capital a greener, cleaner place.

London Cemeteries (londoncemeteries.co.uk). A comprehensive site with information and photos of over 100 historic London cemeteries.

London Gardens Online (londongardensonline.org.uk). Set up by the London Parks and Gardens Trust (see below), the website serves as an inventory of the 2,500 plus green spaces across Greater London.

London Parks and Gardens Trust (londongardenstrust.org). Independent charitable trust established in 1994 which aims to increase the public's knowledge and appreciation of London's open spaces, and to conserve them for our education and enjoyment. LPGT organises regular events, including lectures and walks, study days and conferences.

Green Space (green-space.org.uk). This charity's mission is to achieve a network of safe, accessible, attractive and welcoming parks, gardens and green spaces throughout the UK.

London Wildlife Trust (wildlondon.org.uk). Charity dedicated to protecting the capital's wildlife and wild spaces, engaging London's diverse communities through access to its nature reserves, campaigning, volunteering and outdoor learning.

Metropolitan Public Gardens Association (mpga.org.uk). Long-established charity – its roots go back to 1882 – which has played a vital role in the preservation and improvement of countless gardens, neglected sites and green open spaces across London.

National Gardens Scheme (ngs.org.uk). A charity that arranges for thousands of gardens, most privately owned, to open to the public each year (most are open just a few times a year) in aid of charity. The NGS publishes *The Yellow Book*, a guide to over 3,700 gardens.

National Trust (nationaltrust.org.uk). A leading conservation organisation that seeks to protect the heritage of England, Wales and Northern Ireland, including historic buildings, forests, beaches, parks, gardens, ancient monuments and nature reserves.

Natural England (www.naturalengland.org.uk). The government's advisor on the natural environment, Natural England provides practical and scientific advice on safeguarding the country's natural resources.

Open Spaces Society (oss.org.uk). The country's oldest national conservation body (dating from 1865), the OPS is a campaign group which protects public access to open spaces, e.g. common land, village greens and public paths, across England and Wales.

Open Squares (opensquares.org). Open Garden Squares Weekend is an annual two-day event (see website for dates), organised by the London Parks and Gardens Trust, during which community gardens and private squares across the capital welcome visitors. One ticket provides access to all gardens.

Parks and Gardens (parksandgardens.org). A leading online resource for information about historic parks, gardens and designed landscapes.

Royal Horticultural Society (rhs.org.uk). The UK's leading gardening charity dedicated to advancing horticulture and promoting good gardening. The RHS organises two of the world's foremost flower shows, both in London: the Chelsea Flower Show and the Hampton Court Palace Flower Show.

Royal Parks (royalparks.org.uk). Manages and conserves London's Royal Parks: Bushy Park, Green Park, Greenwich Park, Hyde Park, Kensington Gardens, Regent's Park, Richmond Park and St James's Park.

Sites of Special Scientific Interest (sssi.naturalengland.org.uk). England has more than 4,100 Sites of Special Scientific Interest (SSSIs), notable for their geology and wildlife; all are regulated by Natural England and listed on this site.

Trees for Cities (treesforcities.org). A charity that inspires people to plant and look after trees in cities across the world, including London.

Walk London (walklondon.org.uk). Part of the Walk England organisation, dedicated to getting people on their feet, Walk London provides maps and information about London's seven major walking routes: the Capital Ring, Green Chain, Jubilee Greenway, Jubilee Walkway, Lea Valley Walk, London Outer Orbital Path (LOOP) and Thames Path.

Wikipedia (en.wikipedia.org/wiki/parks_and_open_spaces_in_london). Wikipedia's pages on London's parks and open spaces.

Wild About Britain (wildaboutbritain.co.uk). Charity and home to hundreds of thousands of pages about British wildlife, the environment and the great outdoors.

Wildlife Trusts (wildlifetrusts.org). Website of the Royal Society of Wildlife Trusts, an umbrella body for the 47 individual Wildlife Trusts, including the London Wildlife Trust (wildlondon.org.uk), which covers the UK and manages around 2,300 nature reserves.

Woodland Trust (woodlandtrust.org.uk). The UK's leading woodland conservation society, dedicated to maintaining Britain's native woods and trees. Its Visit Woods website (visitwoods.org.uk) provides information about woods that are open to the public, including many in Greater London.

Worshipful Company of Gardeners (gardenerscompany.org.uk). One of the City's ancient livery companies (66th in order of precedence), the Gardeners' Company was first recorded in 1345 and received a Royal Charter in 1605. It's still dedicated to promoting the art and practice of good gardening throughout the UK and, especially, in London.

INDEX OF ATTRACTIONS & AMENITIES

Farm

Fishing

Community Garden

Cricket Pitch

Tennis Courts

Where to Live in London

ISBN: 978-1-907339-13-4

David Hampshire & Graeme Chesters

Essential reading for newcomers planning to live in London, containing detailed surveys of all 33 boroughs including property prices and rental costs, schools, health services, shopping, social services, crime rates, public transport, parking, leisure facilities, local taxes, places of worship and much more. Interest in living in London and investing in property in London has never been higher, both from Britons and foreigners.

£15.95

Living and Working in London

ISBN: 978-1-907339-50-9, 6th editon

Graeme Chesters & David Hampshire

Living and Working in London, is essential readi for anyone planning to live or work in London an the most up-to-date source of practical informati available about everyday life. It's guaranteed to hasten your introduction to the British way of life, and, most importantly, will save you time, trouble and money! The best-selling and most comprehensive book about living and working in London since it was first published in 1999, containing up to twice as much information as some similar books.

£14.95

INDEX

London Sketchbook

ISBN: 978-1-907339-37-0, 96 pages, hardback.

Jim Watson

London Sketchbook is a unique guide to the most celebrated landmarks of one of the world's major cities. In ten easy walks it takes you on a fascinating journey around the most famous of London's huge variety of vistas, with identification of the panoramic views and relevant historical background along the way.

Jim Watson's illustration technique is traditional line and wash, but his approach is that of a curious neighbour, seeking out the scenes which give each area its individual character – while keeping a keen eye open for the quirky and unusual.

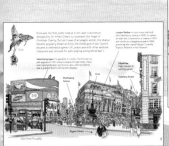

London's Secrets

LONDON'S HIDDEN SECRETS

ISBN: 978-1-907339-40-0, £10.95

Graeme Chesters

A guide to London's hidden and lesser-known sights not found in standard guidebooks. Step beyond the chaos, cliches and queues of London's tourist-clogged attractions to its quirkier side.

Discover its loveliest ancient buildings, secret gardens, strangest museums, most atmospheric pubs, cutting-edge art and design, and much more: some 140 destinations in all corners of the city.

LONDON'S HIDDEN SECRETS VOL 2

ISBN: 978-1-907339-79-0, £10.95

Graeme Chesters & David Hampshire

Hot on the heels of London's Hidden Secrets comes another volume of the city's largely undiscovered sights, many of which we were unable to include in the original book. In fact, the more research we did the more treasures we found, until eventually a second volume was inevitable.

Written by two experienced London writers, LHS 2 is for both those who already know the metropolis and newcomers wishing to learn more about its hidden and unusual charms.

LONDON'S SEC WALKS

ISBN: 978-1-907339-51-6

Graeme Chesters

London is a great city f walking – whether for p exercise or simply to ge to B. Despite the city's sive public transport sy walking is also often the quickest and most enjo way to get around – at the centre – and it's als and healthy!

Many attractions are beaten track, away fror major thoroughfares ar transport hubs. This fav walking as the best way explore them, as does fact that London is a vi interesting city with a w of stimulating sights in 'nook and cranny'.

320 PAGES, PRINTED IN COLOUR

NDON'S SECRET PLACES

8-1-907339-92-9, £10.95

Chesters & David Hampshire

is one of the world's
tourist destinations
ealth of world-class
ns: amazing museums
eries, beautiful parks
dens, stunning palaces
nd houses, and much,
ore. These are covered
rous excellent tourist
and online, and need no
tion here. Not so well
are London's numerous
attractions, most of which
lected by the throngs who
d upon the tourist-clogged
ghts. What London's
Places does is seek out
s lesser-known, but no
thy, 'hidden' attractions.

LONDON'S SECRETS: MUSEUMS & GALLERIES

ISBN: 978-1-907339-96-7, £10.95

Robbi Atilgan & David Hampshire

London is a treasure trove for
museum fans and art lovers
and one of the world's great
art and cultural centres, with
more popular museums and
galleries than any other world
city. The art scene is a lot like
the city itself – diverse, vast,
vibrant and in a constant state of
flux – a cornucopia of traditional
and cutting-edge, majestic and
mundane, world-class and run-of-
the-mill, bizarre and brilliant.

So, whether you're an art lover,
culture vulture, history buff or just
looking for something to entertain
the family during the school
holidays, you're bound to find
inspiration in London. All you need
is a comfortable pair of shoes, an
open mind – and this book!

LONDON'S SECRETS: PUBS & BARS

ISBN: 978-1-907339-93-6, £10.95

Graeme Chesters

British pubs and bars are world
famous for their bonhomie,
great atmosphere, good food
and fine ales. Nowhere is this
more so than in London, which
has a plethora of watering
holes of all shapes and sizes:
classic historic boozers and
trendy style bars; traditional
riverside inns and luxurious
cocktail bars; enticing wine
bars and brew pubs; mouth-
watering gastro pubs and
brasseries; welcoming gay
bars and raucous music
venues. This book highlights
over 250 of the best.

320 PAGES, PRINTED IN COLOUR

A Year in London:
Two Things to Do Every Day of the Year

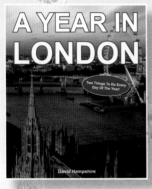

ISBN: 978-1-908282-69-1, 256 pages

David Hampshire

London offers a wealth of things to do, from exuberant festivals and exciting sports events to a plethora of fascinating museums and stunning galleries, from luxury and oddball shops to first-class restaurants and historic pubs, beautiful parks and gardens to pulsating nightlife and clubs. Whatever your interests and tastes, you'll find an abundance of things to enjoy – with a copy of this book you'll never be at a loss for something to do in one of the world's greatest cities.

Published December 2013

£12.95

London's Secrets: Bizarre & Curious

ISBN: 978-1-908282-58-2, 320 pages

Graeme Chesters

London is a city with 2,000 years of history, ove which it has accumulated a wealth of odd and strange buildings, monuments, statues, street trivia and museum exhibits, to name just a few examples. This book seeks out the city's most bizarre and curious sights and tells the often fascinating story behind them, from the Highga vampire to the arrest of a dead man, a legal brothel and a former Texas embassy to Roman bikini bottoms and poetic manhole covers, from London's hanging gardens to a restaurant whe you dine in the dark. This book is guaranteed to keep you amused and fascinated for hours.

£11.95

Published January 2014